BLACK & DECKER®

THE COMPLETE GUIDE TO
HOME CARPENTRY

Carpentry Skills & Projects
for Homeowners

CREATIVE
PUBLISHING
international

MINNETONKA, MINNESOTA

www.howtobookstore.com

Contents

Copyright © 2000
Creative Publishing international, Inc.
5900 Green Oak Drive
Minnetonka, Minnesota 55343
1-800-328-3895
www.howtobookstore.com
All rights reserved

Printed on American Paper by:
QuebecorWorld
10 9 8 7 6 5 4 3

President/CEO: David D. Murphy
Vice President/Retail Sales & Marketing: Kevin Haas

Executive Editor: Bryan Trandem
Creative Director: Tim Himsel
Managing Editor: Michelle Skudlarek
Editorial Director: Jerri Farris

Lead Editor: Daniel London
Editors: Paul Currie, Paul Gorton, Phil Schmidt
Copy Editor: Jennifer Caliandro
Senior Art Director: Kevin Walton
Mac Designers: Jon Simpson, Kari Johnston
Illustrator: Rich Stromwall
Technical Photo Editor: Keith Thompson
Technical Photo Assistant: Sean Doyle
Project Manager: Julie Caruso
Photo Researcher: Angela Hartwell
Studio Services Manager: Marcia Chambers
Studio Services Coordinator: Carol Osterhus
Photo Team Leader: Chuck Nields
Photographers: Andrea Rugg, Tate Carlson
Scene Shop Carpenters: Christopher Kennedy,
  Dan Widerski, David Johnson
Director of Production Services: Kim Gerber
Production Manager: Stasia Dorn

THE COMPLETE GUIDE TO HOME CARPENTRY
Created by: The Editors of Creative Publishing international, Inc.,
in cooperation with Black & Decker. Black & Decker is a trademark
of The Black & Decker Corporation and is used under license.

Library of Congress
Cataloging-in-Publication Data

The complete guide to home carpentry :
carpentry skills & projects for homeowners
    p. cm.
At head of title: Black & Decker.

Includes index.
ISBN 0-86573-577-8 (softcover)
1. Carpentry—Amateurs' manuals.
2. Dwellings—Maintenance and repair—
Amateurs' manuals. I. Creative Publishing
international. II. Black & Decker Manufac-
turing Company (Towson, Md.)

TH5607.C65 2000
694—dc21   00-031539

Portions of *The Complete Guide to Home Carpentry*
are taken from *Carpentry: Remodeling, Carpentry:
Tools, Shelves, Walls & Doors, Exterior Home
Repairs & Improvements, The Complete Photo
Guide to Home Repair, The New Everyday Home
Repair,* and *Workshop Tips & Techniques.* Other
titles from Creative Publishing international include:

*Decorating With Paint & Wallcovering, Basic Wiring
& Electrical Repairs, Advanced Home Wiring,
Landscape Design & Construction, Bathroom*

*Remodeling, Built-In Projects for the Home, Refinish-
ing & Finishing Wood, Home Masonry Repairs &
Projects, Building Porches & Patios, Flooring Pro-
jects & Techniques, Advanced Home Plumbing,
Remodeling Kitchens, Stonework & Masonry Pro-
jects, The Complete Guide to Home Plumbing, The
Complete Guide to Home Wiring, The Complete
Guide to Decks, The Complete Guide to Painting &
Decorating, The Complete Guide to Creative Land-
scapes, The Complete Guide to Home Masonry*

Introduction

Begin any carpentry project by making pencil drawings of the project you have in mind. As you refine the project idea, add as much detail as possible to the drawing, so you can anticipate issues such as what tools and materials the project will require and how the project will affect your living space.

Planning a Carpentry Project

A carpentry project can be fun and rewarding, but it requires more than just a knack for cutting lumber and pounding nails. In fact, your natural ability with tools may not affect the finished product as much as your attention to details, materials, costs, and local building codes. Address these issues in the planning stages so you can use your time efficiently once you start to cut. Start any project by asking yourself the questions below. Once you've addressed each question, you can feel confident about the project you're about to start.

Is a permit required? Most building departments require a permit if your carpentry project will significantly alter your home's condition. You'll probably need a permit for anything more extensive than replacing a rotted window. Permits are required for adding or replacing beams, posts, joists, rafters; for building additions; for converting a basement or attic; and for many other projects. Ask your building department for any literature on carpentry projects. If a permit is required, you'll need to show an inspector a detailed diagram and a list of building materials before you begin.

How will the project affect my living space? Building a wall or installing a new window may drastically change your living environment. Make sure you consider the pros and cons each project will produce before starting.

What types of materials will work best for my project? To maintain a common theme throughout a room, choose building materials that match your existing living space. Always choose well-crafted materials that meet the requirements of local building codes.

Which tools do I need? Each carpentry project in this book includes a list of tools, including portable power tools. Some tools, such as a power drill and circular saw, should be considered essential. Others, such as a power miter saw or router, simplify the job, but are not essential. Dado cuts for shelves can be made using a circular saw, instead of a router. Making miter cuts with a back saw and miter box is also possible. Using different tools to complete specific tasks usually takes extra time, but you'll be able to enjoy a sense of craftsmanship that using hand tools brings to a project.

Tips for Planning a Carpentry Project

Lay out the project using 2" masking tape on the floor to indicate the boundaries of the project. An actual-size layout will help you visualize the end result and can often draw your attention to issues that aren't obvious from a scale drawing.

Examine the areas directly below and above the project before cutting into a wall to determine the location of water lines, ductwork, and gas pipes. In most cases, pipes, utility lines, and ductwork run through the wall vertically between floors. Original blueprints for your house, if available, usually show the locations of the utility lines.

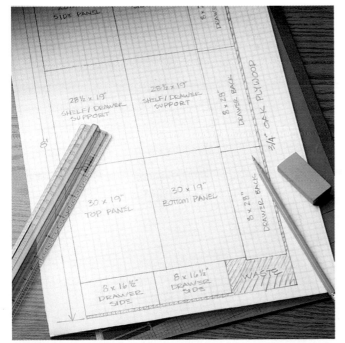

Draw cutting diagrams to help you make efficient use of materials. Make scale drawings of sheet goods on graph paper, and sketch cutting lines for each part of your project. When laying out cutting lines, remember that the cutting path (kerf) of a saw blade consumes up to ⅛" of material.

Make a list of materials, using your plan drawings and cutting diagrams as a guide. Photocopy the materials list, and use it to organize your work and estimate costs.

Project Safety

Your personal safety when working on carpentry projects depends greatly on what safety measures you take. The power tools sold today offer many safety features, such as blade guards, locks to prevent accidental starts, and double insulation to reduce the risk of shock in the event of a short circuit. It's up to you to take advantage of these safety features. For example, never operate a saw with the blade guard removed. You risk injury from flying debris as well as from being cut by the blade.

Follow all precautions outlined in the owner's manuals for your tools and make sure you protect yourself with safety glasses, ear plugs, and a dust mask or respirator to filter out dust and debris.

Keep your work environment clean. A cluttered work area is more likely to result in accidents. Clean your tools and put them away at the end of every work period, and sweep up dust and debris.

Some materials emit dangerous fumes or particles. Keep such materials stored away from heat sources and out of the reach of children; always use these products in a well-ventilated area.

Maintaining safety is an ongoing project. Take the time to update your first-aid kit and evaluate your work space, tools, and safety equipment on a regular basis. To avoid accidents, repair and replace old and worn-out parts before they break.

Read the owner's manual before operating any power tool. Your tools may differ in many ways from those described in this book, so it's best to familiarize yourself with the features and capabilities of the tools you own. Always wear eye and ear protection when operating a power tool. Wear a dust mask when the project will produce dust.

Some walls may contain asbestos. Many homes built or remodeled between 1930 and 1950 have older varieties of insulation that included asbestos. Consult a professional for removal of hazardous pollutants like asbestos, and if you find asbestos or materials that may contain asbestos, do not attempt to remove them on your own. Even if you determine that no asbestos is present, it is a good idea to wear a particle mask and other safety gear when doing demolition.

Tips for Project Safety

Assemble a first-aid kit. Cuts from a hand or power tool can be serious and require prompt and thoughtful attention. Be prepared for such situations with a well-equipped first aid kit that is easy to find. Record any emergency telephone numbers on the first aid kit or by the nearest phone so they are available in an emergency.

Equip your kit with a variety of items (photo right), including bandages, needles, tweezers, antiseptic ointment, cotton swabs, cotton balls, eye drops, a first-aid handbook, a chemical-filled cold pack, elastic bandages, first aid tape, and sterile gauze.

For puncture wounds, cuts, burns, and other serious injuries, always seek medical attention as soon as first aid—such as washing and wrapping of cuts—has been provided.

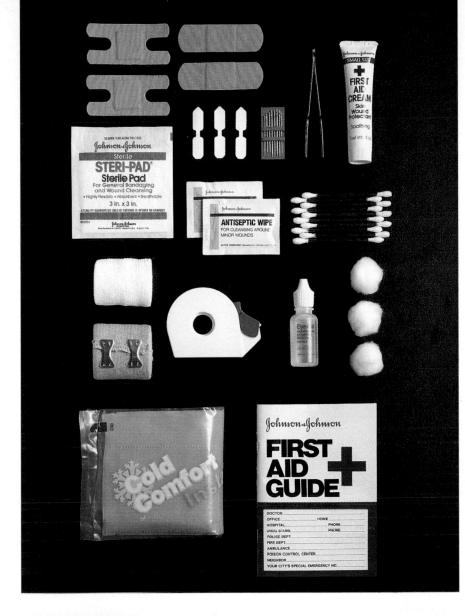

Keep your tools sharp and clean. Accidents are more likely when blades are dull and tools are filled with sawdust and dirt.

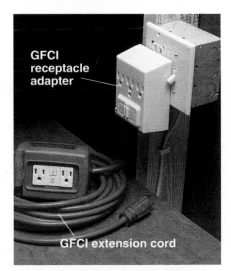

Use a GFCI receptacle, adapter, or extension cord to reduce the risk of shock while operating a power tool outdoors or in wet conditions.

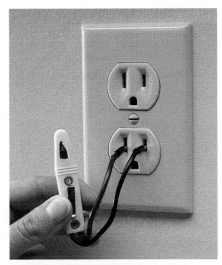

Check with a neon circuit tester to make sure the power is off before removing cover plates, exposing wires, or drilling or cutting into walls that contain wiring.

A carpenter's workshop should be a well-lighted space that's large enough to keep common tools, hardware, and equipment easily accessible and well organized. A workbench is convenient for various tasks. To operate a table saw or other large power equipment, you'll need plenty of space for handling large lumber and sheet goods.

Workshop Basics

Whether your workshop is in a basement utility room, a shed, or a garage, it should be a comfortable place to work and should provide convenient space for organizing your tools and equipment. Your workshop should include a generous benchtop at a comfortable height, plenty of well-directed lighting, and ample floor space to operate a table saw or other stationary power tools. If you plan to store paints or solvents, make sure the room has plenty of ventilation and is equipped with a smoke detector and fire extinguisher.

Your workshop should have enough electrical circuits to supply power to the lights and several pieces of equipment without overloading a circuit. Calculate your shop's circuit capacity (opposite page) and contact an electrician if you need to add a circuit.

There are many devices for hanging tools on workshop walls, but the most versatile is still a sheet of pegboard with tool hooks hung from it (opposite page). Pegboard allows you to organize the hooks to suit your needs.

Deep, sturdy shelves provide a great place to store tool boxes, buckets, and portable power tools. Ready-to-assemble shelf units are available at home centers. Or, you can build your own adjustable-height utility shelves (pages 228 to 231).

If your workshop is in the house, you may want to add hollow-core tiles to the inside of the workshop door to reduce sound transmission and a door sweep to block noise and keep dust from traveling under the door.

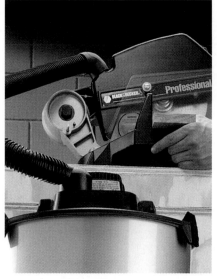

Mount a sturdy bench vise with a swivel base on the end of your workbench (pages 94 to 97) to brace materials for cutting, or to use as a clamp when gluing or assembling parts. Select a vise that adjusts easily and has a minimum jaw opening of about 4".

Use a wet/dry shop vacuum for quick clean up. Many power tools have attachments that allow you to connect the vacuum's hose to the tool, so most debris is sucked directly into the cannister. Buy a vacuum with durable parts and a powerful motor.

Hang a pegboard tool rack on a masonry wall by first attaching 1 × 2s to the wall to provide a gap for inserting tool hooks. Attach the 1 × 2s with masonry nails, then attach the pegboard to the 1 × 2s, using 1" screws and washers.

How To Assess Your Workshop's Electricity Supply

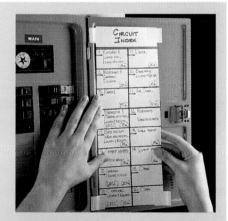

To know whether your workshop circuitry is sufficient to run your power tools and other equipment safely, first determine the circuit's safe capacity—the maximum load, or wattage that it can handle without overheating. Locate the correct circuit on your service panel and check the amperage rating (right, top). Multiply that number by 120 volts, then subtract 20% to find the safe capacity. Next, find the wattage of each tool or appliance that will use that circuit. All tools and appliances are labeled with their amperage and voltage ratings (right, bottom) Calculate wattage by multiplying the amperage by the voltage. Add together the wattages of all of the tools and appliances you're likely to use simultaneously to find out whether they are within the circuit's safe capacity. The chart shows wattages for some common power tools and appliances. If the circuit's safe capacity is not high enough to handle the load, you may need another circuit in the workshop. Ask an electrician to inspect your service panel. You can probably add a circuit to the service panel and additional receptacles to your workshop.

Typical Wattage Ratings

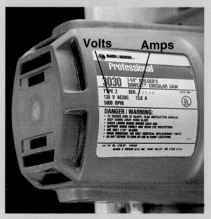

Appliance	Amps	Watts
Circular saw	10 to 12	1200 to 1440
Drill	2 to 4	240 to 480
Fan (portable)	2	240
Heater (portable)	7 to 12	840 to 1440
Router	2 to 5	240 to 600
Sander	2 to 5	240 to 600
Table saw	7 to 10	840 to 1200
Shop vacuum	6 to 11	720 to 1320

Materials

Lumber

Lumber for structural applications such as walls, floors and ceilings is usually milled from strong softwoods and is categorized by grade, moisture content, and dimension.

Grade: Characteristics such as knots, splits, and grain slope affect the strength of the lumber and determine the grade (chart, opposite page).

Moisture content: Lumber is also categorized by moisture content. S-DRY (surfaced dry) is the designation for lumber with a moisture content of 19 percent or less. S-DRY lumber is the least likely to warp or shrink and is a good choice for framing walls. S-GRN (surfaced green) means the lumber contains a moisture content of 19 percent or more.

Exterior lumber: Lumber milled from redwood or cedar is naturally resistant to decay and insect infestation, and is a good choice for exterior applications. The most durable part of a tree is the heartwood, so specify heartwood for pieces that will be in contact with the ground.

Treated lumber: Lumber injected with chemicals under pressure is resistant to decay and is generally less expensive than decay-resistant heartwoods, such as redwood and cedar. For outdoor structures like decks, use treated lumber for posts and joists, and more attractive redwood or cedar for decks and railings.

Dimension lumber: Lumber is sold according to its nominal size, such as 2 × 4. Its actual size (chart, page 17) is smaller. Always use actual sizes for measuring and estimating.

Check lumber visually before using it. Stored lumber can warp from temperature and humidity changes.

The Steel Framing Alternative

Lumber is not the only material available for framing walls. Metal studs and tracks offer an attractive—if less common—choice for new construction. Steel-framed walls can be installed faster than wood stud walls—the parts are attached by crimping and screwing the flanges—and the channels are precut to accommodate electrical and plumbing lines. Steel framing is also lighter in weight, easy to recycle, fireproof, and comparable in price to lumber. If you are interested in using steel framing for a new wall in a wood-framed home, consult a professional for information about electrical, plumbing, and load-bearing safety precautions. Steel framing is available at most home centers.

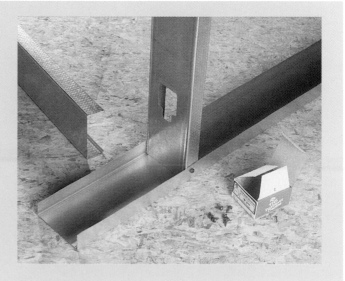

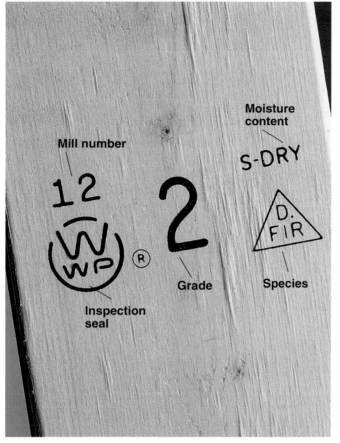

Grade stamps provide valuable information about a piece of lumber. The lumber's grade is usually indicated by the largest number stamped on the wood. Also stamped on each piece of lumber are its moisture content, species, and lumber mill of origin.

Lumber Grading Chart

Grade	Description, uses
Clear	Free of knots and defects.
SEL STR or Select Structural 1,2,3	Good appearance, strength and stiffness. 1,2,3 grades indicate knot size.
CONST or Construction STAND or Standard	Both grades used for general framing. Good strength and serviceability.
STUD or Stud	Special designation used in any stud application, including load-bearing walls.
UTIL or Utility	Economical choice for blocking and bracing.

Much of today's lumber is still fairly wet when it is sold, so it's hard to predict how it will behave as it dries. But a quick inspection of each board at the lumber yard or home center will help you disqualify flawed boards. Lumber that is *cupped, twisted,* or *crooked* should not be used at full length. However, you may be able to cut out good sections for use as blocking or other short framing pieces. If a board is slightly *bowed,* you can probably flatten it out as you nail it. *Checks, wanes,* and *knots* are cosmetic flaws that seldom affect the strength of the board. The exception is a knot that is loose or missing. In this case, cut off the damaged area. Sections with *splits* should also be cut off. Splits are likely to spread as the wood dries.

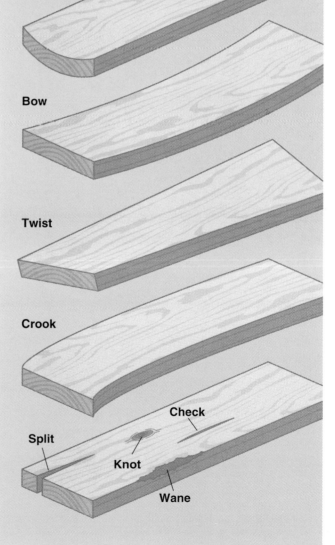

How to Select the Right Materials for a Project

Picking the right wood for a project is a decision that will affect the durability and attractiveness of the final product. Some woods are more prone to warping than others, some are more resistant to decay, and some are superior when it comes to holding a coat of paint. Matching styles and wood varieties will help to create a common theme throughout your home.

Lumber sizes such as 2 × 4 are *nominal dimensions,* not actual dimensions. The actual size of lumber is slightly smaller than the nominal size. When it is originally milled, lumber is cut at the nominal size, however, the boards are then planed down for a smoother finish, producing the actual dimensions you buy in the store. See the chart on the opposite page for nominal and actual dimensions.

Softwood	Description	Uses
Cedar	Easy to cut, holds paint well. Heartwood resists decay.	Decks, shakes, shingles, posts, and other decay-prone surfaces.
Fir, larch	Stiff, hard wood. Holds nails well. Some varieties are hard to cut.	Framing materials, flooring, and subflooring.
Pine	Lightweight, soft wood with a tendency to shrink. Holds nails well. Some varieties resist decay.	Paneling, trim, siding, and decks.
Redwood	Lightweight, soft wood that holds paint well. Easy to cut. Heartwood resists decay and insect damage.	Outdoor applications, such as decks, posts, and fences.
Treated lumber	Chemically treated to resist decay. Green in hue. Wear protective eye wear and clothing to avoid skin, lung, and eye irritation.	Ground-contact and other outdoor applications where resistance to decay is important.

Hardwood	Description	Uses
Birch	Hard, strong wood that is easy to cut and holds paint well.	Painted cabinets, trim, and plywood.
Maple	Heavy, hard, strong wood that is difficult to cut with hand tools.	Flooring, furniture, and countertops.
Poplar	Soft, light wood that is easy to cut with hand or power tools.	Painted cabinets, trim, tongue-and-groove paneling, and plywood cores.
Oak	Heavy, hard, strong wood that is difficult to cut with hand tools.	Furniture, flooring, doors, and trim.
Walnut	Heavy, hard, strong wood that is easy to cut.	Fine woodwork, paneling, and mantelpieces.

Type	Description	Common Nominal sizes	Actual sizes
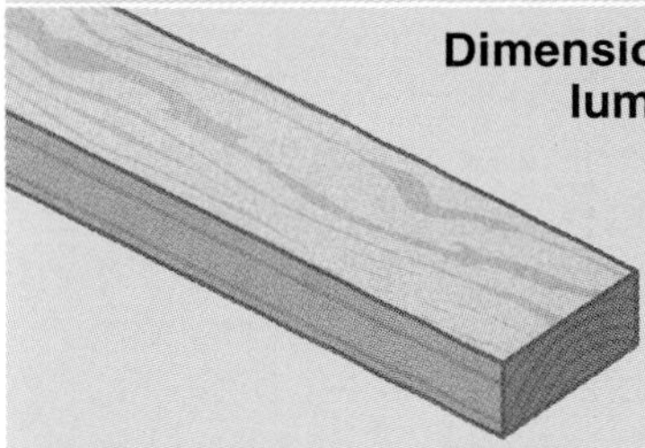 **Dimensional lumber**	Used in framing of walls, ceilings, floors, and rafters, structural finishing, exterior decking, fencing, and stairs.	1 × 4 1 × 6 1 × 8 2 × 2 2 × 4 2 × 6 2 × 8	¾" × 3½" ¾" × 5½" ¾" × 7¼" 1½" × 1½" 1½" × 3½" 1½" × 5½" 1½" × 7¼"
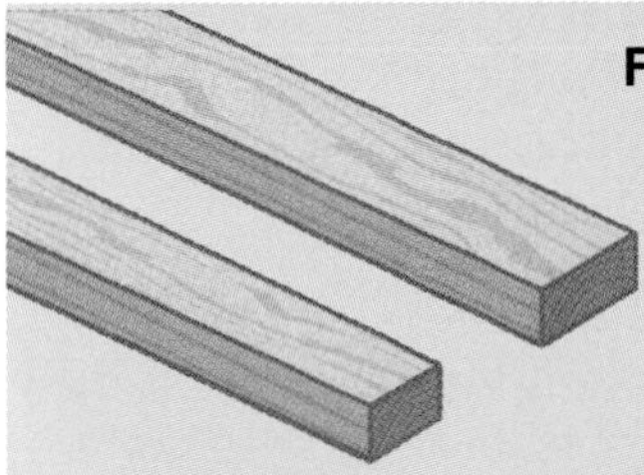 **Furring strips**	Low-grade dimensional lumber used to level uneven surfaces or framing, create an air space, or prepare surfaces for installing finish materials.	1 × 2 1 × 3	¾" × 1½" ¾" × 2½"
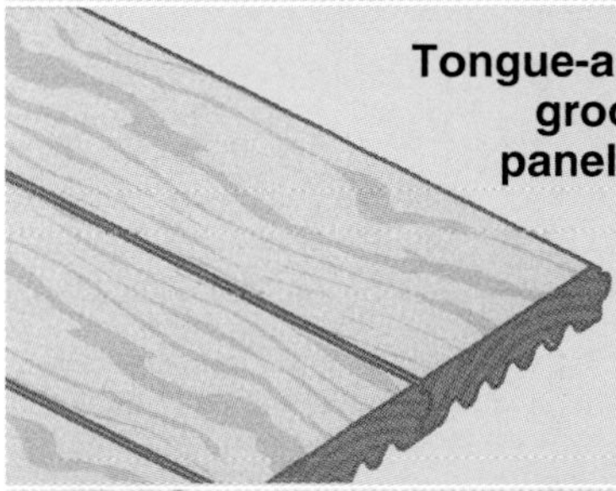 **Tongue-and-groove paneling**	Boards used in wainscoting and full-length paneling of walls and ceilings.	5⁄16" × 4 1 × 4 1 × 6 1 × 8	Varies, depending on milling process and application.
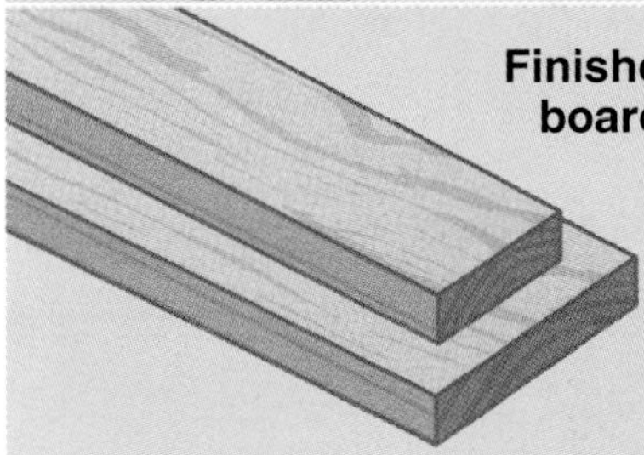 **Finished boards**	Used in trim, shelving, cabinetry, and other applications where a fine finish is required.	1 × 4 1 × 6 1 × 8 1 × 10 1 × 12	¾" × 3½" ¾" × 5½" ¾" × 7¼" ¾" × 9¼" ¾" × 11¼"
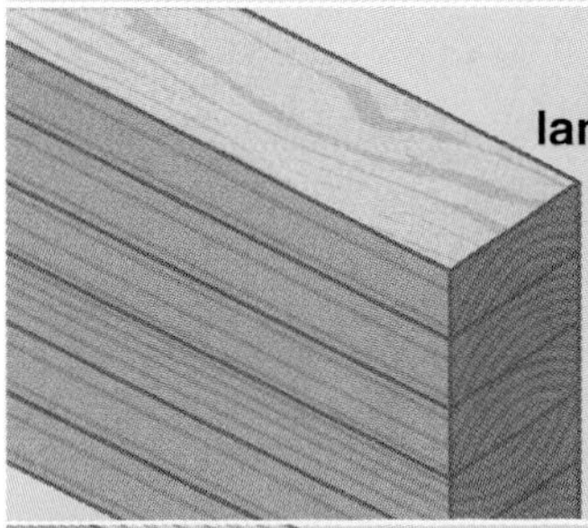 **Glue laminate**	Beam composed of layers of lumber laminated to form a solid piece. Used for beams and joists.	4 × 10 4 × 12 6 × 10 6 × 12	3½" × 9 3½" × 12 3½" × 9 3½" × 12
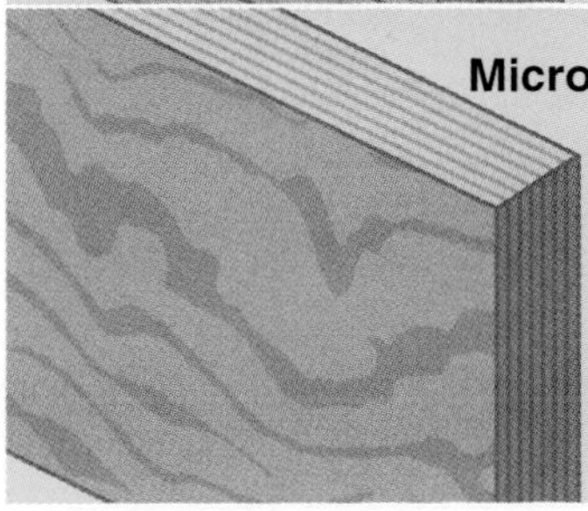 **Micro-lam®**	Beam composed of thin layers glued together for use as joists and beams.	4 × 12	3½" × 11⅜"

Finish plywood

Sheathing plywood

Strandboard

Plastic laminate
(bonded to particleboard)

Waferboard

Particleboard

Plywood & Sheet Goods

There are many different types of sheet goods, but plywood is the most widely used. Plywood is an extremely versatile sheet material that is made up of thinly sliced layers or *plies* of wood. Plywood is available in thicknesses ranging from 3/16" to 3/4" and is graded A through D, depending on the quality of the wood in its outer plies. It is also graded for interior or exterior usage. Classifications for plywood are based on the wood species used for the face and back veneers. Group 1 species are the strongest and stiffest, Group 2 is the next strongest.

Finish plywood is graded either A-C, meaning it has a finish-quality wood veneer on one side and a utility-grade ply on the other side, or A-A, indicating it has a finish veneer on both sides.

Sheathing plywood is graded C-D with two rough sides, and features a bond between plies that is waterproof. Plywood rated EXPOSURE 1 is for use where some moisture is present, and plywood rated EXTERIOR is used in applications that are permanently exposed to weather. Sheathing plywood also carries a thickness rating and a roof and floor span index, which appear as two numbers separated by a diagonal slash. The first number, for roofing application, indicates the maximum spacing for rafters. The

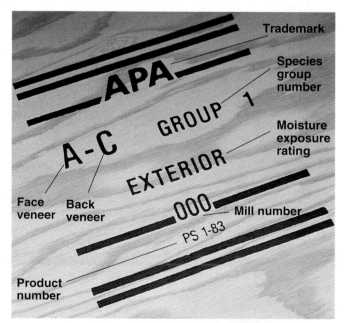

The finish plywood grading stamp shows the grade of face and back veneers, species group number, and a moisture exposure rating. Mill numbers and product numbers are for manufacturer's use.

second number specifies the joist spacing when plywood is used for subflooring. Some plywood is stamped "sized for spacing." This means that the actual dimensions are slightly smaller than 4 × 8 ft. to allow space for expansion between sheets after installation.

Plastic laminates make durable surfaces for countertops and furniture. Plastic laminates are sometimes bonded to particleboard for use in shelving, cabinets, and countertops.

Strand-, particle-, and waferboard are made from waste chips or inexpensive wood species and are used for shelving and floor underlayment.

Foam insulating board is lightweight and serves as insulation for basement walls.

Cementboard is used behind ceramic wall tiles and in other high-moisture areas.

Wallboard, also known as drywall, Sheetrock, and plasterboard, comes in panels 4-ft. wide and 2, 4, 8, 10, or 12-ft. long, and in ⅜", ½", and ⅝" thicknesses.

Pegboard and hardboard are made from wood fibers and resins bonded together under high pressure, and are used for tool organization with a workbench and as shelf backing.

Plastic foam insulating board

Cementboard

Wallboard

Pegboard

Hardboard

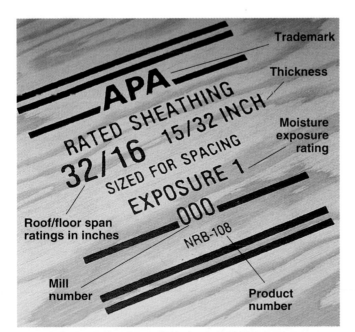

APA
RATED SHEATHING
32/16   15/32 INCH
SIZED FOR SPACING
EXPOSURE 1
000
NRB-108

Trademark

Thickness

Moisture exposure rating

Roof/floor span ratings in inches

Mill number

Product number

Sheathing plywood grading stamp shows thickness, roof or floor span index, and exposure rating, in addition to manufacturer's information.

Decorative moldings give a finished appearance to a carpentry project. Other finish materials include door and window casings, baseboard, and other types of trim.

Trim Moldings

Trim moldings give character and definition to many carpentry projects. In addition, you can sometimes use them to cover up carpentry mistakes, such as hiding small gaps in wall corners when the wallboard hasn't been cut perfectly.

It's important to measure and cut moldings precisely so that when installed, they fit together snugly without gaps. Predrilling moldings is recommended, especially when hardwoods such as oak are used. Predrilling makes nailing easier, reduces splitting during installation, and makes it easier to set nails cleanly.

Most moldings should be painted or stained before installation. Cove moldings and wainscoting, can be purchased with a factory coat of white paint. Care must be taken to ensure that paint or stain does not interfere with installation (see "Installing Tongue-and-groove Wainscoting," page 162). Pine and poplar are good choices if you plan to paint. For stained surfaces, use a hardwood with a pleasing grain, such as oak.

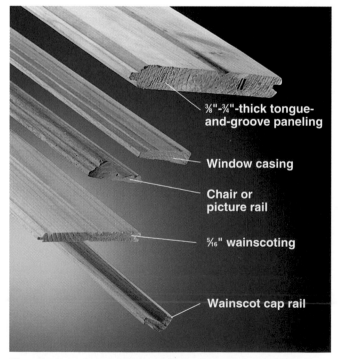

⅜"-¾"-thick tongue-and-groove paneling

Window casing

Chair or picture rail

⁵⁄₁₆" wainscoting

Wainscot cap rail

Use the same wood species whenever possible in selecting trim materials for walls, doors, windows, and built-ins. Similar materials will provide visual consistency throughout a room.

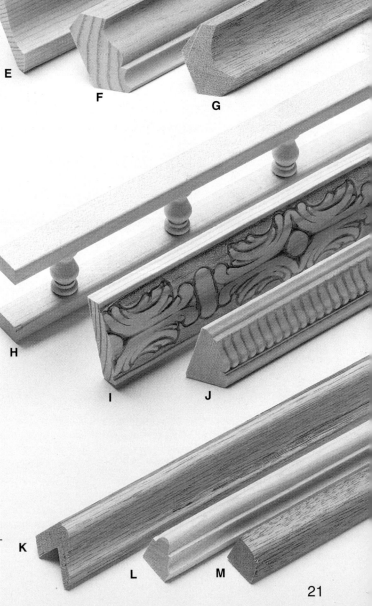

Trim moldings are both functional and decorative. They can be used to conceal gaps at the base and around the sides of a carpentry project, to hide the edges of plywood surfaces, or simply to add visual interest to the project. Moldings are available in dozens of styles, but the samples shown here are widely available at all home improvement centers.

Synthetic trim moldings, available in many styles, are less expensive than hardwood moldings. Synthetic moldings are made of wood composites (A) or rigid foam (B) covered with a layer of melamine.

Baseboard molding (C) is used to trim the bottom edge of a wall along the floor line. Choosing molding that matches the baseboard elsewhere in your home helps your project fit in with its surroundings.

Hardwood strips (D) are used to construct face frames for carpentry projects, and to cover unfinished edges of plywood shelves. Maple, oak, and poplar strips are widely available in 1 × 2, 1 × 3, and 1 × 4 sizes.

Crown moldings (E, F) cover gaps between the top of a wall and the ceiling. They can also add a decorative accent to other projects.

Cove molding (G) is a simple, unobtrusive trim for covering gaps.

Ornamental moldings, including spindle and rail (H) and embossed moldings (I, J), give a distinctive look to many projects.

Door-edge molding (K), also called cap molding, is only available in specialty stores, in some areas. It is used with finish-grade plywood to create panel style-doors and drawer faces.

Shelf-edge molding (L), also called base cap molding, provides a decorative edge to plywood shelves or can be used to create a wider baseboard molding.

Base-shoe molding (M) covers gaps around the top, bottom, and sides of a wall. Because it bends easily, base-shoe molding works well to cover irregular gaps caused by uneven walls and loose floors.

21

Types of Nails

Common nail for heavy-duty framing

Box nail for light work or edge nailing

Cement-coated sinker nail for outside sheathing

Finish nail for fastening wood trim

Galvanized casing nail for outside trim

Spiral flooring nail for subflooring

Cement nail for fastening wood to concrete

Masonry nail for brick and concrete

Galvanized ring-shank siding nail

Galvanized spiral siding nail

Aluminum cedar siding nail

Aluminum cedar fence nail

Galvanized roofing nail

Self-sealing galvanized roofing nail for metal roofs

Wallboard nail

Duplex nail for temporary construction

Nails

The wide variety of nail styles and sizes makes it possible to choose exactly the right fastener for each job. Nails are identified by their typical purpose, such as casing, flooring, or roofing nails; or by a physical feature, such as galvanized, coated, or spiral. Some nails come in both a galvanized and non-galvanized version. Use galvanized nails for outdoor projects and non-galvanized indoors. Nail lengths may be specified in inches or by numbers from 4 to 60 followed by the letter "d," which stands for "penny" (See "Nail Sizes," opposite page).

Some of the most popular nails for carpentry projects include:

Common and box nails for general framing work. Box nails are smaller in diameter, which makes them less likely to split wood. Box nails were designed for constructing boxes and crates, but they can be used in any application where thin, dry wood will be nailed close to the edge of the piece. Most common and box nails have a cement or vinyl coating that improves their holding power.

Finish and casing nails, which have small heads and are driven just below the work surface with a nail set. Finish nails are used for attaching moldings and other trim to walls. Casing nails are used to fasten door jambs and exterior trim. They have a slightly larger head than finish nails for better holding power.

Brads, similar to small finish nails, are used in finish carpentry and woodworking. They have a small head designed for countersinking, unlike the broader, flat heads of wire nails.

Flooring nails, which are often spiral-shanked for extra holding power to prevent floor boards from separating or squeaking. Spiral flooring nails are sometimes used in other applications, such as installing tongue-and-groove paneling on ceilings.

Galvanized nails, which have a zinc coating that resists rusting. They are used for outdoor projects.

Wallboard nails, once the standard fastener for wallboard, are less common today because of the development of Phillips-head wallboard screws that drive quickly with a screw gun or drill and offer superior holding power (page 24).

Nail Sizes

The penny weight scale that manufacturers use to size nails was developed centuries ago as an approximation of the number of pennies it would take to buy 100 nails of that size. The range of nail types available today (and what they cost) is much wider, but the scale is still in use. Each penny weight refers to a specific length (see chart, below), although you will find slight variations in length from one nail type to the next. For example, box nails of a given penny weight are roughly ⅛" shorter than common nails of the same weight.

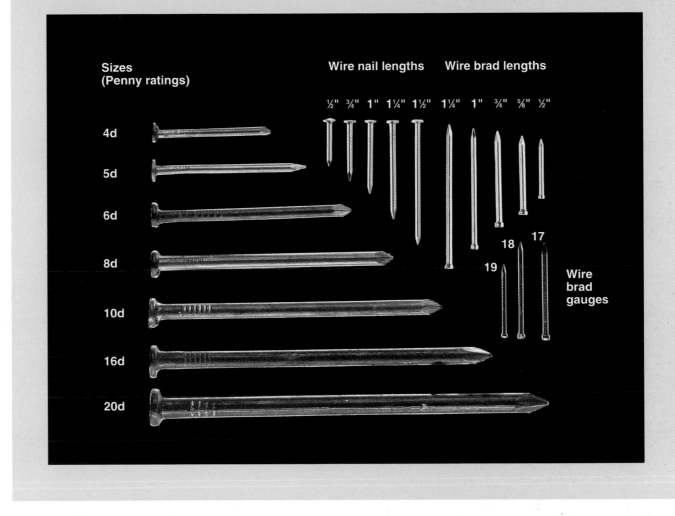

How to Estimate Nail Quantities

Estimate the number of nails you'll need for a project, then use the chart to determine approximately how many pounds of nails to purchase.

NOTE: Sizes and quantities not listed are less common, although they may be available through some manufacturers.

Penny wt.		2d	3d	4d	5d	6d	7d	8d	10d	12d	16d	20d
Length (in.)		1	1¼	1½	1⅝	2	2⅛	2½	3	3¼	3½	4
Common		870	543	294	254	167		101	66	61	47	29
Box	Nails per lb.	635	473	406	236	210	145	94	88	71	39	
Cement-Coated				527	387	293	223	153	111	81	64	52
Finish		1350	880	630	535	288		196	124	113	93	39
Masonry				155	138	100	78	64	48	43	34	

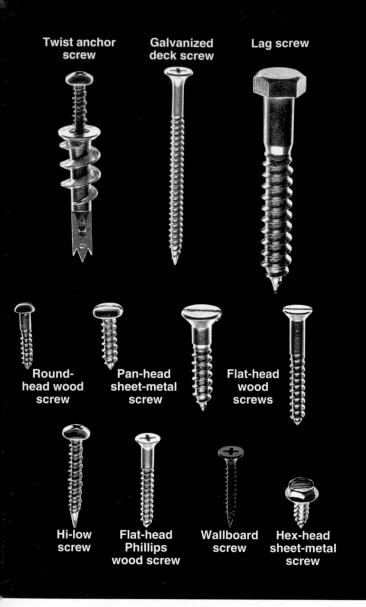

Twist anchor screw

Galvanized deck screw

Lag screw

Round-head wood screw

Pan-head sheet-metal screw

Flat-head wood screws

Hi-low screw

Flat-head Phillips wood screw

Wallboard screw

Hex-head sheet-metal screw

Screws & Other Hardware

The advent of the screwgun and numerous types of driver bits for drills have made screws a mainstay of the carpentry trade. With literally hundreds of different screws and types of fastening hardware available, there is a specific screw for almost every job. But, for most carpentry jobs you will only need to consider a few general purpose types. Although nails are still preferred for framing jobs, screws have replaced nails for hanging wallboard, installing blocking between studs, and attaching sheathing and flooring. Screws are also used to attach a workpiece to plaster, brick, or concrete, which requires an anchoring device (opposite page, top).

Screws are categorized according to length, slot style, head shape, and gauge. The thickness of the screw body is indicated by the gauge number. The larger the number, the larger the screw. Large screws provide extra holding power; small screws are less likely to split a workpiece. There are various styles of screw slot, including Phillips, slotted, and square. Square drive screwdrivers are increasing in popularity because they grip the screwhead tightly, but Phillips head screws are still the most popular.

Wallboard Screws & Deck Screws

Deck screws

Wallboard screw

Fine thread wallboard screw

Use wallboard screws for general-purpose, convenient fastening. Easily recognizable by their bugle-shaped heads, wallboard screws are designed to dimple the surface of wallboard without ripping the facing paper. However, they are often used for non-wallboard projects because they drive easily with a drill or screw gun, don't require pilot holes, and seldom pop up as wood dries. In soft wood, the bugle-shaped heads allow the screws to countersink themselves. Deck screws are corrosion-resistant wallboard screws made specifically for outdoor use.

Using Masonry & Wall Anchors

Cement anchors

Lag screw/lead shield combinations

Plastic plugs

Use wall anchors to attach hardware or lumber to plaster, concrete, or brick. Choose an anchor that is equal in length to the thickness of the wall's surface material. Plastic plugs are used for anchoring in hollow walls.

To install a wall anchor, drill a pilot hole equal in diameter to the plastic anchor. Insert the anchor in the hole and drive it flush with the wall surface. Insert the screw and tighten it; as the anchor expands, it will create a tight grip.

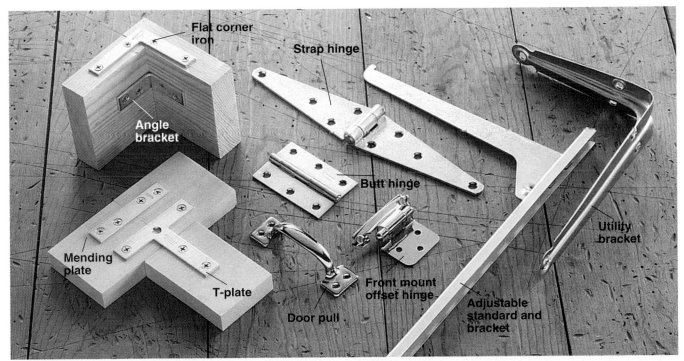

Flat corner iron

Strap hinge

Angle bracket

Butt hinge

Utility bracket

Mending plate

T-plate

Door pull

Front mount offset hinge

Adjustable standard and bracket

Specialized hardware is used for many different carpentry applications. Braces and plates provide extra support to wood joints. Install them during assembly of a project for added support or to mend a broken joint.

Use hinges to attach cabinet faces, doors, and lids. Building shelves with brackets saves time and creates strong, well mounted units.

Carpentry adhesives include (clockwise from top right): clear adhesive caulk, for sealing gaps in damp areas; waterproof construction adhesive, for bonding lumber for outdoor projects; multi-purpose adhesive, for attaching paneling and forming strong bonds between lumber pieces; electric hot glue gun and glue sticks, for bonding small decorative trim pieces on built-ins; wood glues and all-purpose glue, for many woodworking projects.

Glues & Adhesives

When used properly, glues and adhesives can be stronger than the materials they hold together. Use hot glue in lightweight woodworking projects, carpenter's glue for wood joints, and carpentry adhesive for preliminary installation of thin panels and lumber. Panel adhesive, a thinner formula that can be applied from a tube or with a brush, is used to install paneling, wainscoting, and other lightweight tongue-and-groove materials. Most caulk is applied with a caulk gun, but some types are available in squeeze tubes for smaller applications. Caulks are designed to permanently close joints, fill gaps in woodwork, and hide subtle imperfections. Different caulks are made of different compounds and vary greatly in durability and workability. While silicone caulks last longer, they are not paintable and are difficult to smooth out. Latex caulks are less durable than silicone, but are much easier to work with, especially when used to hide gaps. Many caulks are rated on scales of 1 to 4 to indicate how well they bond to masonry, glass, tile, metals, wood, fiberglass, and plastic. Read the label carefully to choose the right caulk for the job.

Tips for Using Adhesives & Glues

Strengthen floors and decks and reduce squeaks with joist and deck adhesive. For outdoor applications, make sure you choose a waterproof adhesive.

Place wax paper between a pipe clamp or C-clamp and the workpiece to prevent any glue seeping out of the wood joints from bonding to the clamp.

How to Reglue Loose Veneer

1 Use a putty knife to gently pry up the edge of the loose veneer. Carefully scrape away the old glue.

2 Apply a thin coat of yellow carpenter's glue to the surface, using a cotton swab or craft stick. Press the veneer in place, and wipe away any excess glue with a damp cloth.

3 Cover the glued area with wax paper or a scrap of rubber, and clamp it with a block of wood and a C-clamp. Let the glue dry overnight.

Tools & Skills

Carrying Your Tools

There are two basic types of tool belts: apron-style and side-mounted bags (shown here). Side bags don't get in your way when you crouch, and make the tools easier to reach. However, it is easier to get between studs while wearing an apron-style belt.

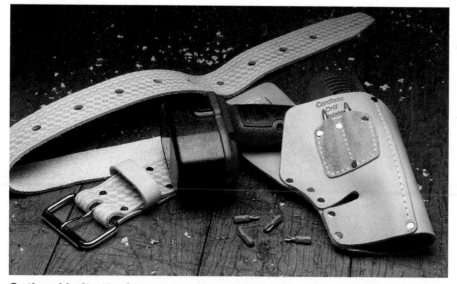

Optional belt attachments, such as holsters for drills, help organize your tool load. They can be worn alone or with other tool bags.

Carpentry jobs are easier when your tools are organized in a tool belt, because you spend less time searching for the right tool.

Standard features for tool belts include slots for screwdrivers, files, a carpenter's pencil, and a utility knife; at least one hammer loop; and a deep pouch or two for carrying nails and screws. Many belts also have a slot for a tape measure and a hook for hanging a small level.

Think about the tools you most often use, and choose a tool belt that has the right number of slots, pockets, or loops for your tool load. The more varied the tasks you'll be handling, the more elaborate your belt should be. If you'll only be framing, a simple canvas nailing apron with a hammer loop may be all you need.

If you carry a lot of tools on your belt, a pair of suspenders can be useful. Suspenders release some of the weight from your hips. Several companies offer suspenders designed to attach to your tool belt.

For projects that require tools you can't fit into your belt, consider using a bucket apron (page opposite).

If you plan to carry a drill, you may want to purchase a separate drill holster with slots for commonly used bits.

Use a tool bucket for larger or less frequently needed tools and a tool belt for quick access to small tools. The bucket apron is a convenient way to carry specialty tools that will not fit into your tool belt, such as a long level or a caulk gun. The tool bucket also allows several people to share tools.

Prying Tools

Prying tools are an essential part of any carpenter's tool arsenal, because many carpentry projects start with the removal of existing materials. With the right tools, you can often remove nails without damaging the lumber, so that it can be used again.

Pry bars are available in many sizes. Choose quality pry bars forged from high-carbon steel in a single piece. Forged tools are stronger than those made from welded parts.

Most pry bars have a curved claw at one end for pulling nails and a chisel-shaped tip at the opposite end for other prying jobs. You can improve leverage by placing a wood block an inch or two away from the material you're trying to pry loose.

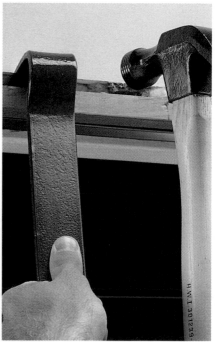

A flat bar is made of flattened, slightly flexible steel. This tool is useful for a variety of prying and demolition jobs. Both ends can be used for pulling nails.

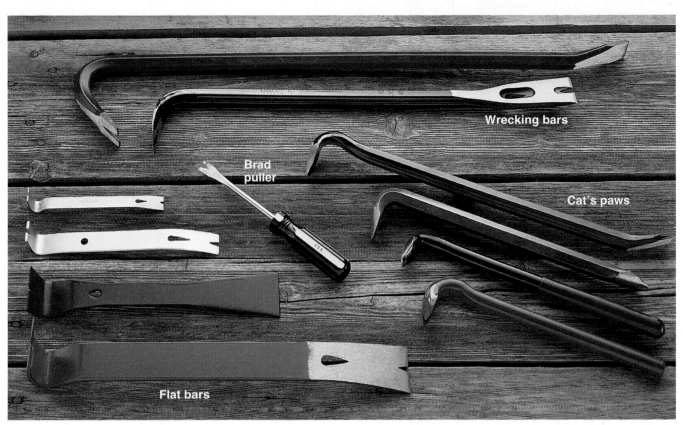

Prying tools include wrecking bars for heavy demolition work, cat's paws for removing nails, and a brad puller. Flat bars are made of flattened steel and come in a variety of sizes for light- and heavy-duty use.

A wrecking bar, sometimes called a crowbar, is a rigid tool for demolition and heavy prying jobs. Use scrap wood under the bar to protect surfaces.

A cat's paw has a sharpened claw for removing stubborn nails. Use a hammer to drive the claw into the wood under the nail head, then lever the tool to pull up the nail.

Tape Measures

An important step in every carpentry project is measuring accurately. Buy a 25-ft. steel tape measure with a ¾"-wide blade for general use. Most tape measures are retractable, so the tape returns easily. Make sure your tape has a locking mechanism, so you can keep it extended to a desired length. A belt clip is also essential.

Wider tapes normally have a longer *standout*—the distance a tape can be extended before it bends under its own weight. A long standout is an extremely useful feature when you're measuring without a partner to support the far end of the tape. Open a tape in the store and extend it until it bends. It should have a standout of at least 7 ft.

Tape measures are commonly set in ¹⁄₁₆" increments along the top edge and ¹⁄₃₂" increments for the first six inches across the bottom. Select one with numbers that are easy to read. "Easy reader" tapes feature a fractional readout for people who have difficulty reading measurement calibrated with dash marks. Most tape measures feature numbers that are marked or labeled every 16" for easy marking of studs. A high-quality tape measure also has a two- or three-rivet hook to control the amount of play in the tape, ensuring your measurements are as accurate as possible.

Buy a 25-ft. retractable steel tape for general carpentry projects. If you are working on a large project like a deck, patio, or retaining wall, consider purchasing a 50-ft. reel-type tape.

"Bury an inch." The end hook on a tape measure has a small amount of play, and should not be used when an extremely accurate measurement is required. For precise measurements, use the 1" mark as your starting point (called burying an inch), then subtract 1" from your reading.

Use only one tape measure, if possible, while working on a project. If you must work with two tapes, make sure they record the same measurement. Different tape measures do not always measure equally. A slight difference in the end hooks can create an error of 1/16" or more between two tapes, even if they are of the same brand and style.

Simplify the task of making straight, horizontal cuts in wallboard. Lock a tape measure at the desired width and position a utility knife blade under the tape hook. Hold the tape body in one hand and the knife and tape hook in the other as you slide the blade along the wallboard.

Check for square when building frames, boxes, cabinets, drawers, and other projects where fit is important. Hold a tape measure across the diagonals of the workpiece (A-C, B-D). The measurements will be identical if the workpiece is square.

Plumb Bobs & Chalk Lines

The plumb bob is a simple, yet extremely precise tool used to establish a line that is plumb—or exactly vertical. Plumb bobs are commonly used to find marking points to position a sole plate when building a wall. Plumb can be a hard concept to visualize. Plumb refers to a hypothetical line running to the exact center of the earth. Another way to conceptualize plumb is to think of it as a line that is exactly perpendicular to a level surface.

The chalk line is a tool used to mark straight lines on flat surfaces for layout or to mark sheet goods and lumber for cutting. A chalk line is more accurate than a pencil when marking over longer distances. Typical chalk lines contain 50-100 ft. of line wound up in a case filled with chalk. Always tap the box lightly to fully coat the line with chalk before pulling it out. To mark a line, extend it from the case, pull it taut, and snap it using the thumb and forefinger. Chalk lines have a crank that is used to reel in the line when the job is complete, and a locking mechanism to help keep the line taut during marking.

Most of today's chalk lines (sometimes called chalk boxes) double as plumb bobs for general use (see photos, opposite page, bottom). A chalk box isn't quite as accurate as a plumb bob for establishing a verticle lines. However, if you don't own a plumb bob, using a chalk box is an easy alternative.

Buy powdered chalk refills of blue or red chalk. Do not overfill your chalk box or the string will be difficult to pull out and wind in. Keep moisture out of your chalk box or the chalk will clump together, causing uneven coverage of the line.

To make a clean chalk mark, place the hook over the edge of the work surface or hang it on a nail. At your endpoint, hold the line taut against the work surface, then pull the chalk line away from the surface with your thumb and fore-finger. Release it so the line snaps quickly back, leaving a clear, straight line of chalk. To make a chalk line longer than 12 ft., pin the line down in the center, then snap it once on each side of the midpoint. If your chalk line is faint, it may be time to reload the line, or you may have moisture in your box. Tapping the box a few times against your hammer before pulling out the line should ensure that it is fully coated with chalk. If not, you have moisture in your box. To dry out your line, pull the entire line out at the end of the day and set it near a heat source overnight.

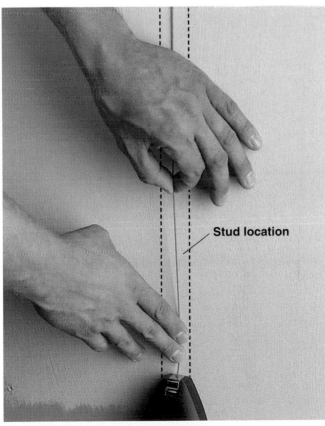

Stud location

To snap a chalk line over a very short distance, pin the string down with the edge of your palm, then use your thumb and forefinger on the same hand to snap the line. When snapping lines to mark stud locations, make sure you snap over the center of the studs, so you will know where to drive screws or nails.

To position a sole plate, hang a plumb bob from the edge of the top plate so that it nearly touches the floor. When it hangs motionless, mark the floor di-rectly below the point of the plumb bob. Repeat the process at each end of the new wall space to deter-mine the proper sole plate position.

Carrying case

Carpenter's levels

Torpedo level

You should own at least two levels, a 2-ft. carpenter's level for checking studs, joists, and other long construction surfaces, and a 8 to 9" *torpedo* level that is easy to carry in a tool belt and is perfect for checking shelves, and other small workpieces. A 4-ft. version of the carpenter's level is most useful for framing projects. Consider purchasing a level with a protective carrying case.

Levels

Levels are essential to virtually every carpentry project. They help you build walls that are perfectly vertical (plumb), shelves, countertops, and steps that are level, and roofs that incline at a correct and consistent pitch.

Take care of your levels. Do not throw them into a tool bucket or box. Unlike some other tools, a level is a finely tuned instrument that is easily broken. Before you buy a level, test it on a level surface to make sure the vials are accurate (opposite page).

Most levels contain one or more bubble gauges—sealed vials with a single small air bubble suspended in fluid—that indicate the level's orientation in space at any moment. As the level is tilted, the bubble shifts its position in-

side the vial to reflect the change. This type of level is sometimes referred to as a *spirit level* because of the use of alcohol inside the gauge. There are also several types of electronic levels that offer digital readouts instead of using a bubble gauge.

Most carpenter's levels contain three gauges: one for checking level (horizontal orientation) one for plumb (vertical orientation), and one for 45° angles. Some levels include pairs of gauges with opposing curves to improve readability.

Top quality carpenter's levels contain screw-in or snap-in vial cases that can be replaced if they become damaged, heavy glass lenses to protect each vial or set of vials, and shock-absorbing rubber end caps for additional protection.

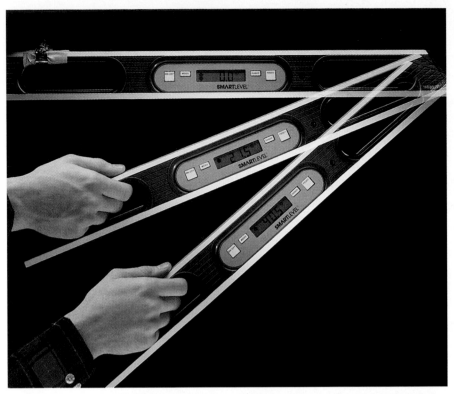

Battery-powered digital levels represent the latest advance in level design. Digital levels provide very accurate digital readouts, so you don't have to trust your eye judging bubble position within a vial. Digital levels also measure slope and offer rise/run ratios, which are useful when building stairs. The electronic components are contained in a module that can be used alone as a torpedo level, or inserted into frames of varying lengths.

Build a leveling jig to check warped and bowed lumber by cutting a straightedge on a table saw, and attaching short 2 × 4 blocks to the ends. The straightedge should be slightly shorter than the lumber you are checking. Tape or clamp a level to the straightedge on the side opposite the 2 × 4 blocks. Hold the blocks against the lumber and read the level to check for plumb or level. If your project requires it, you can install a short support piece, called a *cripple,* that will force bowed lumber into line at the warped or bowed location, before you nail it in place.

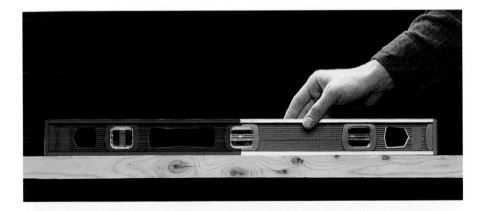

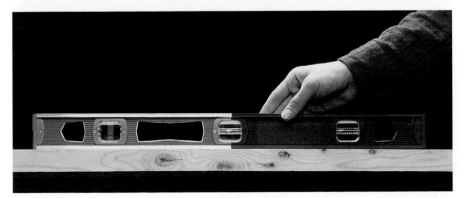

Make sure your level is accurate. Hold one side of the level against a flat, even surface (top photo), mark the location, and read the bubble gauge carefully. Pivot the level 180° (bottom photo) and read the gauge again. Next, flip the level over and read the gauge. The bubble should give the same reading each time. If not, adjust the mounting screws to calibrate the bubble, or buy a new level.

Squares

Squares come in many shapes and sizes, but they are all designed with one general purpose: to help you mark lumber and sheet goods for cutting.

There are, however, distinct differences between the various types of squares. Some are made for marking straight cuts on sheet goods, while others are best for making quick crosscuts on 2 × 4s or marking angles on rafters. Using the right tool will speed your work and improve the accuracy of your cuts.

Familiarize yourself with the different types of squares and their uses so you can choose the right tool for the job.

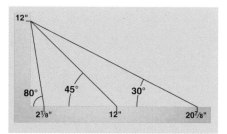

A framing square is commonly used to mark right angles on sheet goods and other large surfaces, but it can also be used to establish other angles by using different measurements along the body (long arm) and the tongue (short arm). The tool has gradations marked in tiny increments, and many come with detailed tables to help you make angles.

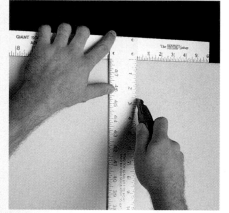

A wallboard T-square simplifies the task of marking and cutting straight lines on sheets of wallboard. The top of the T hooks over the edge of the wallboard while the leg is used as a straightedge. A T-square is also handy for marking cutting lines on plywood and other sheet goods. Some models have an adjustable T that can be set to common angles.

Common Framing Square Angles

Angle	Tongue	Body
30°	12"	20⅞"
45°	12"	12"
60°	12"	6¹⁵⁄₁₆"
70°	12"	4⅜"
75°	12"	3⁷⁄₃₂"
80°	12"	2⅛"

The chart above shows the markings to use on the framing square to obtain commonly required angles. If you want to make a line at a 30° angle, mark the workpiece at 12" on the tongue and 20⅞" on the body and connect the marks with a straight line.

How to Use a Combination Square

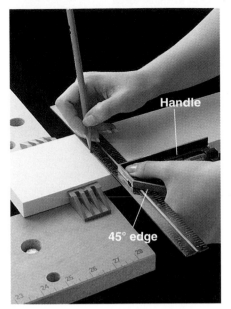

To mark a board for crosscutting, hold the square against the edge of the workpiece, then use the edge of the blade to guide your pencil. Use the handle's 45° edge to mark boards for miter cuts.

To mark a line parallel to the edge of a board, lock the blade at the desired measurement, then hold the tip of the pencil along the edge of the blade as you slide the tool along the work piece. This is useful when marking reveal lines on window and door jambs (pages 152 to 155).

To check for square, set the blade of a square flush with the end of the workpiece and the handle flush with one edge. If the end is a true 90°, there will not be a gap between the blade and the workpiece.

How to Use a Rafter Square

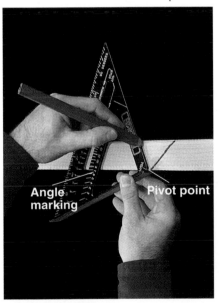

To mark angle cuts, position the rafter square's pivot point against the edge of the workpiece and set the tool so the desired angle marking is aligned with the same edge. Scribe a line to mark the angle on the workpiece. Flip the tool over to mark angles in the opposite direction.

To mark crosscuts, place a rafter square's raised edge flush with one edge of the board and use the perpendicular edge to guide your pencil. On wide boards, you'll need to flip the square to the board's other edge to extend the line across the board.

To guide a circular saw when making crosscuts, first align the blade of the saw with your cutting line. As you cut, hold the raised edge of the square against the front edge of the workpiece and the perpendicular edge flush with the foot of the saw.

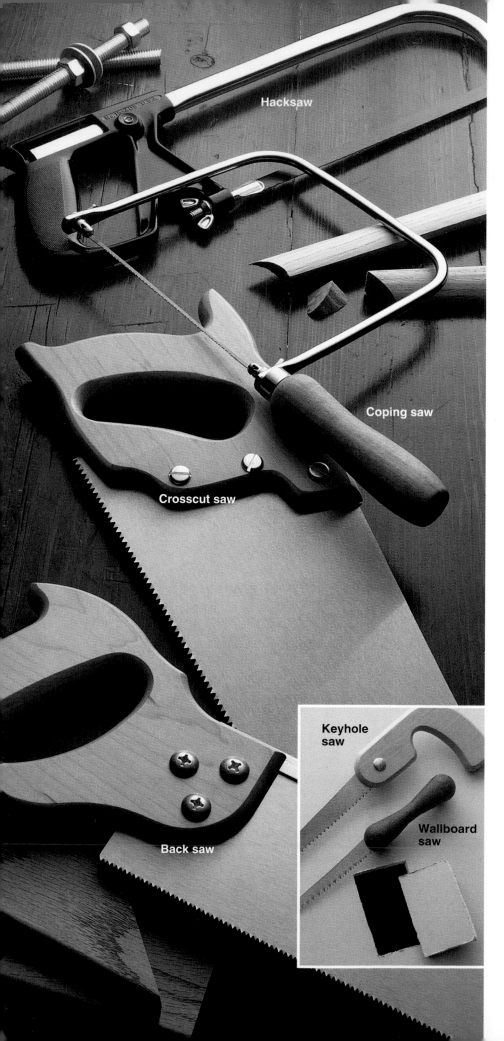

Hacksaw

Coping saw

Crosscut saw

Back saw

Keyhole saw

Wallboard saw

Handsaws

For every portable power saw available today, there is also a handsaw available that was originally used to make the same type of cut. Although you will probably use a circular, jig, or miter saw for most cutting, there are times when using a hand saw is easier, more convenient, and produces better results. Handsaws also provide the do-it-yourselfer a cost-effective alternative to the higher price of power tools.

There are many differences between handsaws. When you shop for a saw, look for one that's designed for the type of cutting you plan to do. Differences in handle design and the number, shape, and angle (set) of the teeth make each saw work best in specific applications.

For general carpentry cuts, use a crosscut saw with 8 to 10 teeth per inch. Crosscut saws have pointed teeth designed to slice through wood on the forward stroke and to deepen the cut and remove sawdust from the kerf on the back stroke.

Always use a handsaw for its intended purpose. Misuse of a handsaw will only damage the tool, dull the blade, or lead to injury.

When saw blades become dull, take them to a professional blade sharpener for tuning. It's worth the extra cost to ensure the job is done right.

Making a cutout by hand requires a saw with a narrow, tapered blade that fits into confined spaces. Use a keyhole saw for making cutouts in plywood, paneling, and other thin materials, and a wallboard saw for making fixture cutouts in wallboard. For tips on using these saws see page 47.

Choosing the Right Handsaw

A crosscut saw comes in handy for single-cut projects or in confined spaces where power tools won't fit. At the end of a cut, saw slowly, and support waste material with your free hand to prevent splintering.

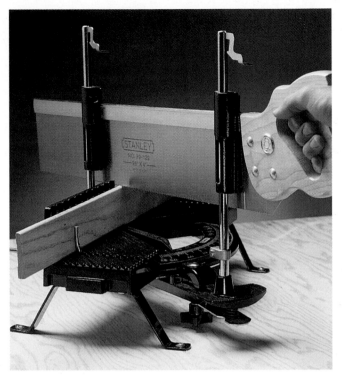

A backsaw with a miter box cuts precise angles on moldings and other trim. Clamp or hold the workpiece in the miter box and make sure the miter box is securely fastened to the work surface.

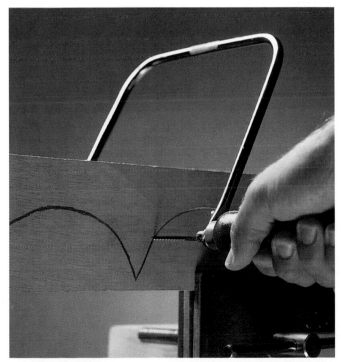

A coping saw has a thin, flexible blade designed to cut curves. It is also essential for making professional-looking joints in trim moldings. The blade of a coping saw breaks easily when under heavy use. Buy extra blades.

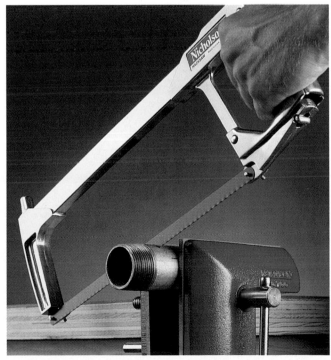

A hacksaw has a flexible, fine-tooth blade designed to cut metal. Carpenters use hacksaws to cut plumbing pipe or to cut away stubborn metal fasteners. To avoid breaking the blade, stretch the blade tight in the hacksaw frame before cutting.

Wood

Rigid foam

Garden hose

Protect handsaw teeth and prevent accidents by covering the edge with a protective sheath when the saw is not in use. A saw sheath can be made from a narrow strip of wood, rigid foam, or an old garden hose. Cut a lengthwise slot into one edge of the sheath, then fit it over the saw teeth.

Develop a proper stance for sawing. Always take the time to get comfortable before sawing, and make sure your hand, elbow, and shoulder are directly in line with the saw blade. Use your thumb to guide the saw as you start. Saw with a steady rhythm, applying slight pressure on the push strokes and relaxing on the pull strokes.

Begin a handsaw cut with an upward stroke to establish the cut line, then make long, smooth strokes with the blade at a 45° angle. Remember: A saw blade consumes from ¹⁄₁₆" to ⅛" of wood. Start your cut just wide of the marked cutting line to avoid cutting off too much material. As you start the cut, guide the saw with the side of your thumb.

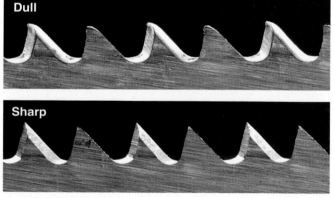

Dull

Sharp

Frequently examine handsaws for sharpness. On dull saws, the teeth show wear and are visibly rounded (top). Sharp saws have pointed teeth with clean, smooth edges. Dull saws should be sharpened by a professional. Check the yellow pages under "Saws, Sharpening."

Tips for Using Handsaws

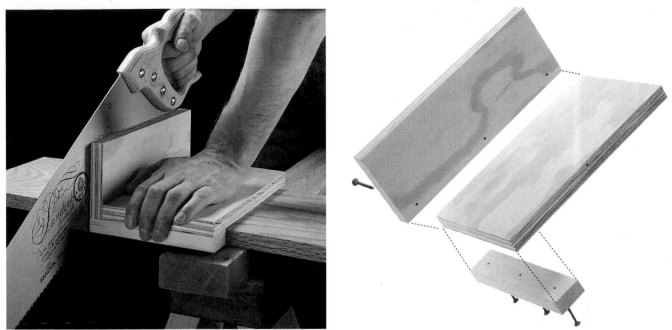

Keep handsaw cuts square to the face and sides of a workpiece. Make this job easier by building a squaring guide from scrap hardwood or ¾" plywood. Use a combination square to make sure each piece is square before assembling the guide. Join the pieces with carpenter's glue and 1¼" wallboard screws; check the final assembly again to make sure it is square.

Choose a Cutting Style

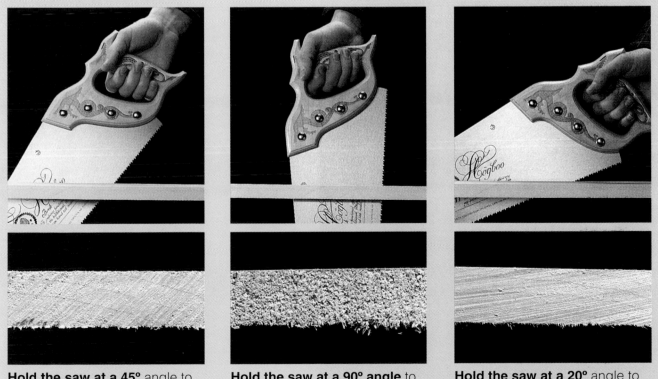

Hold the saw at a 45° angle to the workpiece for most cutting jobs. This angle produces a fairly smooth cut.

Hold the saw at a 90° angle to the workpiece to make fast cuts. This technique leaves a rough-edged cut.

Hold the saw at a 20° angle to the workpiece to make very smooth cuts. Sawing at this angle requires extra cutting time.

Tips for Using a Wooden Miter Box

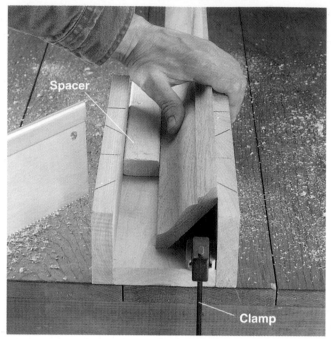

Clamp the wooden miter box tightly to your workbench before cutting stock. Use a spacer if necessary to help brace the material so it doesn't shift during cutting.

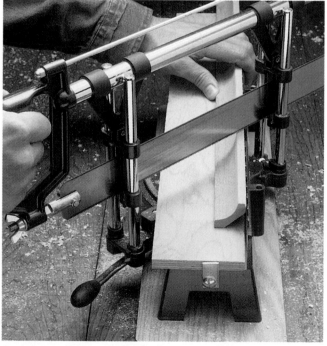

Think of the base of the miter box as the ceiling and the fence as the wall when positioning cove moldings. This will remind you to place the molding in the miter box upside down and sprung at a 45° angle.

Tips for Using a Swivel-type Miter Box

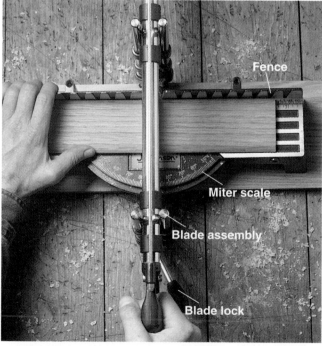

Use a swivel-type miter box to make cuts up to 45° in either direction. Swivel the blade assembly to the exact angle you need to cut, using the miter scale as a guide, and set the blade lock to hold the blade in place during cutting. Make sure the material is flush with the fence before you begin cutting.

Position cove moldings against the fence just as you would on a wood miter box, upside down and sprung at a 45° angle. The backsaw fits into a rigid assembly that slides up and down, so you can insert and remove materials as necessary. To support wide stock and to protect the miter box base, mount a piece of hardboard or particleboard on the base.

How to Make a Coped Joint

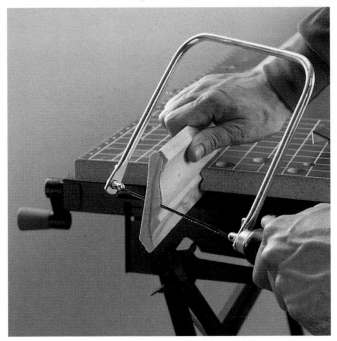

1 Coped joints form neat inside corners when installing baseboards or ceiling trim. Install the first corner piece with square-cut ends. Bevel-cut the second piece at a 45° angle, then cope along the exposed grain to form an edge that will overlap the first piece.

2 Test-fit the pieces to make sure the coped piece fits snugly against the profile of the first piece. If necessary, make small adjustments by using sandpaper to smooth irregular cuts.

Tips for Cutting Out Sheet Goods

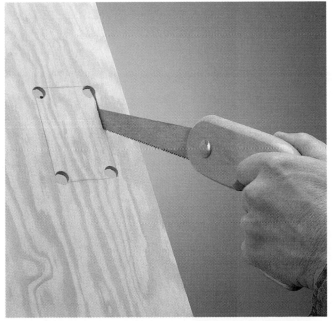

Use a keyhole saw to cut out plywood and other sheet goods for receptacles, fixtures, and other small openings. Mark the cutting lines with a pencil, then drill pilot holes at the corners, and insert the saw to cut along the cutting lines.

Use a wallboard saw to cut small openings in wallboard. Mark cutting lines, then push the point of the saw through the wallboard and saw along the cutting line.

Jig Saws

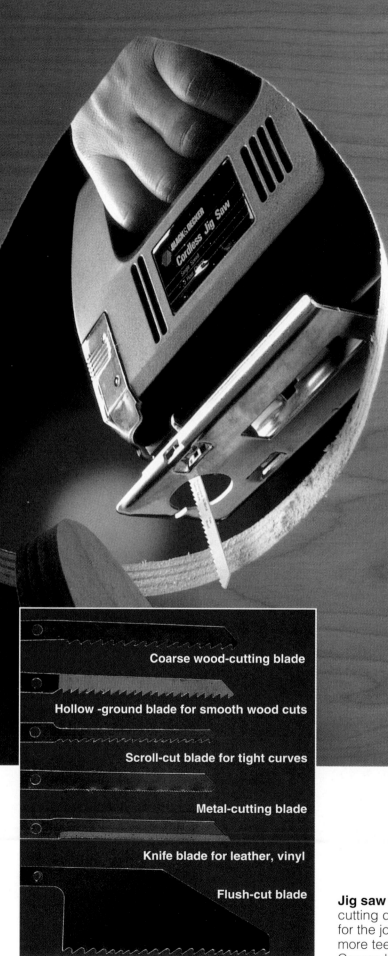

The jig saw is a very good portable power tool for cutting curves. The cutting capacity of a jig saw depends on its power and the length of its blade stroke. Choose a saw rated to cut 2"-thick softwood and ¾"-thick hardwood stock. Many jig saws have a pivoting baseplate that can be locked so you can make bevel cuts as well.

A variable-speed jig saw is the best choice, because different blade styles require different cutting speeds for best results. In general, faster blade speeds are used for cutting with coarse-tooth blades and slower speeds with fine-tooth blades.

Jig saws vibrate more than other power saws because of the up-and-down blade action. However, top-quality jig saws have a heavy-gauge steel baseplate that reduces vibration to help you hold the saw tightly against the workpiece for better control.

Because jig saw blades cut on the upward stroke, the top side of the workpiece may splinter. If the wood has a good side to protect, cut with this surface facing downward.

Coarse wood-cutting blade

Hollow-ground blade for smooth wood cuts

Scroll-cut blade for tight curves

Metal-cutting blade

Knife blade for leather, vinyl

Flush-cut blade

Jig saw blades come in an array of designs for cutting different materials. Choose the right blade for the job. With fine-tooth blades that have 14 or more teeth per inch, set the saw at a low speed. Coarse blades require faster blade speeds.

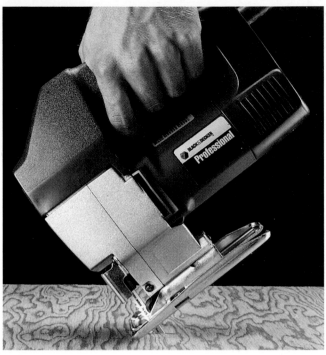

Do not force blades. Jig saw blades are flexible and may break if forced. Move the saw slowly when cutting bevels or tough material like knots in wood.

Make plunge cuts by tipping the saw so the front edge of the baseplate is held firmly against workpiece. Start the saw, and slowly lower it to a horizontal position, letting the blade gradually cut through the workpiece.

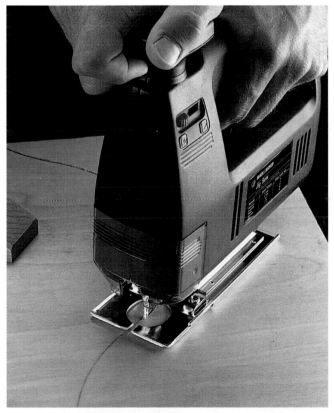

Use a narrow blade to make scroll or curved cuts. Move the saw slowly to avoid bending the blade. Some jig saws have a scrolling knob that allows you to turn the blade without turning the saw.

Cut metals with a fine-tooth metal-cutting blade and select a slow blade speed. Support sheet metals with thin plywood to eliminate vibration. Use emery paper or a file to smooth burred edges left by the blade.

Circular Saws

A portable circular saw has become the most frequently used cutting tool for do-it-yourselfers. With the right set of blades, you can use a circular saw to cut wood, metal, plaster, concrete, or other masonry materials. An adjustable baseplate lets you set the blade depth for your workpiece, and also pivots from side to side for bevel cuts.

Most professional carpenters use a 7¼"-blade circular saw. For home carpentry, 7¼"-blade and 6½"-blade models are the most popular. A smaller blade means a smaller, lighter saw body, but bear in mind that a smaller saw is usually less powerful, and is limited when cutting bevel cuts or material that is thicker than 2× stock.

Cordless circular saws have 5⅜"-wide blades—wide enough to cut through sheet goods or to make square cuts on 2× lumber. Cordless models are useful in situations where a power cord gets in the way. However, most cordless circular saws aren't powerful enough to be the primary cutting tool for big projects.

Because circular saw blades cut in an upward direction, the top face of the workpiece may splinter. To protect the finished side of the workpiece, mark measurements on the back side and place the good side down for cutting.

Get the most out of your saw by inspecting your blade regularly and changing it as needed (pages 52 to 53). You can also improve your results with a straightedge guide (page 57), which makes it easier to cut long stock precisely.

7¼"-blade worm-drive saw. Some carpenters prefer the worm-drive saw for heavy-duty cutting. Worm-drive saws offer more torque at any given speed. As a result, they are less likely to slow, bind, or kick back when subjected to a heavy load.

7¼"-blade standard-drive saw. Standard-drive circular saws are the most popular choice among do-it-yourselfers and are widely used by professional carpenters. This model has a sawdust-release pipe that connects to a collection bag.

Sawdust-release pipe

Viewing window

Viewing window

5⅜"-blade cordless trim saw. Cordless trim saws are convenient for cutting trim and other thin stock, especially when the work site is outdoors or away from an electrical receptacle.

Viewing window

6½"-blade standard-drive saw. Do-it-yourselfers looking for a lightweight saw may want to consider a standard-drive saw with a 6½ blade. This model has a convenient window for an easy view of the line while cutting.

51

Panel blade

Hollow ground planer blade

Carbide-tipped combination blade

Masonry blade

Metal-cutting blade

Selecting & Maintaining Circular Saw Blades

To get full use out of your circular saw, you'll need an assortment of blades. Your collection should include at least one carbide-tipped combination blade and a panel blade for cutting plywood. Buy additional blades based on the type of cutting you plan to do:

• A panel blade has small teeth designed to cut through plywood and other veneer panels without chipping them.

• A hollow-ground planer blade has a tapered surface that reduces friction for smoother cuts in fine woodworking.

• A carbide-tipped combination blade is a general purpose blade designed for fast, semi-smooth woodcutting in any direction.

• A masonry blade is used to score or cut masonry.

• A metal-cutting blade is used to cut through metal pipes, studs, sheet metal, and fasteners. Both masonry and metal cutting blades wear down quickly with heavy use.

You can keep a saw blade in good condition by using it only for the material that it's designed to cut, cleaning it if it becomes dirty, and avoiding cutting through nails and other fasteners. Nails and screws can break a blade, cause saw kickback, or project metal fragments. Clean a blade with kerosene and steel wool, then dry the blade and coat it lightly with machine oil as a protectant against rust.

A dull blade puts undue strain on the saw's motor. Replace blades that are dull, or have them sharpened by a professional. Never use a blade with cracked or chipped teeth.

How to Set the Blade Depth

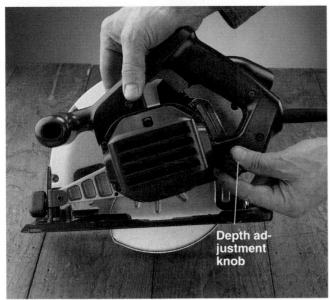

Depth adjustment knob

Blade guard lever

1 The blade on a circular saw does not move when you set the blade depth. Instead, on most circular saws, the saw baseplate pivots up and down, changing the amount of blade that is exposed. Unplug the saw, then pull out the depth adjustment lever and slide it up or down to adjust the blade depth.

2 Pull up on the blade guard lever to expose the blade, then position the blade flush with the edge of the workpiece to check the setting. The blade should extend beyond the bottom of the workpiece by no more than the depth of a saw tooth. Release the knob to lock the blade. NOTE: Some saws have a baseplate that drops rather than pivots. When the knob is pulled out, the entire baseplate can be moved up or down.

How to Change the Blade

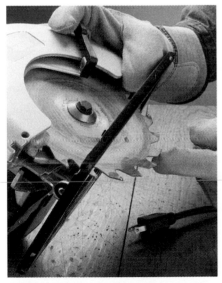

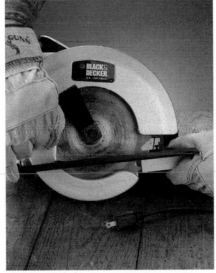

1 Unplug the saw and inspect the blade, wearing gloves to protect your hands. Replace the blade if you find worn, cracked, or chipped teeth. Remove the blade for cleaning if sticky resin or pitch has accumulated.

2 To loosen the blade, first depress the arbor lock button or lever to lock the blade in position, then loosen the bolt with a wrench and slide the bolt and washer out of the assembly. NOTE: On older models with no arbor lock, insert a wood block between the blade and baseplate to keep the blade from turning as you loosen the bolt.

3 Install a new blade. Or, if the old blade is soiled but in otherwise good condition, clean and reinstall it. Use the directional markings on the side of the blade as a guide when attaching a blade. Insert the bolt and washer, then tighten the bolt with a wrench until the bolt is snug. Do not overtighten.

53

How to Make Crosscuts

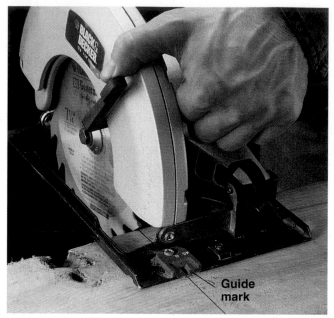

Guide mark

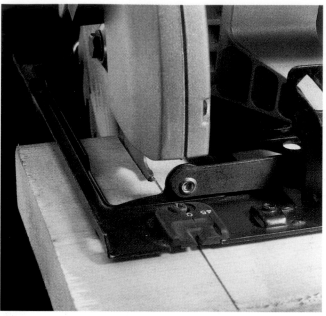

1 Secure the workpiece with clamps and position the baseplate with the blade approximately 1" from the edge. Align the guide mark with the cutting line. NOTE: The saw will remove a small amount of material on each side of the blade. If your project requires exact cuts, make your first cut in the waste-area. You can make a second pass with the saw, as necessary, to remove more material.

2 While holding the saw with two hands, squeeze the trigger and guide the blade into the work-piece, following the cutting line with the guide mark and applying steady pressure as you push the saw forward. The guide mark on every saw is different. If you will be cutting material with someone else's saw, make a few practice cuts to familiarize yourself with the new saw.

How to Make Plunge Cuts

1 Support the workpiece by clamping it down on sawhorses. Clamp a 2 × 4 on the edge as a guide. Retract the blade guard and position the saw so the front edge of the foot, not the blade, is against the workpiece,

2 Hold the saw with two hands as you make the cut. Start the saw, and slowly lower the blade into the workpiece, keeping the baseplate against the 2 × 4.

54

How to Make Rip Cuts

Attach a commercial straightedge guide to the baseplate of your circular saw. For greater stability, attach a straight 8" strip of hardwood to the base of the guide, using panhead screws. For even more reliable edges, build your own straightedge guide (page 57).

Cut timbers that are thicker than the maximum depth of your circular saw by setting the blade depth to slightly more than half the timber thickness and making matching cuts from opposite sides. Take care to keep the cuts straight.

Tips for Making Rip Cuts

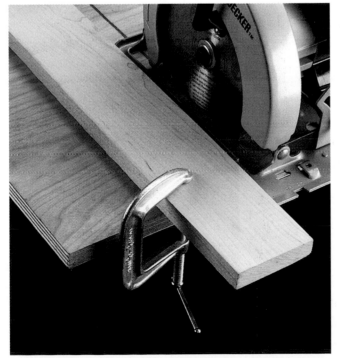

Clamp a straightedge to your workpiece for straight, long cuts. Keep the baseplate tight against the straightedge and move the saw smoothly through the material.

Drive a wood shim into the kerf after you have started the cutting workpiece to keep your saw from binding. For longer cuts, stop the saw and position the shim about 12" behind the baseplate.

How to Make Bevel Cuts

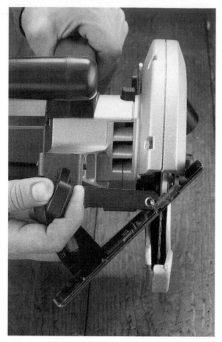

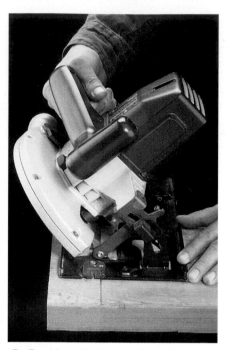

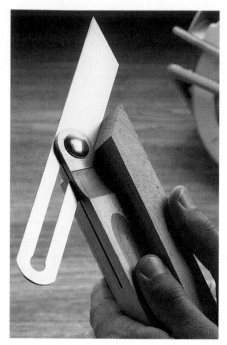

1 Loosen the bevel adjustment knob and slide the knob to the required setting. NOTE: Some models have a setscrew for common angles such as 90° (no bevel) and 45°. Tighten the knob.

2 Position the baseplate of your saw on the workpiece. As you cut, sight down the blade to ensure it remains aligned with the cutting line on the waste side of the workpiece.

TIP: Copy existing angles with a T-bevel. Transpose the cutting line to your workpiece and adjust the angle of your circular saw to cut on the line.

How to Cut Dadoes

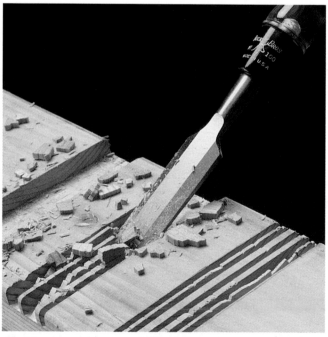

1 To cut dadoes with a circular saw, set the blade depth to ⅓ the desired depth of the dado, and mark the outside edges where you want the dado. Secure the workpiece with a clamp and cut the outside lines using a straightedge. Make several parallel passes between the outside cuts, every ¼".

2 Clean out the material between the cuts with a wood chisel. To avoid gouging the workpiece apply hand pressure or tap the chisel with the bevel side up with a mallet. For more information on chisels see page 85.

Building a Straightedge Guide

Making straight and accurate rip cuts or cutting long sheets of plywood or paneling is a challenge. Even the best carpenter can't always keep the blade on the cutline, especially over a longer span. A straightedge guide or jig solves the problem. As long as you keep the saw's baseplate flush with the edge of the cleat as you make the cut, you're assured of a straight cut on your workpiece.

The guide's cleated edge provides a reliable anchor for the baseplate of the circular saw as the blade passes through the material. For accurate cutting, the cleat must have a perfectly straight edge.

A straightedge guide overcomes the difficulty of making square rip cuts and other square cuts on long workpieces. The guide is built square, ensuring that any cuts made with it will be square as well.

Everything You Need:

Tools: C-clamps, pencil, circular saw.

Materials: ¼" finish plywood base (10 × 96"), ¾" plywood cleat (2 × 96"), carpenter's glue.

How to Build a Straightedge Guide

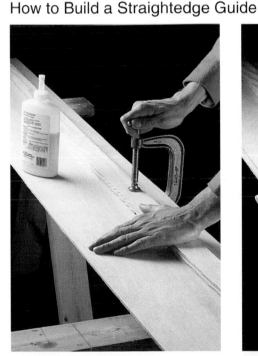

1 Apply carpenter's glue to the bottom of the ¾" plywood cleat, then position the cleat on the ¼" plywood base, 2" from one edge. Clamp the pieces together until the glue dries.

2 Position the circular saw with its foot tight against the ¾" plywood cleat. Cut away the excess portion of the plywood base with a single pass of the saw to create a square edge.

3 To use the guide, position it on top of the workpiece, so the guide's square edge is flush with the cutting line on the workpiece. Clamp the guide in place with C-clamps.

Table Saws

For any serious do-it-yourself carpenter, a table saw is one of the most useful of all tools. Table saws make miter, rip, cross, and bevel cuts. They can also produce dadoes, dovetails, rabbets, and tenon joints for countless carpentry projects.

Several hand-made accessories can improve your results and minimize the risk of injury when using a table saw. Pushsticks and straddlesticks (page 60) make it easier to push stock through the blade's path while keeping your hands at a safe distance. Fingerboards (page 61) help keep your stock flat and straight during cutting.

If you want to add a table saw to your workshop but don't have the money or enough space for a full-size model, consider buying a portable table saw. Although they are smaller, these saws have most of the capabilities of a full-size table saw.

For general carpentry work, use a combination blade. If you plan to do a lot of ripping or cross-cutting and want the most accurate cuts possible, switch to a blade that's designed exclusively for that purpose.

NOTE: Using a table saw requires extra caution because of the exposed position of the blade. Remember that your hands and fingers are vulnerable, even with a safety guard in place. Read the owner's manual for specific instructions on how to operate your saw and always wear eye and ear protection when using a table saw.

Tips for Using a Table Saw

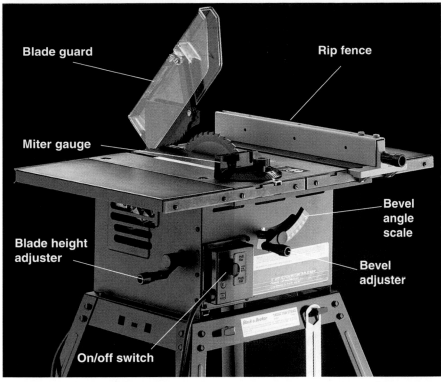

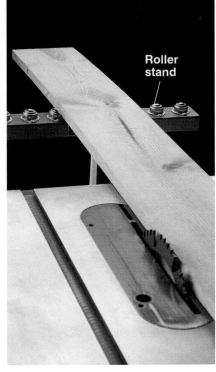

Learn what the parts and accessories of a table saw do before operating one. This portable table saw includes: blade guard; rip fence, for aligning the cutting line on the workpiece with the blade; blade height adjuster and bevel angle scale; on/off switch; bevel adjuster; and miter gauge, for setting miter angles.

Use a roller stand to hold long pieces of stock at the proper height when cutting them on a table saw. A roller stand allows you to slide the material into the cutting blade without letting the workpiece fall to the floor.

How to Set Up a Table Saw

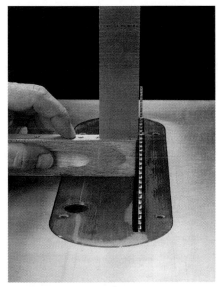

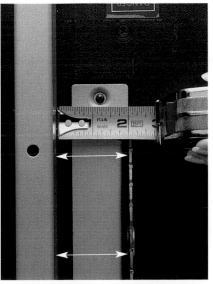

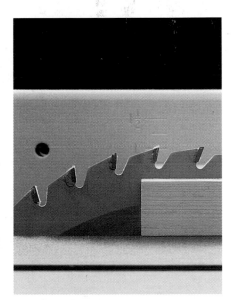

Check the vertical alignment of a table saw blade by adjusting the bevel to 0° and holding a try square against it. The blade and square must be flush. If not, adjust the blade according to the instructions in the owner's manual.

Check the horizontal blade alignment by measuring the distance between the blade and the rip fence at both ends of the blade. If the blade is not parallel to the fence, it may cause binding or kickback. Adjust the saw according to the owner's manual.

Set the blade so it extends no more than ½" above the surface of the workpiece. This minimizes strain on the motor and produces better cutting results.

59

How to Change a Table Saw Blade

  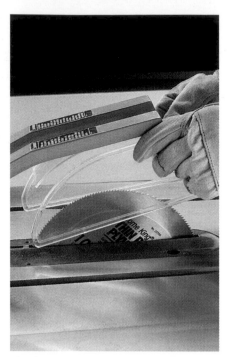

1 Unplug the table saw. Remove the blade guard and the table insert, then turn the blade height adjustment knob clockwise to raise the blade to its maximum height.

2 Wearing gloves, hold the blade stationary with a piece of scrap wood. Loosen and remove the arbor nut by turning it clockwise. (An arbor wrench is supplied with most saws).

3 Carefully remove the old blade, and install the new blade so the teeth curve toward the front of the saw. Don't overtighten the arbor nut. Replace the table insert and the blade guard.

Using Pushsticks & Straddlesticks

Use a pushstick to guide your workpiece without placing your fingers near the blade. The pushstick shown has notches to accommodate different thicknesses of wood.

Use a straddlestick for added safety when cutting boards. A straddlestick is a pushstick that fits over the top of the rip fence. Straddlesticks and pushsticks can be made with a piece of plywood, or purchased at woodworking stores or home centers.

How to Make a Fingerboard

1 Fingerboards help guide a workpiece through the blade of a table saw safely and precisely. Select a piece of straight 1 × 4 that is free of knots and cracks; mark a stop line 8" from the end of the board. Mark a series of parallel lines ¼" apart from the end of the board to the stop line.

2 Mark the end of the board at a 20° angle and clamp the workpiece firmly with the end line overhanging the work surface. Cut off the end of the board using a jig saw.

3 Make a series of parallel cuts from the end of the board to the stop line, carefully following the cutting lines. Let the blade come to a complete stop before removing it.

TIP: To use a fingerboard, set the workpiece 4" in front of the saw blade. Clamp the fingerboard slightly over the edges of the workpiece so they apply light pressure, forcing the workpiece against the rip fence and the table. The "fingers" should flex slightly as the workpiece travels forward.

Power Miter Saws

Power miter saws are versatile, portable tools that are used to cut angles in trim, framing lumber, and other narrow stock.

The blade assembly of a power miter saw swivels up to 45° in either direction, allowing it to make straight, mitered, and beveled cuts. However, when the assembly is turned to a 45° angle, the cutting depth is considerably shortened.

If you are considering buying or renting a power miter saw for a specific project, such as building a deck, don't assume that every saw will have the capacity to cut wider boards at a 45° angle. Ask the sales person about the maximum cutting capacity for each saw at a 45° angle and make sure the saw you choose can make clean cuts through the stock you use most frequently.

A compound miter saw (opposite page, top) has a second pivot point on the blade assembly that makes it possible to cut a bevel and miter angle at the same time. This option is useful when cutting cove moldings. See page 69 for more information about compound miter cuts.

The biggest limitation of a power miter saw is cutting extra-wide stock. A sliding compound miter saw (opposite page, bottom) eliminates this limitation. The entire blade assembly is mounted on a sliding carriage, giving the saw a much greater cutting capacity than a standard or compound miter saw. For tips on cutting extra-wide boards without a sliding compound miter saw, see page 67.

Variations of Power Miter Saws

Dust collection bag

Bevel clamp

Trigger

Blade guard

Guide fence

Bevel scale

Sliding Fence

Kerf board

Miter angle release lever

Saw bed

Miter clamp

Miter scale

Extension arm

Sliding carriage

Photo courtesy of Delta Machinery

A compound miter saw cuts bevels and miters at the same time. The miter and bevel scales make it easy to set the saw quickly for precise angles. Before cutting, make sure the material is flush with the guide fence. Otherwise, the angle you cut will be incorrect. Extension arms provide a safe way to hold longer materials in place. Some models also offer stock clamps that secure workpieces to the saw table. Always remove debris or small wood scraps that may be blocking the kerf board before beginning any cut and remember to empty the dust collection bag regularly.

A sliding compound miter saw has all the components of a regular compound miter saw, with the addition of a sliding blade assembly that makes it possible to cut much wider stock.

Types of Blades & Their Applications

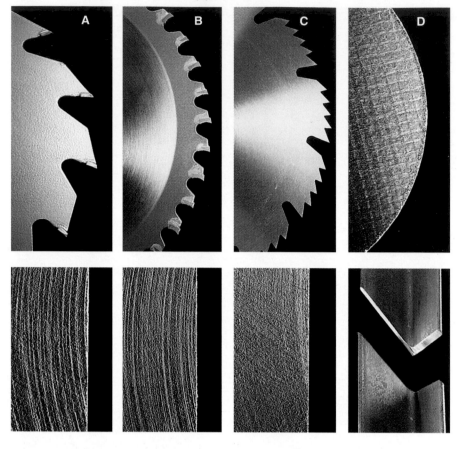

The quality of the cut produced by a power miter saw depends on the blade you use and the speed at which the blade is forced through the workpiece. Let the motor reach full speed before cutting, then lower the blade assembly slowly for the best results.

A 16-tooth carbide-tipped blade (A) cuts quickly and is good for rough-cutting framing lumber.
A 60-tooth carbide-tipped blade (B) makes smooth cuts in both softwoods and hardwoods. It is a good all-purpose blade for general carpentry work.
A precision-ground crosscut and miter blade (C) makes smooth, splinter-free cuts. It is an ideal blade for finish carpentry projects.
An abrasive friction blade (D) makes fast cuts on thin steel, galvanized metals, and iron pipes.

How to Change the Blade on a Power Miter Saw

1 Unplug the saw and inspect the blade: check for dull or damaged teeth.

2 If the blade is dull or is the wrong type for the material you want to cut, depress the arbor lock button and turn the arbor nut on the blade clockwise to remove it.

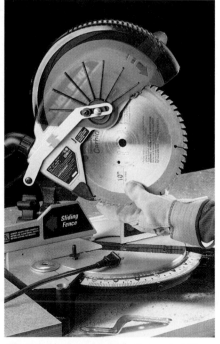

3 When the nut is free, carefully remove the blade and slide the new blade into position. Tighten the arbor nut until snug. Do not overtighten the nut.

Tips For Setting Up a Power Miter Saw

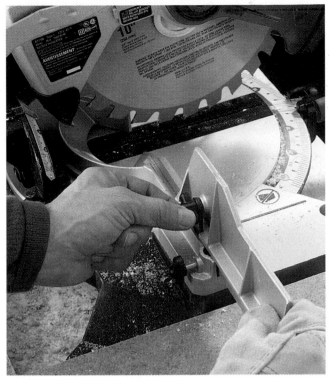

Anchor the saw to a stationary workbench, using C-clamps. To support long moldings or other stock, build a pair of blocks the height of the saw table, using 1× lumber. Align the blocks with the saw fence and clamp them to the workbench.

Position the adjustable fence to support the work piece, then tighten the fence clamp.

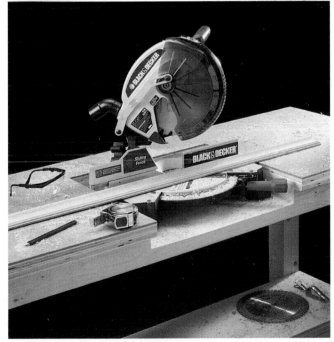

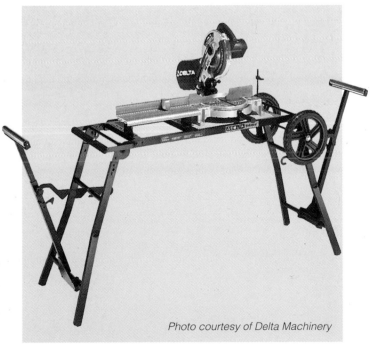

Photo courtesy of Delta Machinery

OPTION: Consider building a cutting table with a recessed area the same depth as the saw bed. The table will support longer stock, eliminating the need for support arms.

OPTION: Rent or buy a portable power miter saw table for extensive cutting of long stock. Or, use a portable workbench and a roller-type support stand (page 59) to support your saw and workpieces.

Tips for Cutting with a Power Miter Saw

To avoid cutting off too much, start out by making a cut about ¼" to the waste side of the cutting line, then "nibble" at the workpiece with one or more additional cuts until you have cut up to the cutting line. Wait until the blade stops before raising the arm on every cut.

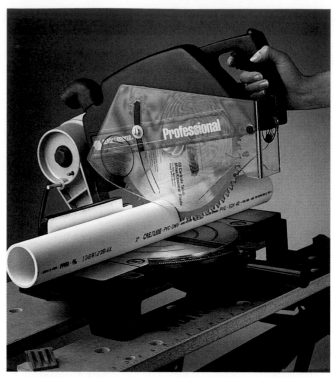

Cut narrow stock, such as PVC pipe, cove moldings, and 2 × 4s on a power miter saw. Check that the saw is anchored to the table properly and hold the workpiece steady while cutting. A standard power miter saw with a 10" blade makes a cut 5¼" long with the blade set at 90°.

Stop block

To cut multiple pieces of stock to the same length, clamp a stop block to your support table at the desired distance from the blade. After cutting the first piece, position each additional length against the stop block and the fence to cut pieces of equal length.

Set the saw assembly in the down position when storing or moving it, or when you won't be using it for a long period of time.

How to Cut Wide Boards

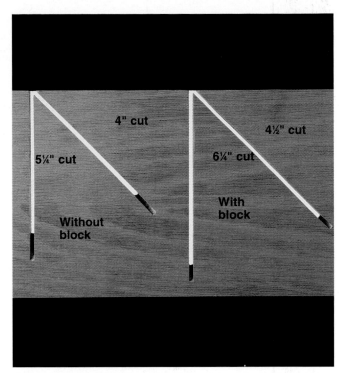

Cut through wider boards by raising the height of the workpiece. Place a scrap 2 × 6 under the workpiece. Elevating the workpiece allows a wider area of the blade to contact the wood. The maximum cutting width when using the block is 6¼" with the blade set at 90° and 4½" at 45°.

How to Cut Extra-wide Boards

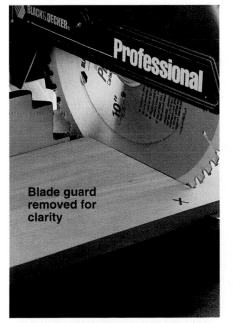

1 Make a full downward cut. Release the trigger and let the blade come to a full stop, then raise the saw arm.

2 Turn the workpiece over and carefully align the first cut with the saw blade. Make a second downward cut to finish the job.

A sliding compound miter saw simplifies cutting wide stock. Loosen the carriage clamp and pull out the carriage, then turn on the saw, lower the blade, and push the carriage in to cut the stock.

Photo courtesy of Delta Machinery

67

How to Cut Case Moldings

1 Mark cutting lines on each piece of molding or other material you plan to cut. On window and door casings, mark a line across the front face of the piece as a reference for the cutting direction. Remember: Only the beginning of the cutting line should actually be used to line up the saw blade. The freehand line across the face of the molding is a directional reference only.

2 Lay door and window casing stock flat on the saw table and set the blade to match the cutting line. If you have a compound saw, set the bevel adjustment to 0°. Anchor the casing with your hand at a safe distance from the blade.

How to Cut Baseboards

Mark a cutting line along the top edge of baseboards to indicate the starting point and direction for each cut. Baseboards and moldings that run the length of a wall are cut by standing the stock against the saw fence.

How to Make Scarf Joints

Join molding pieces for longer spans by mitering the ends at 45° angles. The mitered joint (scarf) cannot open up and show a crack if the wood shrinks.

How to Miter Cove Moldings on a Compound Miter Saw

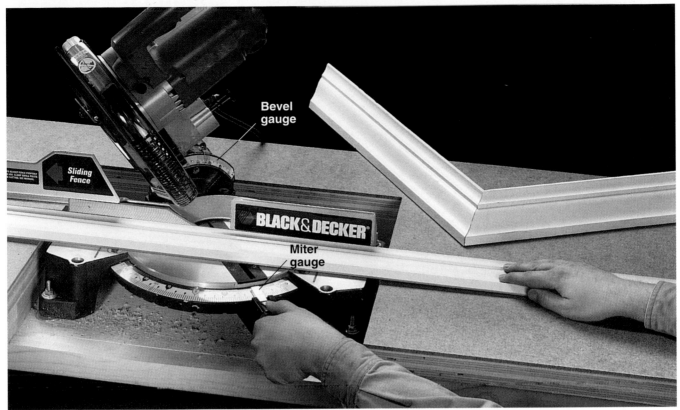

Lay the molding flat on the saw table and set the miter and bevel angles. For cove moldings, the standard settings are 33° (miter) and 31.62° (bevel). On many saws, these settings are highlighted for easy identification. If the walls are not perpendicular, you will need to experiment to find the correct settings.

How to Miter Cove Molding With a Standard Miter Saw

1 On a non-compound miter saw, cove moldings must be positioned at an angle for cutting. Position the molding upside-down so the flats on the back of the molding are flush with the saw table and fence.

2 Set the blade at 45° and cut the molding. To cut the molding for an adjoining wall, swivel the miter saw to the opposite 45° setting and make a cut on the second piece, so that it will fit with the first piece to form a corner.

Routers

Cut decorative shapes, make grooves, and trim laminates with a router. A router is a high-speed power tool that uses bits to perform a wide variety of cutting and shaping tasks. The two main types of routers available are the plunge router and the standard router.

A standard router is good for edging work and is easier to use when mounted on a router table (page 73).

A plunge router has a spring-loaded base that allows you to position the bit above the work-piece and "plunge" into a exact spot. Plunge routers are particularly well suited to making mortise and dado cuts.

Routers rotate at speeds up to 30,000 revolutions per minute, and range from ½ to 3 horse-power.

For general purpose routing, choose a router that is rated at 1½ horsepower or more. Other features to look for include a conveniently placed ON/OFF switch, a clear plastic chip guard, and a built-in work light.

Router bits spin in a clockwise direction, causing the tool to pull to the left. For best results, feed the router from left to right so that the cutting edge of the bit feeds into the wood.

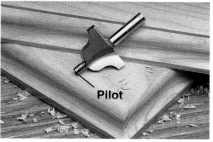

Decorative edging is usually made with a bit that has a pilot at the tip. The round pilot rides against the edge of the workpiece to guide the cut.

Common Router Bits

A corner rounding bit makes simple finish edges on furniture and wood moldings.

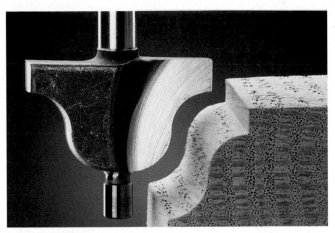

An ogee bit cuts traditional, decorative shapes in wood. Ogee bits are often used to create wood moldings and to shape the edges of furniture components.

A rabbet bit makes step-cut edges. Rabbeted edges are often used for woodworking joints and for picture frame moldings.

Ball-bearing pilot

A laminate trimmer bit cuts a finished edge on plastic laminate installation. A ball-bearing pilot prevents the bit from scorching the face of the laminate.

A straight bit cuts a square, flat-bottomed groove. Use it to make woodworking joints or for freehand routing.

A dovetail bit cuts wedge-shaped grooves used to make interlocking joints for furniture construction and cabinetwork.

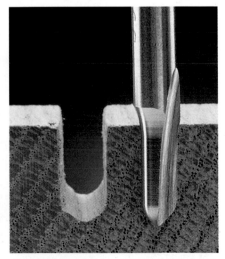

A veining bit is a round-bottomed cutter used for free-hand decorative carving and lettering.

How to Set Up a Plunge Router

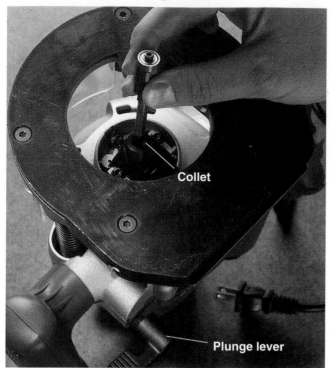

1 Unplug the router and insert the desired bit into the collet until it reaches the bottom of the shaft. Then, slide the bit out approximately ⅛" so the collet does not become damaged as the bit expands.

2 Depress the shaft lock button, then tighten the collet with a wrench. If your model doesn't have a shaft lock, use a second wrench to hold the shaft while you turn the collet.

3 Plunge the router down until the tip of the bit touches the workpiece. Lock the plunge lever. With the control bar resting on the router base, slide the depth indicator to "0" on the bit depth scale. Raise the control bar until the indicator is aligned with the desired depth on the scale, and lock the control bar in place by tightening the plunge lever.

4 Use a piece of scrap wood to test the plunge depth before cutting your workpiece. Measure the depth of the desired cut on the scrap wood and mark the cutout area. Adjust the plunge depth as needed.

Tips for Using a Router

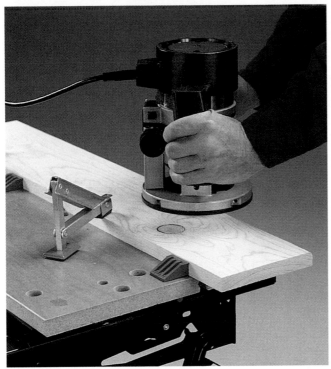

To cut a decorative edge, line up the bit of the router 1" away from the edge of the workpiece. Start the motor and push the bit through the material with even pressure. Edging bits have a pilot tip, so they will cut at an even depth without using a straightedge.

To make straight cuts easier, mark a cutting line on the workpiece and clamp down a straightedge guide. Keep the base of the router firmly against the straightedge when passing through the workpiece.

Keep the router base flat when cutting a decorative edge, by clamping a piece of scrap lumber the same thickness as the workpiece to the surface of the workbench.

Use a router table to increase your control of the workpiece and decrease set up time. You can build your own router table or buy a factory model like the one shown.

Hammers

Hammer loop

Finish hammer

Mallet

Sledgehammer

Framing hammer

Selecting the right hammer for a task depends mainly on finding one that feels comfortable and manageable, but that also has enough weight to get the job done. For general carpentry, choose a hammer with a smooth finish, a high-carbon steel head, and a quality handle made of hickory, fiberglass, or solid steel. Less expensive steel handles often have hollow cores that are not as efficient at transmitting force to the head.

For light-duty nailing, a 16-ounce, curved-claw finish hammer is a popular choice. It is designed for driving, setting, and pulling nails.

A mallet with a non-marking rubber or plastic head is the best tool for driving chisels without damaging the tools. Mallets are also useful for making slight adjustments to a workpiece without marring the surface of the wood.

A sledgehammer or maul is effective for demolishing old construction or adjusting the position of framing members.

Straight-claw framing hammers—usually with a 20-ounce or heavier head (opposite page)—are used for framing walls and other heavy-duty tasks. The extra weight helps drive large nails with fewer swings. Most framing hammers are too heavy for finish carpentry, where control is of primary importance.

Framing hammers vary in size, length, and handle material. Handle types include fiberglass, solid steel, hollow core, and wood. Hammers typically range in length from 14" to 18". Most framing hammers have a head weighing at least 20 ounces, but lighter and heavier models are available. Some heads feature a waffle pattern across the face that increases the hammer's hold on the nail for more efficiency and accuracy. Framing hammers have straight claws for prying boards.

Use a sledgehammer to demolish wall framing and to drive spikes and stakes. Sledgehammers vary in weight from 2 to 20 pounds, and in length from 10 to 36".

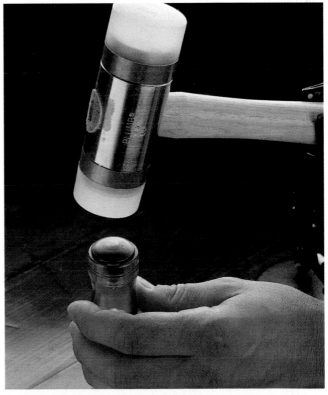

A mallet with a rubber or plastic head drives woodworking chisels. A soft mallet face will not damage fine woodworking tools.

Shopping for a Hammer

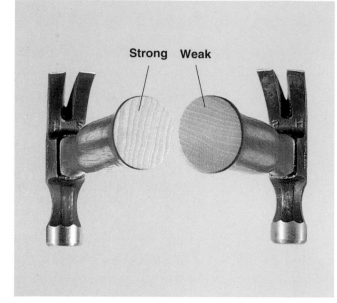

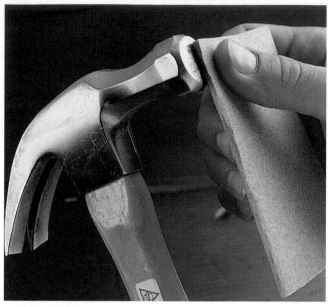

The strongest wooden tool handles have wood grain that runs parallel to the tool head (left). Handles with the grain running perpendicular to the tool head (right) are more likely to break. Check the end grain before buying a new tool or tool handle. Tool handles that are cracked or loose should be replaced. Wood handles absorb more shock than fiberglass or metal.

A new hammer may have a very smooth face that tends to slip off the heads of nails. Rough up the face with sandpaper to increase friction between the hammer and the nail. For finish hammering, you may want to stick with a smooth-face hammer. NOTE: You can also use fine sandpaper to remove wood resins and nail coatings that build up on the face of your hammers.

How to Pull Nails with a Hammer

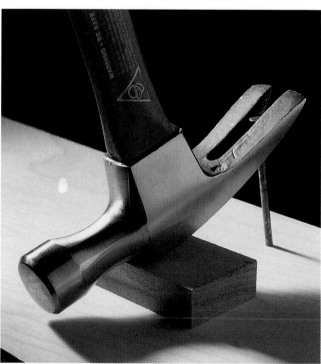

Remove stubborn nails by placing a block of wood under the hammer head for added leverage. To avoid damage to the workpiece use a block big enough to evenly distribute pressure from the hammer head.

Pull large nails by wedging the shank of the nail tightly in the claws and levering the hammer handle sideways.

How to Drive Nails with a Hammer

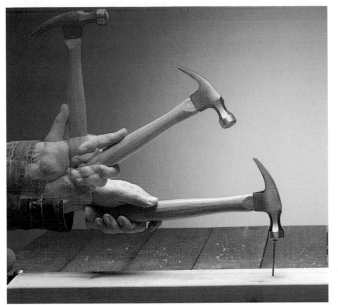

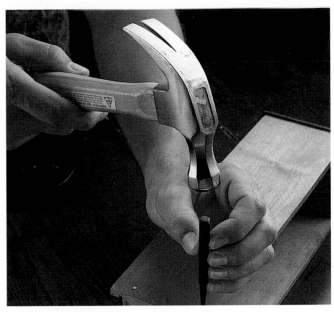

Hold the hammer with a relaxed grip: Take advantage of the hammer's momentum and weight by releasing your wrist at the bottom of the swing as if you were throwing the head of the hammer onto the nail. Hit the nail squarely on the head, repeating the motion until the nail head is flush with the work surface.

To set a finish nail below the surface, position the tip of a nail set on the nail head and strike the other end with a hammer.

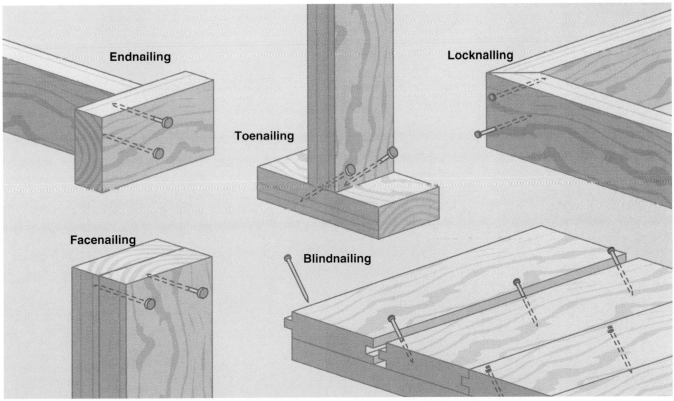

Endnailing

Toenailing

Locknailing

Facenailing

Blindnailing

Use the proper nailing technique for the task. Endnailing is used to attach perpendicular boards when moderate strength is required. Toenail at a 45° angle for extra strength when joining perpendicular framing members. Facenail to create strong headers for door

and window openings. Blindnail tongue-and-groove boards to conceal nails, eliminating the need to set nails and cover them with putty before painting or staining. Locknail outside miter joints in trim projects to prevent gaps from developing as the trim pieces dry.

Screwdrivers

Every carpenter should own several Phillips and slotted screwdrivers. Even though the drill-mounted screw bit has become the standard for large projects, screwdrivers are still essential for a variety of carpentry tasks. Look for quality screwdrivers with hardened-steel blades and handles that are easy to grip. Other features to look for include insulated handles to protect against electrical shock and oxide-coated tips for a strong hold on screw heads. For working in tight spots, a screwdriver with a magnetic tip can also be helpful.

Cordless power screwdrivers save time and effort. For small projects, they are an inexpensive alternative to a cordless drill or screwgun. Most models include a removable battery pack and charger, so you can keep one battery in the charger at all times. Cordless power screwdrivers have a universal ¼" drive and come with a slotted bit and a #2 Phillips bit. Other bits, such as Torx and socket bits are also available.

NOTE: Always use the correct screwdriver for the job. Screwdrivers should fit the slot of the screw tightly so you can avoid stripping the head of the screw or damaging the workpiece.

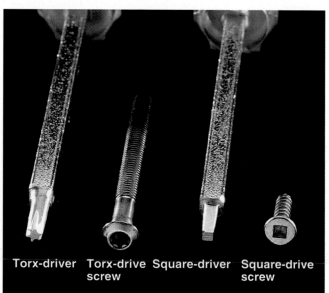

Torx-driver Torx-drive Square-driver Square-drive
screw screw

Other driving options include square-drive and Torx-drive screws. Square-drive screwdrivers are gaining popularity because square-drive screws are difficult to strip. Torx-drivers are used in electronics and automotive applications.

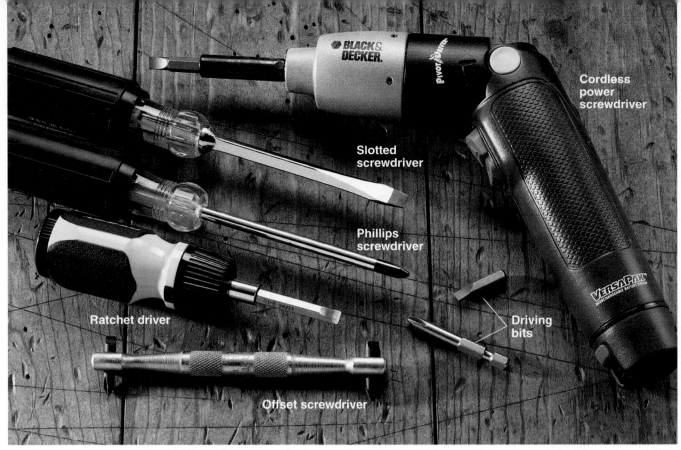

Common screwdrivers include: slotted screwdriver with insulated handle, Phillips screwdriver with insulated handle and oxide tip for better control, ratchet driver with interchangeable bits, offset screwdriver for driving in tight places, and cordless power screwdriver with battery pack and pivoting shaft.

Tips for Using Screwdrivers

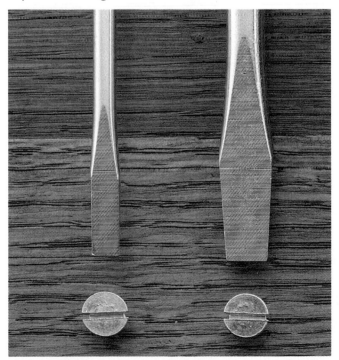

Use a screwdriver or screw bit that closely matches the screw head. A tip that's too big or too small will damage the screw and the driver, and make the screw hard to remove later.

Recondition a slotted screwdriver on a bench grinder if the tip becomes damaged. Dip the tip of the screwdriver in cold water periodically to keep it from getting too hot during grinding.

Drills & Bits

The power drill is one of the most popular and versatile power tools. Thanks to a host of improvements in its design, today's drills have many more functions than just drilling holes. Most of today's drills are variable-speed reversing (VSR) drills, making them convenient for driving and removing screws, nuts, and bolts, as well as for drilling, sanding, and stirring paint. The keyless chuck on most new drills makes it easy to swap bits or quickly convert a drill into a grinder, sander, or paint mixer. Newer models allow you to adjust the drill's clutch for drilling or for driving into various materials, so the clutch will automatically disengage before screw heads strip or sink too far into the material.

Drills are commonly available in ¼", ⅜", and ½" sizes. The size refers to the diameter of the bits and other accessories that the drill will accept. A ⅜" drill is standard for carpentry projects because it accepts a wide variety of bits and accessories

and runs at a higher speed than ½" models.

Cordless technology has made drills more portable than ever. But it's important to understand the strengths of corded and cordless designs before deciding which one you should own. Most cordless drills operate at slower speeds and with less torque than corded models. Yet, cordless models are convenient because they allow up to several hours of operation between charges and eliminate the need for extension cords. Top-of-the-line cordless drills generate about 1,200 rpm. Corded drills weigh significantly less because they don't require battery packs, and some operate at more than 2,000 rpm. For most jobs, a cordless drill's slower speed is not a problem, but as the battery wears down, drilling becomes difficult and more of a strain on the motor. Spare battery packs can offset this problem. If you own both types of drills, keep your corded model on hand as a backup.

Clutch adjust-
ment dial

Screw bit holder

Variable speed
switch

Trigger lock
and reversing
switch

Keyless
chuck

Voltage
rating

14.4V

Battery
pack

When shopping for a drill, remember that the most powerful tool is not necessarily the best one for the job. This is especially true of cordless drills, because higher voltage ratings require heavier batteries. A more powerful cordless model is useful for heavy-duty drilling, when extra power will allow you to drill holes in thick timbers or masonry more quickly and easily. For driving screws and for light-duty drilling, a medium-voltage cordless model or a corded drill is a better choice. For convenience and versatility, look for features such as a keyless chuck, adjustable clutch, and variable speed and reverse (VSR). Try out several drills so you can compare the feel of the tools under load.

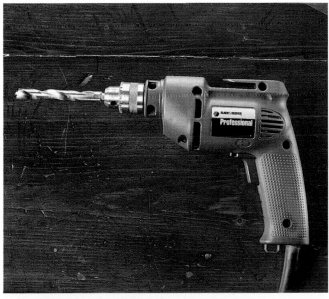

Corded drills are still widely available because they can generate lots of torque and operate at speeds of 2,000 rpm or more. If you want a fast, powerful, lightweight drill, a corded drill may be the right tool for you.

A hammer drill combines the rotary motion of a conventional drill with the impact action of a hammer. It can drill holes in masonry much faster than a regular drill. Hammer drills can also be set for impact motion or rotary motion only, making them useful for general drilling applications as well as carving wood.

81

Tips for Using Drill Bits

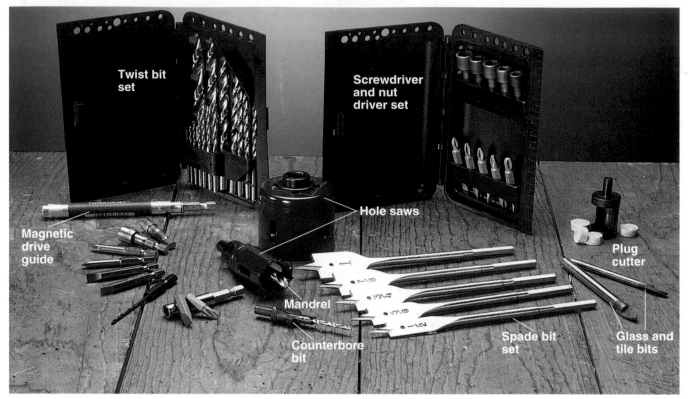

Drill bits include: a magnetic drive guide, twist bit set, screwdriver and nut driver set, plug cutter, glass and tile bits, spade bit set, hole saw bits, and adjustable counterbore bit. These accessories are often sold with a drill or are available separately.

Use a magnetic drive guide when you need to switch back and forth from drilling to screwing. The guide allows you to switch bits quickly and easily without loosening and tightening the chuck.

Prebore holes in hardwood. Start with a small bit, then drill again using a bit of the required size. The extra step will prevent binding and splintering as the larger bit cuts through the wood.

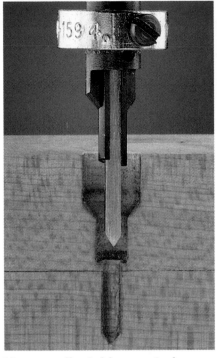

Use an adjustable counterbore bit to pilot, countersink, and counterbore holes with one action. Loosen the setscrew to match the bit to the size and shape of the screw.

Drill holes for door knobs and cylinders with a hole saw (top) and a spade bit (inset). To prevent the door from splintering, drill until the hole saw pilot (*mandrel*) just comes through the other side of the door. Complete the hole from the opposite side. Use a spade bit to drill the latch-bolt hole perpendicular to the door.

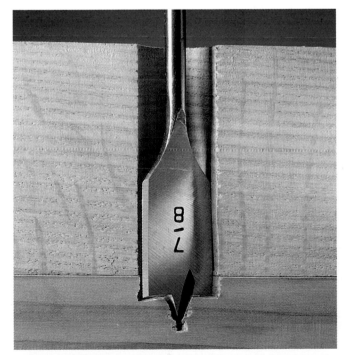

Use a backerboard when drilling holes in hardwood and finish plywood, or any time you want to prevent blemishes. A backerboard placed on the bottom of the workpiece prevents splintering as the bit breaks through.

Remove a broken screw by drilling a pilot hole in the top of the screw and removing it with a properly sized extracting bit. Extracting bits can be used in a drill when it is set on reverse or with a manual extracting tool.

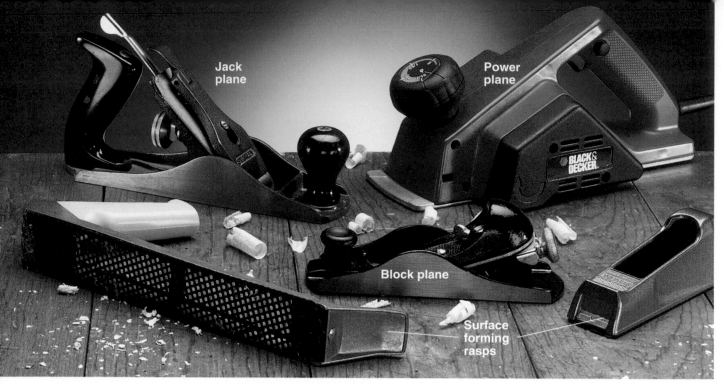

Common carpentry planes include: a jack plane, for trimming framing lumber, doors, and other large workpieces; a power planer, for removing lots of material quickly; a block plane, for shaving material from trim and other narrow workpieces; and surface forming rasps, for trimming flat or curved surfaces.

Planes

Planes are designed for removing material from lumber when a saw would cut off too much material and sanding would remove too little. A hand plane consists of a razor-sharp cutting blade, or *iron*, set in a steel or wood base. Adjusting the blade requires some trial and error. After making an adjustment, test the plane on a scrap piece before using it on your workpiece.

The blade on a surface forming rasp can't be adjusted, but interchangeable blades are available for fine and rough work. Surface forming rasp blades have a series of holes stamped in the metal, so shavings seldom become clogged in the tool's blade.

If you plan on planing many large workpieces, consider purchasing a power planer. A power planer does the job more quickly than a hand plane, and with equally fine results.

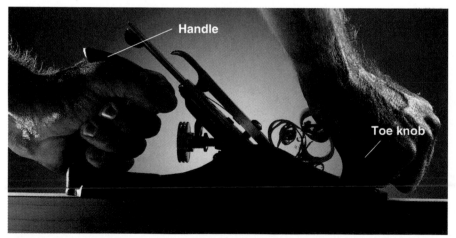

Clamp your workpiece into a vise. Operate the plane so the wood grain runs "uphill" ahead of the plane. Grip the toe knob and handle firmly, and plane with long, smooth strokes. To prevent overplaning at the beginning and end of the board, called *dipping*, press down on the toe knob at the beginning of the stroke, and bear down on the heel at the end of the stroke.

Use a block plane for common jobs, like trimming end grain, planing the edges of particle board and plywood, and trimming laminates.

Chisels

A wood chisel consists of a sharp steel blade beveled on at least one side and set in a wood or plastic handle. It cuts with light hand pressure, or when the end of the handle is tapped with a mallet. A wood chisel is often used to cut hinge and lock mortises.

When creating deep cuts, make several shallow cuts instead of one deep cut. Forcing a chisel to make deep cuts only dulls the tool, and can damage the workpiece.

Sharpen the blades of your chisels often, using a sharpening stone. Chisels are easier and safer to use and produce better results when they are sharp.

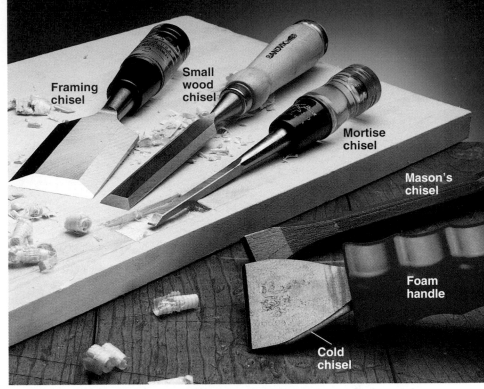

Types of chisels include (from left to right): a framing chisel, used for rough trimming of lumber; a small wood chisel, for light-duty wood carving; a mortise chisel, for framing hinge and lock mortises; a mason's chisel, for cutting stone and masonry; and a cold chisel, which is made of solid steel and is used for cutting through metal.

How to Chisel a Mortise

1 Cut the outline of the mortise. Hold the chisel bevel-side-in and tap the butt end lightly with a mallet until the cut has reached the proper depth.

2 Make a series of parallel depth cuts ¼" apart across the mortise, with the chisel held at a 45° angle. Drive the chisel with light mallet blows to the handle.

3 Pry out waste chips by holding the chisel at a low angle with the beveled side toward the work surface. Drive the chisel using light hand pressure.

Use a sander to remove unwanted material and create a smooth finish. This random-orbital sander is used in general applications that require medium to heavy sanding. The orbital motion combines a circular pattern with side-to-side motion. Unlike disc sanders, random orbit sanders leave no circular markings, and there's no need to follow the grain of the wood. Sanding discs are available with hook-and-loop fasteners or pressure sensitive adhesive. Sponge applicators and accessories are available for buffing and applying paste waxes.

Sanders

Power sanding tools shape and smooth wood and other building materials in preparation for painting and finishing. Carpenters also use them for removing small amounts of material. Finish sanders (opposite page, top) are best for light to medium sanding and for achieving very smooth surfaces. Belt sanders (opposite page, bottom left) are suitable for most work involving rough, fast removal of material. For very small, intricate, or contoured areas, sand by hand with folded sandpaper or a sanding block, or use drill-mounted sanding accessories (opposite page, bottom right).

When sanding a rough workpiece that requires a fine finish, begin sanding with a lower grit sandpaper. Slowly move up to a higher grit to achieve the finish you want. Medium sanding jobs normally consist of three sanding steps; coarse, medium, and fine.

Sanding is painstaking work. Take your time and do it right the first time. If you attempt to cut corners when sanding a project, you will see it in the end result.

NOTE: Sanders create airborne particles of material. Consider buying a sander that has a dust collection bag, and always wear a dust mask and eye protection.

Finish sanders are designed for jobs that require medium- to light-duty sanding to achieve a fine finish. Types of finish sanders include: 3-in-1 sander for finish sanding, medium material removal, and detail work (A); traditional finish sander for finishing larger areas (B); detail sander for detail work (C); and palm sander for smaller-scale finish work and easy corner access (D). The detail sander is also ideal for polishing and scrubbing jobs when fitted with the appropriate accessories.

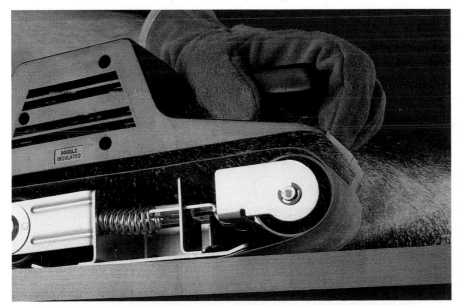

Remove material from large areas quickly with a belt sander. Disposable belts are available ranging from 36 (extra-coarse) to 100 (fine). Most belt sanding is done with the grain. However, sanding across the grain is an effective way to remove material from rough-hewn lumber.

Sanding accessories for power drills include (clockwise from top right): disc sander for fast sanding, sanding drums, and flap sanders to smooth contoured surfaces.

Make your own flap sander for smoothing wood contours, using a 6" length of ⅜" wooden dowel and a 1" strip of cloth-backed sandpaper, such as that used for sanding belts. To make the flap sander, cut a 1" deep slot down the center of the dowel. Hot-glue the strip of cloth-backed sandpaper into the slot. Facing the slotted end of the dowel, wrap the sandpaper strip around the dowel in a clockwise direction. Attach the flap sander to a power drill.

Clean sandpaper with a stiff-bristle brush to remove sawdust and grit that can clog the sandpaper and reduce its effectiveness.

Extend the life of a sanding belt by cleaning it with an old tennis shoe that has a natural rubber sole. Turn the sander on and press the sole of the shoe against the belt for a few seconds. Wood dust trapped between the grit on the sanding belt will cling to the shoe's rubber sole.

A sanding block is helpful for smoothing flat surfaces. For curved areas, wrap sandpaper around a folded piece of scrap carpeting or 2 × 4.

When sanding the edge of a board with a belt sander, clamp it between two pieces of scrap lumber to prevent the belt sander from wobbling and rounding off the edges.

How to Select the Proper Sandpaper for the Job

Use 60-grit coarse sandpaper on hardwood flooring and to grind down badly scratched surfaces. Move sander across the grain for quickest removal.

Use 100-grit coarse sandpaper for initial smoothing of wood. Move the sander in the direction of the wood grain to achieve the smoothest surface.

Use 150-grit fine sandpaper to put a smooth finish on wood surfaces. Use fine sandpaper to prepare wood surfaces for staining or to smooth wallboard joints.

Use 220-grit extra-fine sandpaper to smooth stained wood before varnishing or between coats of varnish.

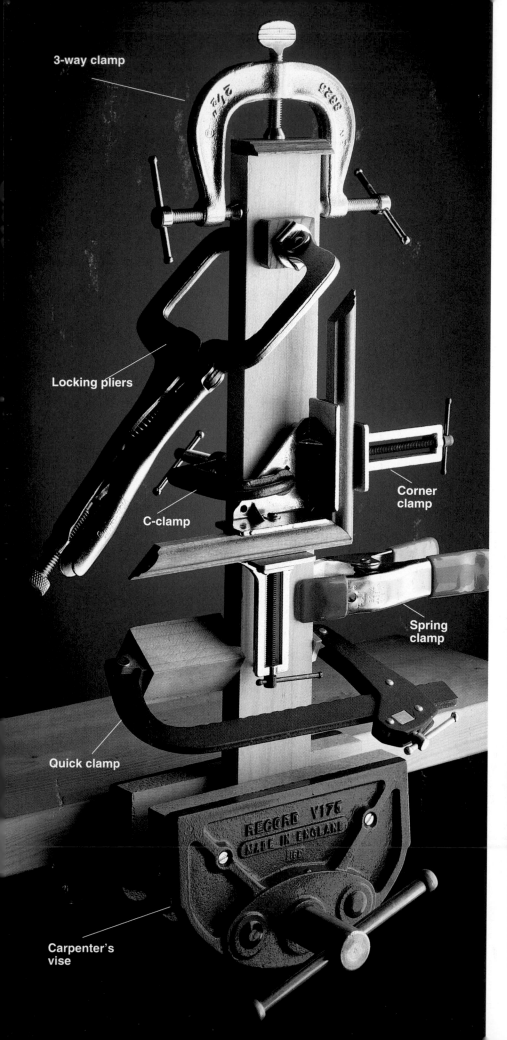

3-way clamp

Locking pliers

C-clamp

Corner clamp

Spring clamp

Quick clamp

Carpenter's vise

Clamps

Vises and clamps are used to hold workpieces in place during cutting or other tasks, and to hold pieces together while glue sets.

Your workbench should include a heavy-duty carpenter's vise. For specialty clamping jobs, a wide variety of clamps are available, including C-clamps, locking pliers, handscrews, web clamps, or ratchet-type clamps.

For clamping wide stock, use pipe clamps or bar clamps (opposite page). The jaws of pipe clamps are connected by a steel pipe. The distance between the jaws is limited only by the length of the pipe.

Protect workpiece surfaces by padding the jaws of clamps. Metal jaws can damage workpieces. Use a hot glue gun to attach protective pads made from felt, plastic caps from film canisters, or small scraps of wood.

Use handscrews to hold materials together at various angles while glue is drying. Handscrews are wooden clamps with two adjusting screws. The jaws won't damage wood surfaces.

Use C-clamps for clamping jobs from 1 to 6". To protect workpieces, place scrap wood blocks between the jaws of the clamp and the workpiece surface.

Clamp edge moldings to the side of shelves, tabletops or other flat surfaces with three-way clamps. A three-way clamp has three thumbscrews. Pad the jaws to protect the workpiece.

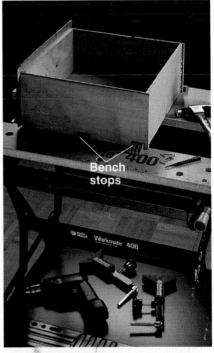

Use ratchet-type clamps to clamp a workpiece quickly and easily. Large ratchet-type clamps can span up to 4 ft., and can be tightened with one hand while supporting the workpiece with the other hand.

Hold large workpieces with pipe clamps or bar clamps. Bar clamps are sold with the bars. Pipe clamp jaws are available to fit ½" or ¾" diameter pipe of any length.

Clamp a workpiece on a portable workbench. Many models have a jointed, adjustable bench top that tightens like a clamp. Accessories, like bench stops, increase the bench's versatility.

Specialty Tools

When a carpentry project calls for a tool that you don't own, you need to decide whether it's worth the investment to buy it. Good quality tools can be expensive, making purchases hard to justify if you won't be using them often. For these types of tools, renting may be a better option.

A wide assortment of tools, including the ones featured on these pages, are available at rental centers at a reasonable cost. Renting gives you an opportunity to try a tool that you're considering buying, and gives you access to tools you would never consider buying, such as a jackhammer, that may make a specific project easier.

When you rent tools, always ask for the accompanying owner's manual and a demonstration of the tool's operation. You'll save time on the job and avoid unsafe or improper use.

Many rental tools are available by the hour rather than by the day. When renting by the hour, prepare your work area prior to picking up the tool to minimize rental costs.

A hammer drill combines impact action with rotary motion for quick boring in concrete and masonry. To minimize dust and to keep bits from overheating, lubricate the drilling site with water. A hammer drill can be used for conventional drilling when the motor is set for rotary action only (page 81).

A pneumatic nailer uses compressed air to drive nails or staples into wood, making it a very efficient carpentry tool. A nailer frees up one hand to hold stock in position while you control the tool with the other hand. Some models are designed for framing; others for finish work.

A reciprocating saw is convenient for making rough cuts in walls or floors, where a circular saw would be difficult to use, or for cutting metals like iron plumbing pipes or ½" lag bolts. Reciprocating saws save time during the demolition stage of a carpentry project. A cordless reciprocating saw offers easy portability and enough power to handle many small jobs.

A powder-actuated nailer quickly drives special hardened-steel nails through furring or studs into concrete. A trigger-activated nail gun (shown) is easiest to use, but a plunger type, activated when the tool is struck with a hammer, is also available. Ask the rental agent to demonstrate proper use of the tool. NOTE: these tools are loud and powerful. Wear hearing protection and eye protection any time you use them.

A screwgun can be used whenever you have a large number of screws to drive, but its main purpose is driving screws into wallboard without tearing the facing paper. The tool's highly sensitive clutch disengages once the screw has dimpled the wallboard's surface, helping you hang wallboard faster, cleaner, and more accurately. If you have a big wallboard project, a screwgun may be a worthwhile investment.

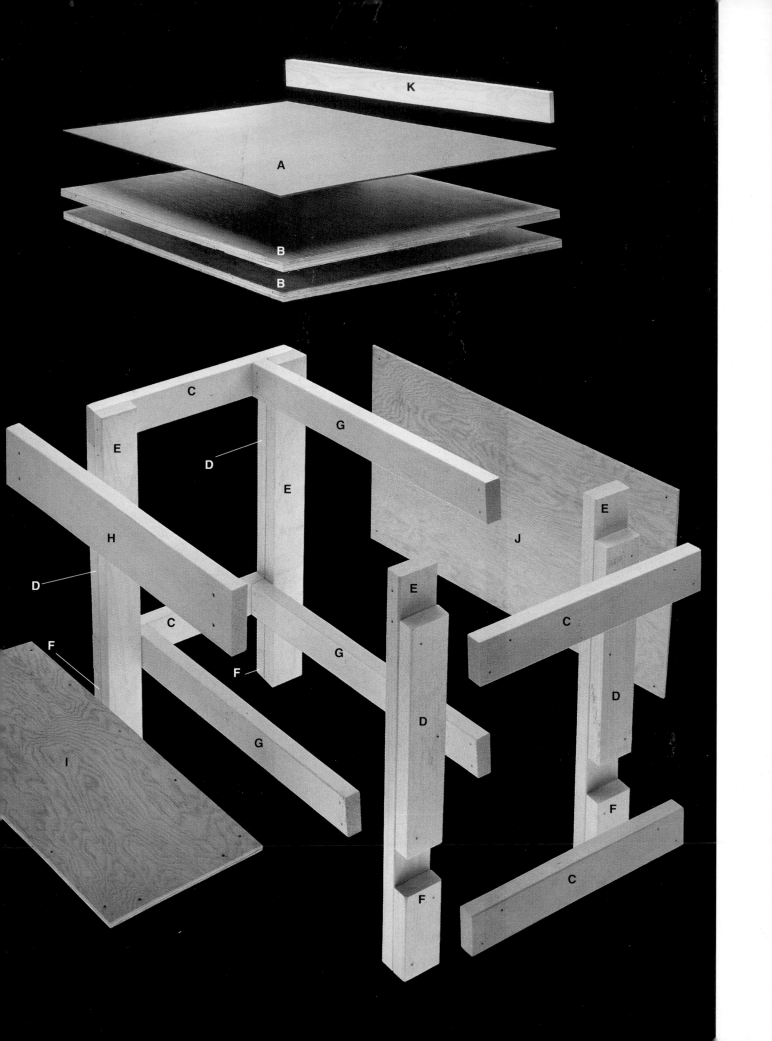

Building a Workbench

This workbench has heavy-duty legs to support big loads and a sturdy double-layer top to withstand pounding. Cover the top with a hardboard surface that can be removed when it becomes damaged. Build a shelf below the work surface for storing power tools. If desired, mount an all-purpose vise on top of the workbench.

Key	Pieces	Size and Description
A	1	⅛" hardboard top, 24 × 60"
B	2	¾" plywood top, 24 × 60"
C	4	2 × 4 crosspieces, 21"
D	4	2 × 4 legs, 19¾"
E	4	2 × 4 legs, 34½"
F	4	2 × 4 legs, 7¾"
G	3	2 × 4 braces, 54"
H	1	2 × 6 front (top) brace, 57"
I	1	½" plywood shelf, 14 × 57"
J	1	½" plywood shelf back, 19¼ × 57"
K	1	1 × 4 backstop, 60"

Everything You Need:

Tools: Circular saw; carpenter's square; drill and bits, including screwdriver bits; ratchet or adjustable wrench; hammer; nail set.

Materials: Wallboard screws (1½", 2½", and 3") lag screws (1½" and 3"), 4d finish nails.

Lumber List: six 8-ft. 2 × 4s, one 5-ft. 2 × 6, one 4 × 8-ft. sheet of ¾" plywood, one 4 × 8-ft. sheet of ½" plywood, one 4 × 8-ft. sheet of ⅛" hardboard.

How to Build a Workbench

1 Cut two pieces of C, D, E, and F for each end of the bench. Assemble them with 2½" wallboard screws.

2 Attach both 2 × 4 rear braces (G, G) inside the back legs of the assembled ends, using 2½" wallboard screws.

3 Attach the 2 × 4 front lower brace (G) inside the front legs of the assembled ends. Secure the bottom shelf (I) and workbench back (J) to the assembled 2 × 4 frame, using 2½" wallboard screws.

4 Drill pilot holes and join the 2 × 6 front upper brace (H) outside the front legs with 3" lag screws.

5 Center the bottom layer of ¾" plywood work surface (B) on top of the frame. Align the plywood with the back edge, draw a reference line for driving the nails, and fasten it in place with 4d nails.

6 Align the bottom and top layers of plywood work surface (B, B), and draw a reference line at least ½" closer to the edge to avoid the nails in the first layer. Drive 3" wallboard screws through both layers and into the bench frame.

7 Nail the hardboard work surface (A) to the plywood substrate (B, B) with 4d finish nails. Set the nails below the surface.

8 Position the vise at one end of the bench. On the bench top, mark holes for the vise base. Bore ¼" pilot holes into the bench top.

9 Attach the vise with 1½" lag screws. Attach the backstop (K) to the back of the bench top, with 2½" wallboard screws.

Sawhorses

Sawhorses provide a stable work surface that can support materials during marking and cutting. They can also form the base for temporary scaffolding to use while installing wallboard or ceiling panels. For scaffolding, place straight 2 × 10s or 2 × 12s across a pair of heavy-duty sawhorses (left). A wide top is best for supporting large loads. Small break-down sawhorses are a good choice if storage space is limited.

Cutting List	
Pcs	**Size and Description**
2	Vertical braces, 2 × 4, 15½"
2	Top rails, 2 × 4, 48"
1	Bottom brace, 2 × 4, 48"
2	Horizontal braces, 2 × 4, 11¼"
4	Legs, 2 × 4, 26"

Everything You Need

Tools: Circular saw, tape measure, screw gun or cordless screwdriver.

Materials: Four 8-ft. 2 × 4s, 2½" wallboard screws.

Easy-storing Sawhorse Options

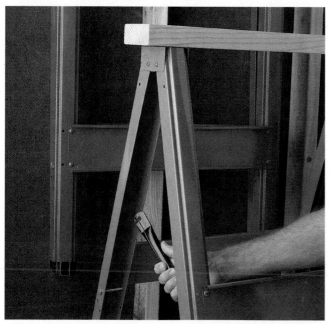

Fold metal sawhorses and hang them on the workshop wall when they are not in use.

Buy brackets made from fiberglass or metal, and cut a 48-inch top rail and four 26" legs from 2 × 4s. Disassemble sawhorses for storage.

How to Build a Heavy-duty Sawhorse

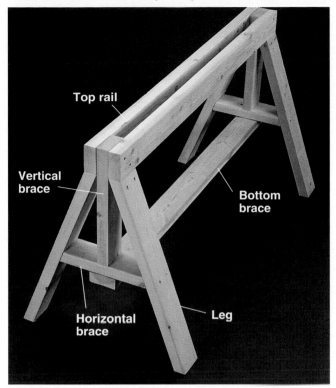

1 Measure and cut the vertical braces, top rails, and bottom brace to the lengths specified in the Cutting List (opposite page) using a tape measure and a circular saw.

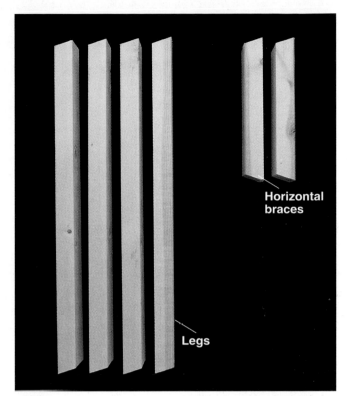

2 Set the circular saw to a 17° bevel angle. (Bevel cuts will match the angle shown above.) Cut the ends of the horizontal braces with opposing angles. Cut the ends of the legs with similar angles.

3 Attach the top rails to the vertical braces, as shown, using 2½" wallboard screws.

4 Attach the horizontal braces to the vertical braces, using 2½" wallboard screws. Attach a pair of legs to the horizontal braces and then to the brace at each end. Complete the sawhorse by attaching the bottom brace to the horizontal braces.

99

Basic Carpentry

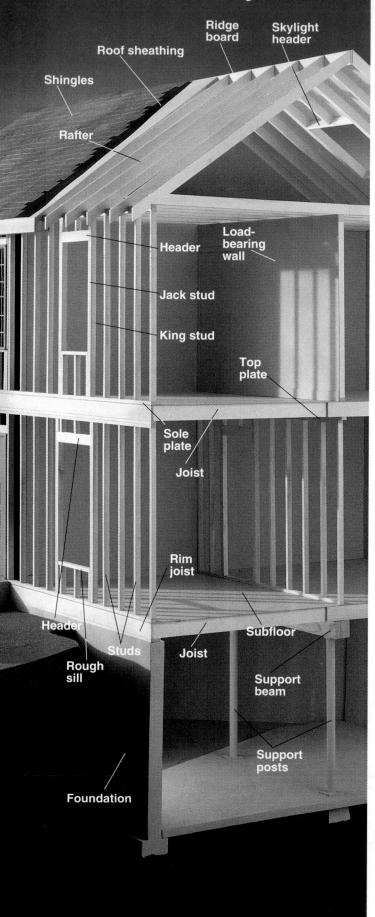

A House With Platform Framing

- Shingles
- Roof sheathing
- Ridge board
- Skylight header
- Rafter
- Header
- Load-bearing wall
- Jack stud
- King stud
- Top plate
- Sole plate
- Joist
- Rim joist
- Header
- Studs
- Subfloor
- Joist
- Rough sill
- Support beam
- Support posts
- Foundation

Anatomy of a House

Before you start a do-it-yourself carpentry project you should familiarize yourself with a few basic elements of home construction and remodeling. Take some time, before you begin, to get comfortable with the terminology of the models shown on the next few pages. The understanding you will gain in this section will make it easier to plan your project, buy the right materials, and clear up any confusion you might have about the internal design of your home.

If your project includes modifying exterior or load-bearing walls, you must determine if your house was built using platform- or balloon-style framing. The framing style of your home determines what kind of temporary supports you will need to install while the work is in progress. If you have trouble determining what type of framing was used in your home, refer to the original blueprints, if you have them, or consult a building contractor or licensed home inspector.

Anatomy of a House With Platform Framing

Platform framing (photos, left and above) is identified by the floor-level sole plates and ceiling-level top plates to which the wall studs are attached. Most houses built after 1930 use platform framing. If you do not have access to unfinished areas, you can remove the wall surface at the bottom of a wall to determine what kind of framing was used in your home.

Framing in a new door or window on an exterior wall normally requires installing a header. Make sure that the header you install meets the requirements of your local building code, and always install cripple studs where necessary.

Floors and ceilings consist of sheet materials, joists, and support beams. All floors used as living areas must have joists with at least 2×8 construction. For modification of smaller joists see page 106.

There are two types of walls: load-bearing and partition. Load-bearing walls require temporary supports during wall removal or framing of a door or window. Partition walls carry no structural load and do not require temporary supports. For more information on determining types of walls, see page 107.

Anatomy of a House With Balloon framing

Balloon framing (photos, right and above) is identified by wall studs that run uninterrupted from the roof to a sill plate on the foundation, without the sole plates and top plates found in platform-framed walls (page opposite). Balloon framing was used in houses built before 1930, and is still used in some new home styles, especially those with high vaulted ceilings.

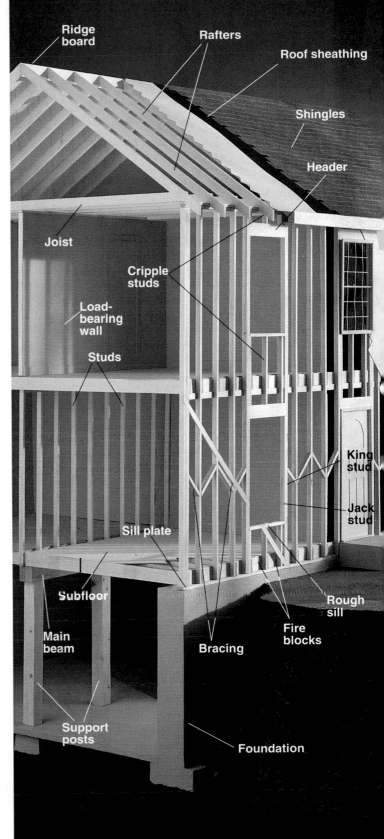

A House With Balloon Framing

Ridge board

Rafters

Roof sheathing

Shingles

Header

Joist

Cripple studs

Load-bearing wall

Studs

King stud

Jack stud

Sill plate

Subfloor

Main beam

Bracing

Fire blocks

Rough sill

Support posts

Foundation

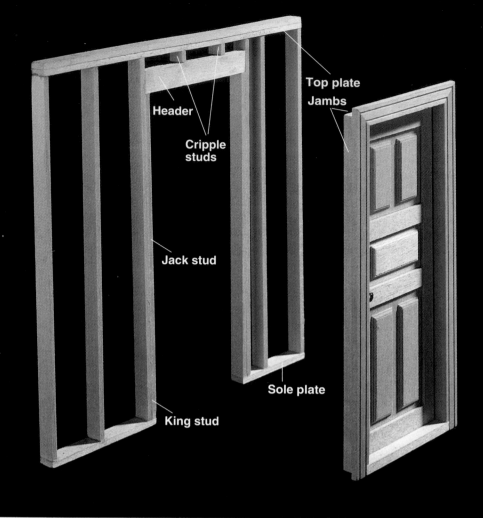

Header

Cripple studs

Top plate

Jambs

Jack stud

Sole plate

King stud

Door opening: The structural load above the door is carried by cripple studs that rest on a header. The ends of the header are supported by jack studs, (also known as *trimmer studs*) and king studs that transfer the load to the sole pate and the foundation of the house. The rough opening for a door should be 1" wider and ½" taller than the dimensions of the door unit, including the jambs. This extra space lets you adjust the door unit during installation.

Anatomy Details

Many remodeling projects, like adding new doors or windows, require that you remove one or more studs in a load-bearing wall to create an opening. When planning your project, remember that new openings require a permanent support beam called a *header*, above the removed studs, to carry the structural load directly.

The required size for the header is set by local building codes and varies according to the width of the rough opening. For a window or door opening, a header can be built from two pieces of 2" dimensional lumber sandwiched around ⅜" plywood (chart, right). When a large portion of a load-bearing wall (or an entire wall) is removed, a laminated beam product can be used to make the new header (page 187).

If you will be removing more than one wall stud, make temporary supports to carry the structural load until the header is installed.

Recommended Header Sizes

Rough Opening Width	Recommended Header Construction
Up to 3 ft.	⅜" plywood between two 2 × 4s
3 ft. to 5 ft.	⅜" plywood between two 2 × 6s
5 ft. to 7 ft.	⅜" plywood between two 2 × 8s
7 ft. to 8 ft.	⅜" plywood between two 2 × 10s

Recommended header sizes shown above are suitable for projects where a full story and roof are located above the rough opening. This chart is intended for rough estimates only. For actual requirements, contact an architect or your local building inspector. For spans greater than 8 ft., see page 187.

Window opening: The structural load above the window is carried by cripple studs resting on a header. The ends of the header are supported by jack studs and king studs, which transfer the load to the sole plate and the foundation of the house. The rough sill, which helps anchor the window unit but carries no structural weight, is supported by cripple studs. To provide room for adjustments during installation, the rough opening for a window should be 1" wider and ½" taller than the window unit, including the jambs.

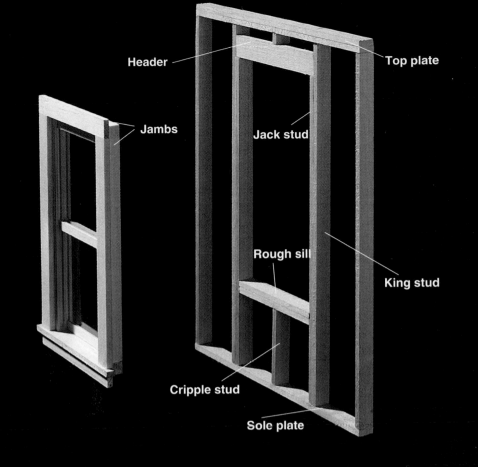

Header

Top plate

Jambs

Jack stud

Rough sill

King stud

Cripple stud

Sole plate

Framing Options for Window & Door Openings (new lumber shown in yellow)

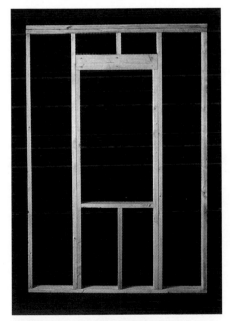

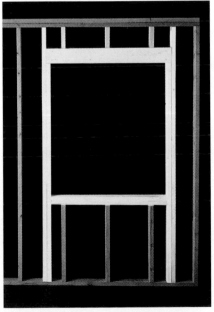

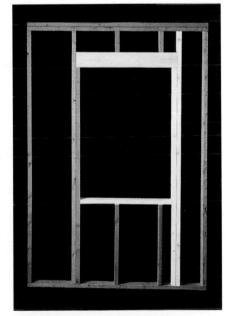

Using an existing opening avoids the need for new framing. This is a good option in homes with masonry exteriors, which are difficult to alter. Order a replacement unit that is 1" narrower and ½" shorter than the rough opening.

Enlarging an existing opening simplifies the framing. In many cases, you can use an existing king stud and jack stud to form one side of the new opening.

Framing a new opening is the only solution when you're installing a window or door where none existed or when you're replacing a unit with one that is much larger.

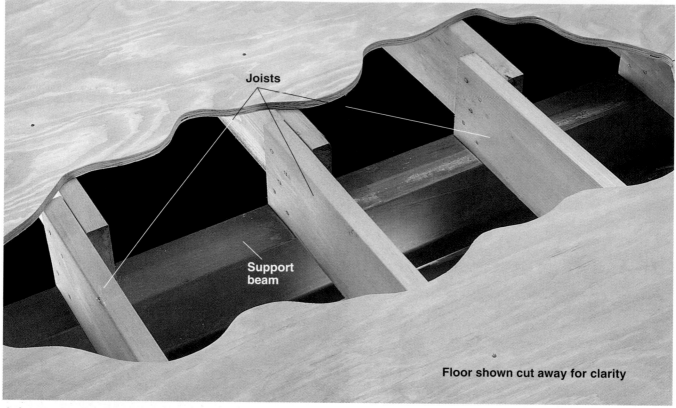

Joists carry the structural load of floors and ceilings. The ends of the joists rest on support beams, foundations, or load-bearing walls. Rooms used as living areas must be supported by floor joists that are at least 2 × 8 in size. Floors with smaller joists can be reinforced with *sister* joists (photos, below).

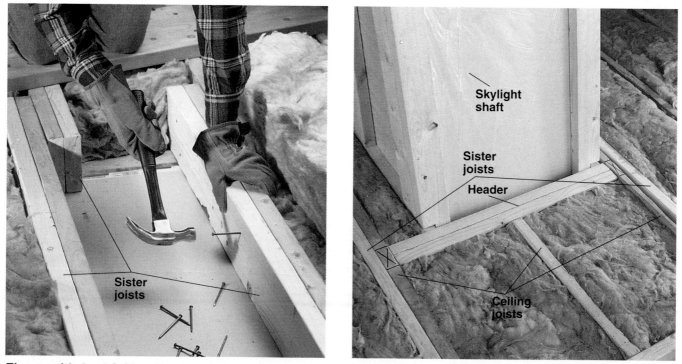

Floors with 2 × 6 joists, like those sometimes found in attics, cannot support living areas unless a sister joist is attached alongside each original joist to strengthen it (above, left). This often is necessary when an attic is converted to a living area. Sister joists also are used to help support a header when ceiling joists must be cut, such as when framing a skylight shaft (above, right).

Roof Anatomy

Rafters made from 2 × 4s or 2 × 6s spaced every 16" or 24" are used to support roofs in most houses built before 1950. If necessary, rafters can be cut to make room for a large skylight. Check in your attic to determine if your roof is framed with rafters or roof trusses (right).

Trusses are prefabricated "webs" made from 2" dimensional lumber. They are found in many houses built after 1950. Never cut through or alter roof trusses. If you want to install a skylight in a house with roof trusses, buy a unit that fits in the space between the trusses.

Wall Anatomy

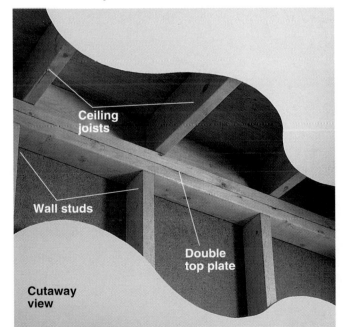

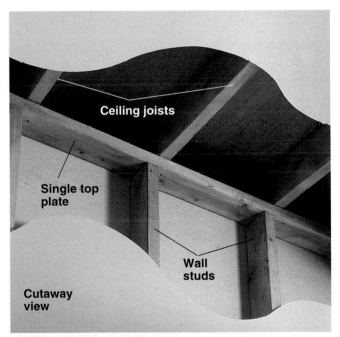

Load-bearing walls carry the structural weight of your home. In platform-framed houses, load-bearing walls can be identified by double top plates made from two layers of framing lumber. Load-bearing walls include all exterior walls and any interior walls that are aligned above support beams.

Partition walls are interior walls that do not carry structural weight of the house. They have a single top plate and can be perpendicular to the floor and ceiling joists but are not aligned above support beams. Any interior wall that is parallel to floor and ceiling joists is a partition wall.

Basic Projects

When planning a carpentry project, you will need to consider and choose from dozens of design and construction options.

Consider hiring professionals if you are unsure of your own skills. For example, if you are removing a long load-bearing wall, you may want to hire a builder to install the heavy permanent header, but do all other work yourself. If your project requires changes to the electrical and plumbing systems, you also may want to leave this work to licensed professionals.

Organize your project into stages, such as layout and planning, permit application (if required), shopping, preparation (opposite page), construction, and inspection. Smaller stages help you work efficiently and let you break large projects into a series of smaller, daily tasks.

If your project requires a permit from the local building inspector (page 6), do not begin work until the inspector has approved your plans and issued the permit. If your project requires plumbing or electrical work, additional permits may be needed. Shopping is easier once you've obtained permits required for the job. Make a detailed material list and make all of your purchases at the outset.

During the preparation phase, try to salvage or recycle materials when possible. Window and door units, moldings, carpeting, and fixtures that are in good shape can be used elsewhere or sold to salvage yards. Most raw metals are accepted at recycling centers. Wallboard and insulation are seldom worth salvaging.

Preparing the Work Area

Most carpentry projects share the same basic preparation techniques and follow a similar sequence. Start by checking for hidden mechanicals in the work area and shutting off and rerouting electrical wiring, plumbing pipes, and other utility lines. If you are not comfortable performing these tasks, hire a professional.

Test all electrical outlets before beginning any demolition of walls, ceilings, or floors. Shovel all demolition debris away from the work area. Clear away the debris whenever materials begin to pile up during the construction of a project. For larger jobs, consider renting a dumpster.

Everything You Need:

Tools: Screwdrivers, broom, trash containers, neon circuit tester, electronic stud finder, flat pry bar, channel-type pliers.

Materials: Drop cloths, masking tape, building paper, plywood.

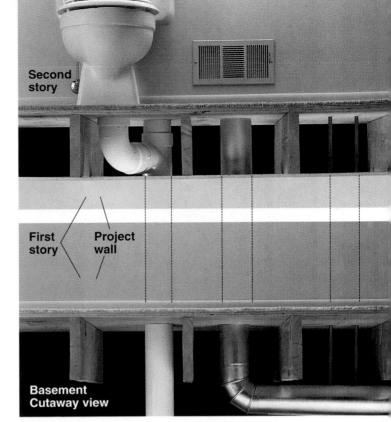

Check for hidden plumbing lines, ductwork, and gas pipes before you cut into a wall. To determine the location of the pipes and ducts, examine the areas directly below and above the project wall. In most cases, pipes, utility lines, and ductwork run through the wall vertically between floors. Original blueprints for your house, if available, usually show the location of the utility lines.

Preparation Tips

Disconnect electrical wiring before you cut into walls. Trace the wiring back to a fixture outside the cutout area, then shut off the power and disconnect the wires leading into the cutout area. Turn the power back on and test for current with a circuit tester before cutting into the walls.

Shovel debris through a convenient window into a wheelbarrow to speed up demolition work. Use sheets of plywood to cover shrubs and flower gardens next to open windows and doors. Cover adjoining lawn areas with sheets of plastic or canvas to simplify cleanup.

Building A Partition Wall: A Step-by-step Overview

This sequence shows the basic steps of building a partition wall, one of the primary carpentry skills. Partition walls divide open spaces into rooms, but do not carry any significant structural weight. They begin with a horizontal top plate nailed to the ceiling, and a sole plate fastened to the flooring. In between the plates, studs are placed every 16" to 24", as specified by local building codes.

To estimate the lumber needed to build a wall, calculate boards for the studs, top and sole plate, ceiling blocking, and door framing materials, if needed.

When adding a wall in a current living space, hang plastic around your project area to contain dust and debris.

1 Install blocking above the ceiling if needed, then install the top plate. If you want to soundproof the walls, see pages 120 to 121.

2 Install the sole plate. Use a plumb bob to align the sole plate directly under the top plate. Take measurements from both ends of the top plate to ensure the sole plate is in the right position.

3 Install the wall studs. Attach the studs with metal connectors, or by toenailing the joints.

4 Frame for a prehung door. Frame the door opening ½" larger on each side than the door unit.

5 Drill holes and run any water pipes or wiring through the framed wall. Protect mechanicals from nail or screw punctures by covering them with flat metal plates.

6 Install the wallboard, using ½" wallboard for most applications. Finish the wallboard.

7 Install a prehung door. Prehung doors come complete with jambs.

8 Cut and install the door casings. Stain or paint the trim pieces as desired.

Building A Partition Wall

The framing techniques used to construct partition walls are simple because the walls are not load-bearing. However, locating the joists beneath finished ceilings and floors may be difficult. If you don't have access to unfinished spaces above and below the work area, use a stud finder to determine the location and direction of the joists.

Interior partition walls usually are built with 2 × 4 lumber, but in some situations it is better to frame with 2 × 6 lumber (photo, left). Before finishing the walls (pages 132 to 139), have the building inspector review your work. The inspector may check to see that any required plumbing and wiring changes are complete.

Use 2 × 6 lumber to frame walls that must hold large plumbing pipes. Where wall plates must be cut to fit pipes, use metal straps to join the framing members. For improved soundproofing, you can also fill walls with fiberglass insulation.

Everything You Need:

Tools: Drill and twist bit, chalk line, tape measure, combination square, pencil, framing square, ladder, plumb bob, hammer.

Materials: Framing lumber, 10d nails.

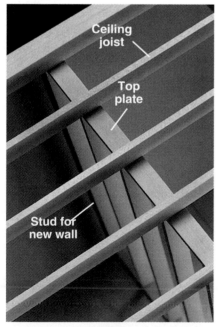

New wall perpendicular to joists: Attach the top plate and sole plate directly to the ceiling and floor joists with 10d nails.

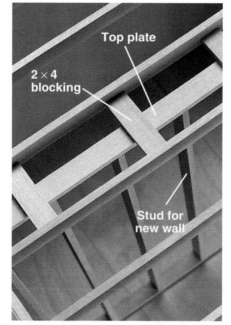

New wall parallel to joists, but not aligned: Install 2 × 4 blocking between the joists every 2 feet, using 10d nails. The bottom of the blocking should be flush with the edges of joists. Anchor plates with 10d nails driven into the blocking.

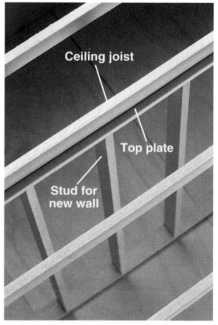

New wall aligned with parallel joists: Attach top plate to ceiling joist and sole plate to the floor, using 10d nails.

How to Build a Partition Wall

1 Mark the location of the new wall on the ceiling, then snap two chalk lines to outline the position of the new top plate. Locate the first ceiling joist or cross block by drilling into the ceiling between the lines, then measure to find the remaining joists.

2 Make the top and sole plates by cutting two 2 × 4s to length. Lay the plates side by side, and use a combination square to outline the stud locations at 16" intervals.

Jack stud marks
King stud marks

3 Mark the position of the door framing members on the top plate and sole plate, using Xs for king studs and Os for jack studs. The rough opening measured between the insides of jack studs should be about 1" wider than the actual width of the door to allow for adjustments during installation.

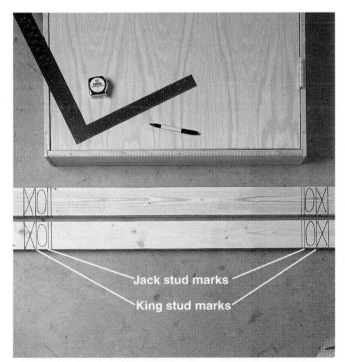

4 Position the top plate against the ceiling between the chalk lines, and use two 10d nails to tack it in place with the stud marks facing down. Use a framing square to make sure the plate is perpendicular to the adjoining walls, then anchor the plate to the joists with 10d nails.

(continued next page)

5 Determine the position of the sole plate by hanging a plumb bob from edge of the top plate near an adjoining wall so the plumb bob tip nearly touches the floor. When the plumb bob is motionless, mark its position on the floor. Repeat at the opposite end of top plate, then snap a chalk line between the marks to show the location of the sole plate.

6 Cut away the sole plate where the door framing will fit, then position the pieces of the sole plate on the outline on the floor. On wood floors, anchor the sole plate pieces with 10d nails driven into the floor joists.

Option: on concrete floors, attach the sole plate with a powder-actuated nailer. This tool, available at rental centers, fires a small gunpowder charge to drive masonry nails through the sole plate into concrete. Wear ear protection when using a powder-actuated nailer.

7 Find the length of the first stud by measuring the distance between the sole plate and the top plate with a tape measure at the first stud mark. Add ⅛" to ensure a snug fit, and cut the stud to length.

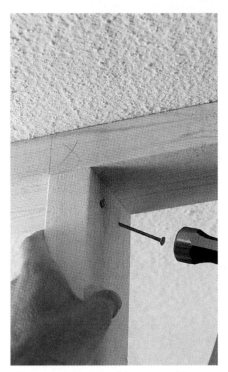

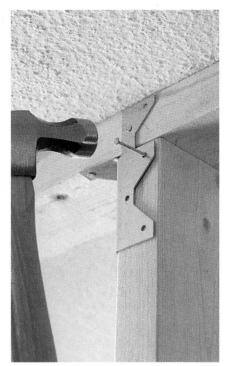

8 Position the stud between the top plate and sole plate so the stud markings are covered.

9 Attach the stud by toenailing through the sides of the stud into the top plate and then the sole plate. Measure, cut, and install all remaining studs, one at a time.

Option: Attach the studs to the top plate and sole plate with metal connectors and 4d nails.

10 Frame the rough opening for the door (see pages 116 to 119).

11 Install 2 × 4 blocking between studs, 4 feet from the floor. Arrange to have the wiring and any other utility work completed, then have your project inspected. Install wallboard and trim the wall as shown on pages 132 to 139.

Top plate

Cripple stud

Door header

King stud

Jack stud

Sole plate

Framing an Opening for an Interior Door

Framing a door opening requires straight, dry lumber, so the door unit fits evenly into the rough opening and won't bind later on. Buy the door or door kit and materials first. The type of door you select will depend on practical and aesthetic considerations. Prehung interior doors, are by far the most common. Most are 32" wide, but other sizes are available. Sliding, or *bypass,* doors and folding doors are popular for closets. Pocket doors, which slide into an enclosure in the wall, are practical in narrow hallways and other cramped spaces.

There are minor differences in the technique for framing the opening for each type of door. Installing, or *hanging,* doors is covered on pages 148 and 149. This section contains instructions for framing a prehung door, bypass or folding doors, and a pocket door (pages 117 to 119). Install the door after installing wallboard.

Everything You Need:

Tools: Tape measure, framing square, hammer, handsaw.

Materials: 2 × 4 lumber, prehung door unit, bypass or folding door kit and doors, or pocket door and kit, metal connectors, 8d common nails.

How to Frame a Prehung Door Opening

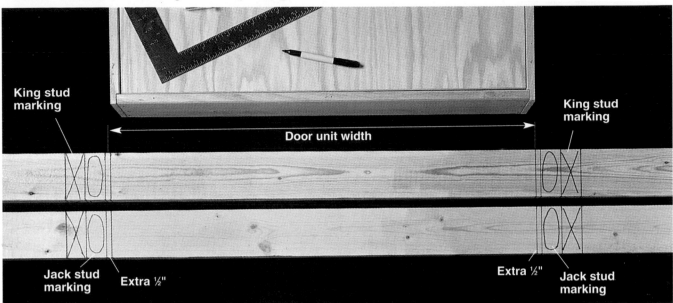

King stud marking

King stud marking

Door unit width

Jack stud marking

Extra ½"

Extra ½"

Jack stud marking

1 Mark the rough opening on the top and sole plates as instructed on page 113, step 3. If you have already marked the rough opening, proceed to step 2.

King stud

2 Measure and cut the king studs and position them at the markings (X). Toenail the joints by driving nails through the king stud and into the header at a 45° angle. Or, attach the studs with metal connectors.

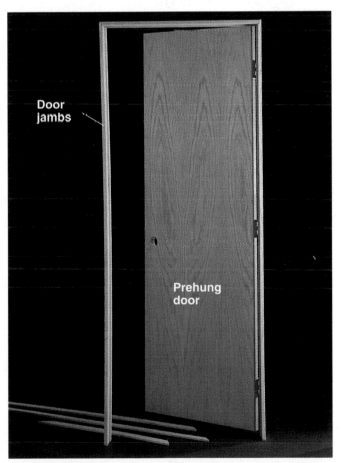

Door jambs

Prehung door

TIP: A prehung door greatly simplifies installation for standard-size openings. Prehung doors are sold with temporary braces in place that support the door jambs during shipping. The braces are removed for installation (pages 148 and 149).

(continued next page)

How to Frame a Prehung Door Opening (continued)

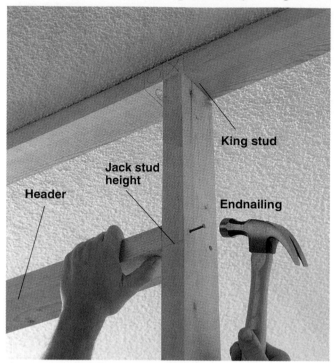

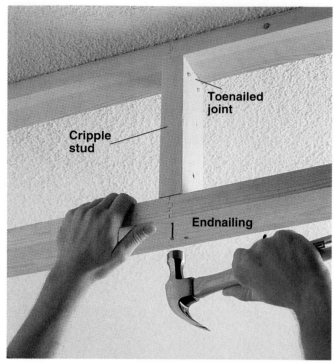

2 Mark the height of the jack stud on each king stud. The height of a jack stud for a standard door is 83½", or ½" taller than the door. Endnail the header to the king stud above the mark for the jack stud.

3 Install a cripple stud above the header, halfway between the king studs. Toenail the cripple stud to the top plate, and endnail through the bottom of the header into the cripple stud.

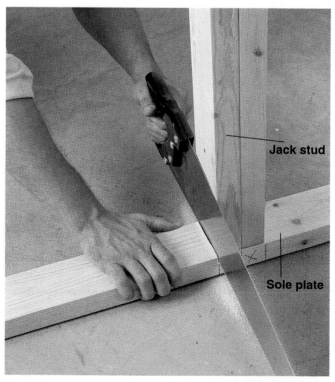

4 Position the jack studs against the insides of the king studs. Endnail through the top of the header down into the jack studs.

5 If the sole plate is still in place, saw through it along the inside edges of the jack studs. Remove the cut portion of the plate.

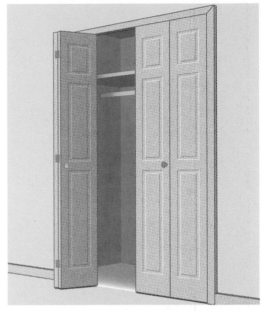

The same basic framing techniques are used, whether you're planning to install a sliding, bifold, pocket, or pre-hung interior door (page 148). The different door styles require different frame openings. You may need to frame an opening 2 to 3 times wider than the opening for standard pre-hung door. Purchase the doors and hardware in advance, and consult the hardware manufacturer's instructions for the exact dimensions of the rough opening for the type of door you select.

Most bifold doors are designed to fit in a 80"-high finished opening. Wood bifold doors have the advantage of allowing you to trim the doors, if necessary, to fit openings that are slightly shorter.

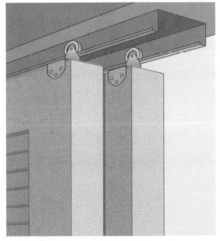

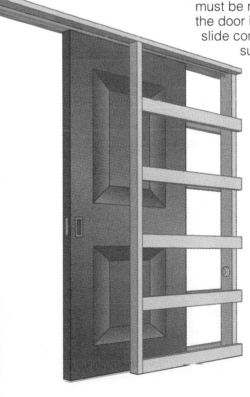

Standard bypass-door openings are 4, 5, 6, or 8 ft.. The finished width should be 1" narrower than the combined width of the doors to provide a 1" overlap when the doors are closed. For long closets that require three or more doors, subtract another 1" from the width of the finished opening for each door. Check the hardware installation instructions for the required height of the opening.

A pocket door's rough opening must be roughly twice the width of the door itself to allow the door to slide completely into the enclosure in the finished wall.

The enclosure is formed by nailing a pocket door cage (available at home centers) to the framing, then adding wallboard and trim. Consult the cage manufacturer's instructions for the dimensions of the rough opening. Note: Replacing a standard door with a pocket door is a major job that's not for the faint of heart. It requires tearing off the existing trim and surface material and reframing the opening. The job can be greatly complicated if the wall is load-bearing or if plumbing or wiring run through the existing wall.

New
wallboard

2 × 4
framing

Old
wallboard

Sound
board

Soundproofing Walls & Ceilings

The best time to soundproof walls and ceilings is during construction, when the framing is accessible and soundproofing materials can be concealed inside the wall. Existing walls can be soundproofed by adding materials such as sound board or a layer of additional wallboard attached to resilient steel channels. Either of these methods will cushion the wall against noise transmission.

Walls and ceilings are rated for sound transmission by a system called Sound Transmission Class (STC). The higher the STC rating, the quieter the house. For example, if a wall is rated at 30 to 35 STC, loud speech can be understood through the wall. At 42 STC, loud speech is reduced to a murmur. At 50 STC, loud speech cannot be heard. Standard construction results in 32 STC rating, while soundproofed walls and

ceilings can carry a rating of up to 48 STC.

TIP: When building new walls, caulk along the floor and ceiling joints to reduce sound transmission.

Everything You Need:

Tools & Materials for new walls: 2 × 6 lumber for top and sole plates, fiberglass batt insulation.

Tools & Materials for existing walls: Sound board, drill, drive bits, resilient steel channels, ⅝" wallboard, construction adhesive, caulk, caulk gun, 1½", and 1" wallboard screws.

Standard & Soundproofed Floor & Ceiling Construction

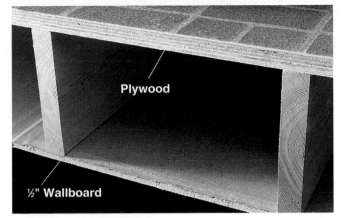

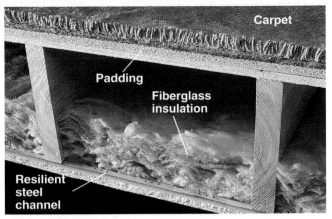

Standard construction, with a wooden subfloor and ½" wallboard on the ceiling below, carries a sound transmission rating of 32 STC.

Soundproofed construction uses carpet and padding on the floor, fiberglass insulation, resilient steel channel screwed to the joists, and ⅝" wallboard on the ceiling. The rating for this system is 48 STC.

How to Soundproof New Walls

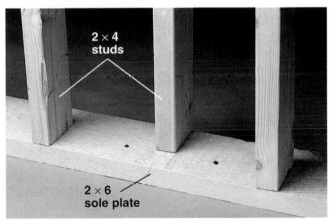

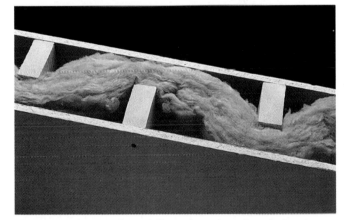

1 Build walls with a 2 × 6 top and sole plates. Position 2 × 4 studs every 12", staggering them flush with the alternate edges of the plates.

2 Weave 3½" unfaced fiberglass batt insulation between the 2 × 4 studs. When covered with ½" wallboard, this wall has a rating of 48 STC.

How to Soundproof Existing Walls & Ceilings

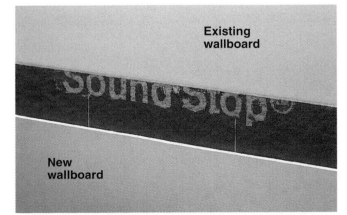

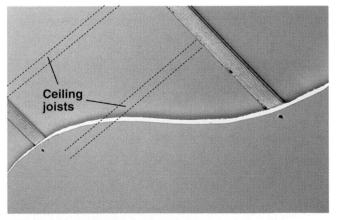

Install ½" sound board over an existing layer of wallboard with 1½" wallboard screws. Glue ½" wallboard over the sound board with construction adhesive. The sound rating for this construction is 46 STC.

Screw resilient steel channels over the ceiling or wall, spaced 24" on center, perpendicular to existing framing. Attach ⅝" wallboard to channels with 1" wallboard screws. The sound rating for this construction is 44 STC.

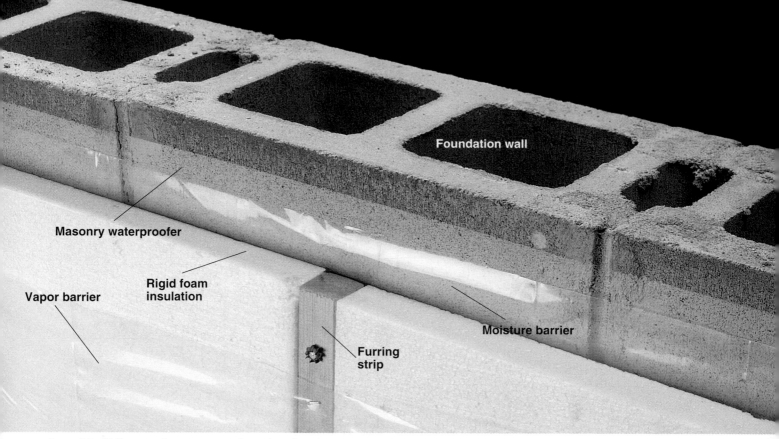

Local building codes may require a barrier to prevent moisture from damaging wood and insulation covering foundation walls. This may be plastic sheeting placed behind or in front of the framing.

Covering Foundation Walls

There are two common methods for covering foundation walls. Because it saves space, the more popular method is to attach 2 × 2 furring strips to the masonry wall. These strips provide a 1½"-deep cavity between strips for insulation and service lines, as well as a framework for attaching wallboard. The other method is to build a complete 2 × 4 stud wall and install it just in front of the foundation wall. This method offers a full 3½" for insulation and lines, and it provides a flat, plumb wall surface, regardless of the foundation wall's condition.

To determine the best method for your project, examine the foundation walls. If they're fairly plumb and flat, you can consider furring them. If the walls are wavy or out of plumb, however, it may be easier to use the stud-wall method. Also check with the local building department before you decide on a framing method. There may be codes regarding insulation minimums and methods of running service lines along foundation walls.

A local building official can also tell you what's recommended—or required—in your area for sealing foundation walls against moisture. Commonly used moisture barriers include a masonry waterproofer that's applied like paint and plastic sheeting installed between the masonry wall and the wood framing. The local building code will also specify whether you need a vapor barrier between the framing and the wallboard.

Before you shop for materials, decide how you'll fasten the wood framing to your foundation walls and floor. The three most common methods are shown on pages 123 and 124. If you're covering a large wall area, it will be worth it to buy or rent a powder-actuated nailer for the job.

Everything You Need:

Tools: Caulk gun, trowel, paint roller, circular saw, drill, powder-actuated nailer, plumb bob.

Materials: Paper-faced insulation, silicone caulk, hydraulic cement, masonry waterproofer, 2 × 2 and 2 × 4 lumber, 2½" wallboard screws, construction adhesive, concrete fasteners, rigid foam insulation.

How to Seal & Prepare Masonry Walls

Insulate the rim-joist cavities (above the foundation walls) with solid pieces of paper-faced fiberglass insulation. Make sure the paper, which serves as a vapor barrier, faces the room. Also apply silicone caulk to the joints between the sill plates and the foundation walls (inset).

Fill small cracks with hydraulic cement or masonry caulk, and smooth the excess with a trowel. Ask the building department whether masonry waterproofer or a plastic moisture barrier is required in your area. Apply waterproofer as directed by the manufacturer or install plastic sheeting to code specifications.

Options for Attaching Wood to Masonry

Masonry nails are the cheapest way to attach wood to concrete block walls. Drive the nails into the mortar joints for maximum holding power and to avoid cracking the blocks. Drill pilot holes through the strips if the nails cause splitting. Masonry nails are difficult to drive into poured concrete.

Self-tapping masonry screws hold well in block or poured concrete, but they must be driven into predrilled holes. Use a hammer drill to drill holes of the same size in both the wood and the concrete after the wood is positioned. Drive the screws into the *web* portion of the blocks (see page 124).

(continued next page)

Options for Attaching Wood to Masonry (continued)

Webs

Powder-actuated nailers offer the quickest and easiest method for fastening framing to block, poured concrete, and steel. They use individual caps of gunpowder—called *loads*—to propel a piston that drives a hardened-steel nail (*pin*) through the wood and into the masonry. The loads are color-coded for the charge they produce, and the pins come in various lengths. Note: Always drive pins into the solid web portions of concrete blocks, not into the voids.

Trigger-type nailers, like the one shown here, are easiest to use, but hammer-activated types are also available. You can buy nailers at home centers and hardware stores or rent them from rental centers. (Ask for a demonstration at the rental center.) Always wear hearing and eye protection when using these extremely loud tools.

How to Install Furring Strips on Masonry Walls

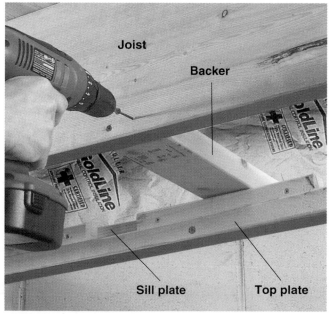

Joist

Backer

Sill plate   **Top plate**

1 Cut a 2 × 2 top plate to span the length of the wall. Mark the furring-strip layout onto the bottom edge of the plate every 16" (so the center of the furring strips will line up with the marks). Attach the plate to the bottom of the joists with 2½" wallboard screws. The back edge of the plate should line up with the front of the blocks.

NOTE: If the joists run parallel to the wall, you'll need to install backers between the outer joist and the sill plate to provide support for ceiling wallboard. Make T-shape backers from short 2 × 4s and 2 × 2s. Install each so the bottom face of the 2 × 4 is flush with the bottom edges of the joists. Attach the top plate to the foundation wall with its top edge flush with the top of the blocks.

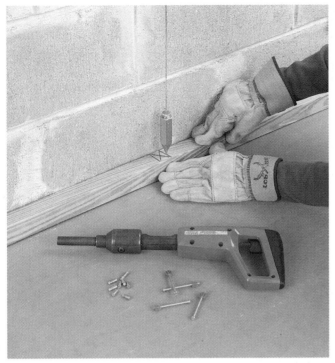

2 Install a bottom plate cut from pressure-treated 2 × 2 lumber so the plate spans the length of the wall. Apply construction adhesive to the back and bottom of the plate, then attach it to the floor with a nailer. Use a plumb bob to transfer the furring-strip layout marks from the top plate to the bottom plate.

3 Cut 2 × 2 furring strips to fit between the top and bottom plates. Apply construction adhesive to the back of each furring strip, and position it on the layout marks on the plates. Nail along the length of each strip at 16" intervals.

Option: Leave a chase for the installation of wires or supply pipes by installing pairs of vertically aligned furring strips with a 2" gap between each pair. NOTE: Consult local codes to ensure proper installation of electrical or plumbing materials.

4 Fill the cavities between furring strips with rigid insulation board. Cut the pieces so they fit snugly within the framing. If necessary, make cutouts in the insulation to fit around mechanical elements, and cover any chases with metal protective plates before attaching the wall surface. Add a vapor barrier, as required by local building code.

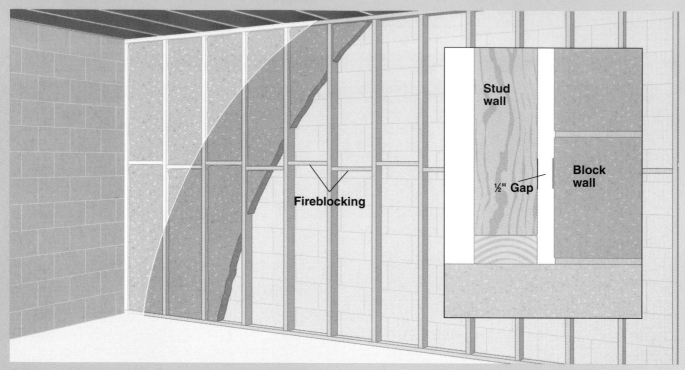

Build a standard 2 × 4 partition wall, following the basic steps on pages 110 to 115. Use pressure-treated lumber for any bottom plates that rest on concrete. To minimize moisture problems and avoid unevenness in foundation walls, leave a ½" air space between the stud walls and the masonry walls (inset). Install all fireblocking required by local code. Insulate the stud walls with fiberglass blankets, and install a vapor barrier, as required by local code.

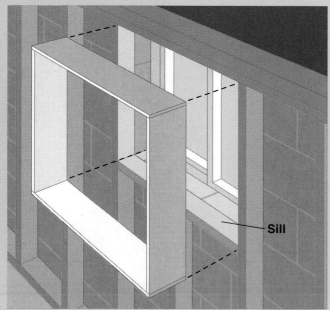

Framing around a window should be flush with the edges of the masonry on all sides. Install a sill at the base of the window, and add a header, if necessary. Fill the space between the framing members and the concrete with fiberglass insulation or non-expanding foam insulation. Install wallboard so it butts against the window frame.

Build a short stud wall to cover a low foundation wall in a walkout or "daylight" basement. Install the top plate flush with the top of the foundation wall. Finish the wall surface with wallboard or other finish, then cap the walls with finish-grade lumber or plywood to create a decorative shelf.

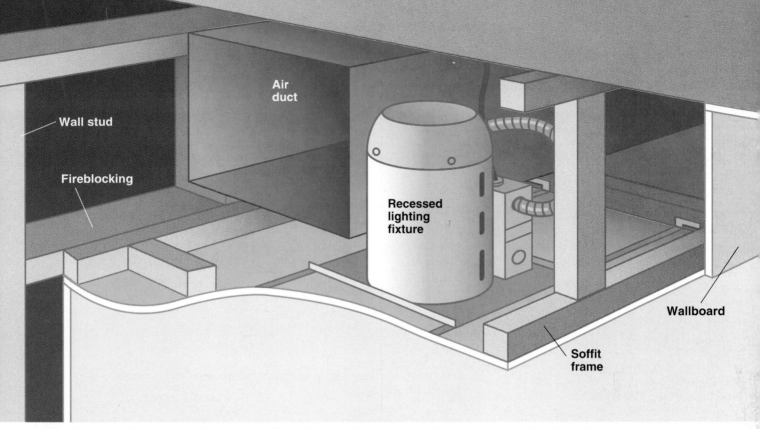

Hide immovable obstructions in a soffit built from dimension lumber and covered with wallboard or other surface material. An extra-wide soffit is also a great place to install recessed lighting fixtures.

Framing Soffits & Chases

Your unfinished basement or attic is sure to have beams, pipes, posts, ductwork, and other elements that are vital to your house but become big obstacles to finishing the space. When you can't conceal the obstructions within walls, and you've determined it's too costly to move them, hide them inside a framed soffit or chase. This can also provide a place to run smaller mechanicals, like wiring and water supply lines.

Soffits and chases are easy to build. A soffit is usually constructed with 2 × 2 lumber, which is easy to work with and inexpensive. You can use 1 × 3s to keep the frame as small as possible and 2 × 4s for large soffits that will house other elements, such as recessed lighting fixtures. Chases should be framed with 2 × 4s.

This section shows you some basic techniques for building soffits and chases, but the design of your framing is up to you. For example, you may want to shape your soffits for a decorative effect, or build an oversized chase that holds bookshelves. Just make sure the framing conforms to local building codes.

There may be code restrictions about the types of mechanicals that can be grouped together, as well as minimum clearances between the framing and what it encloses. And most codes specify that soffits, chases, and other framed structures have fireblocking every 10 ft. and at the intersections between soffits and neighboring walls. Remember, too, that drain cleanouts and shutoff valves must be accessible, so you'll need to install access panels at these locations.

Everything You Need:

Tools: Circular saw, drill, powder-actuated nailer.

Materials: Dimension lumber (1 × 3, 2 × 2, 2 × 4), pressure-treated 2 × 4s, construction adhesive, wallboard, unfaced fiberglass insulation, nails, wood trim, wallboard screws, decorative screws.

(continued next page)

Variations for Building Soffits

Obstructions perpendicular to joists. Build two ladder-like frames for the soffit sides, using standard 2 × 2s. Install 2 × 2 braces (or "rungs") every 16 or 24" to provide nailing support for the seams of the wallboard or other finish material. Attach the side frames to the joists on either side of the obstruction, using nails or screws. Then, install cross pieces beneath the obstacle, tying the two sides together. Cover the soffit with wallboard, plywood, or other finish material.

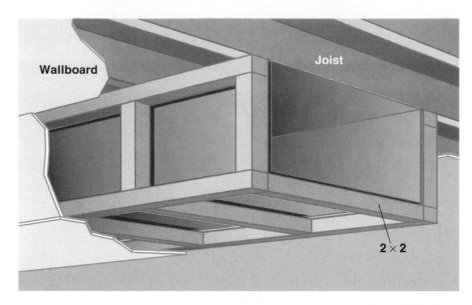

Obstructions parallel to joists. Build side frames as with perpendicular obstructions, but size them to fit in between two joists. This provides nailing surfaces for both the soffit and ceiling finish materials. Attach the frames to the joists with screws, then install cross pieces. NOTE: If you are enclosing a drain pipe, wrap the pipe in unfaced fiberglass insulation to muffle the sound of draining water.

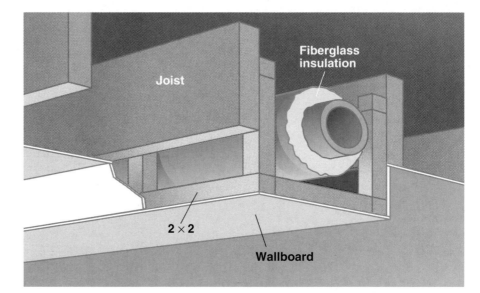

Maximize headroom. In rooms with low ceilings, and where an obstruction is less than 12" wide and the finish material will be wallboard or plywood, build side frames (see above) so that the bottom edges are ⅛" lower than the lowest point of the obstruction. For soffits of this width, the bottom piece of wallboard or plywood stabilizes the structure, so cross pieces between side frames aren't necessary.

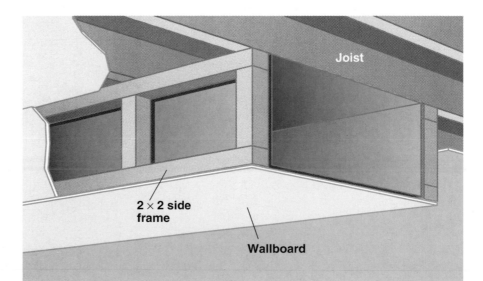

How to Frame a Chase

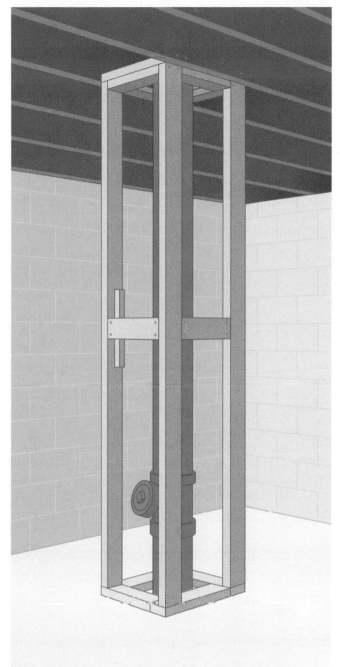

Build chases with 2 × 4s, which tend to be straighter than 2 × 2s and are strong enough to withstand household accidents. Use pressure-treated lumber for bottom plates on concrete floors, attaching them with construction adhesive and powder-actuated nailer fasteners (see page 124). Cut top plates from standard lumber and nail or screw them in place. Install studs to form the corners of the chase, and block in between them for stability. To make the chase smaller, notch the top and bottom plates around the obstruction, and install the studs flat. If you're framing around a vertical drain pipe, leave room around the pipe for soundproofing insulation. Plastic pipes can be especially noisy.

How to Make Access Panels

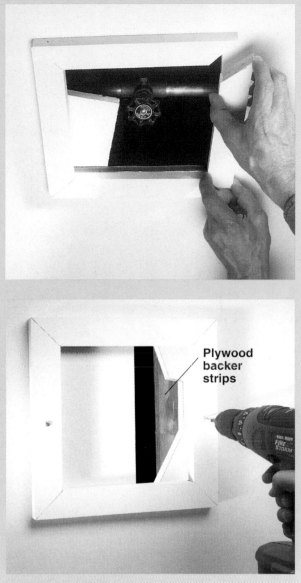

Plywood
backer
strips

After your soffits and chases are framed, note the locations of all access points before you install the wallboard. Make the access panels after the wallboard is installed.

In a horizontal surface (top photo), cut out a square piece of wallboard at the access location. Push the cutout through the opening and slide it to one side so it rests on the inside of the soffit. Glue mitered trim around the opening so it overlaps the opening by approximately ½" on all sides. Position the panel so it rests on the trim and can be moved when necessary.

In a vertical surface (bottom photo), cut an opening in the same fashion, and glue mitered trim to the edges of the cutout. Install plywood backer strips to the back of the wallboard at two sides of the opening. Position the finished panel over the opening so it rests against the strips. Drill pilot holes through the trim, and secure the panel to the backer strips with decorative screws.

Installing wallboard is often the first step in finishing walls and ceilings. Some products, such as suspended ceilings and tongue-and-groove boards, can be installed directly over studs and joists, but check first with your local building department. The building code in your area may require the use of wallboard in some areas as a fire retardant.

Finishing Walls & Ceilings

The first step in finishing walls and ceilings is deciding what types of materials you will use. This decision influences the order in which you complete the project.

Wallboard (pages 132 to 139) is probably the most popular finishing material because it is economical and holds paint and other wallcoverings well. When installed in the proper thickness, wallboard also serves as a firestop or a soundproofing device.

When finishing a ceiling, especially in a basement, take into consideration that you may need occasional access to plumbing or electrical wiring in the ceiling. If so, you may want to install a suspended ceiling (pages 140 to 143) with removable ceiling panels. If you may need

access to mechanicals in a wallboard ceiling, you will have to build access panels (page 129).

In some cases tongue-and-groove boards can be installed directly over framing materials (pages 144 to147). It can also be installed over wallboard, such as tongue-and-groove wainscoting (pages 162 to 167); which can help disguise uneven surfaces.

Door and window casings (pages 152 to 155), cove moldings, baseboard, and other trim (pages 156 to161) are almost always stained before being installed. Painted trim is usually primed prior to installation, then painted afterward. Some people prefer to prime and add one coat of paint before installation, adding the final after the holes have been filled with putty.

Finishing Styles

Select suspended ceilings when easy access to plumbing and electrical wiring is critical. If individual suspended ceiling panels become water damaged or broken, they are easy to replace.

Install tongue-and-groove boards directly over framing, where appropriate and permitted by the building code or install it over wallboard. Holes for light fixtures, switches, outlets, and vents must be measured and cut prior to installation.

Installing wainscoting is easier on walls that are plumb and typically is completed with baseboard and a cap rail, then stained or painted.

Installing Wallboard

Wallboard has become the standard material for finishing most interior walls because it is relatively easy to install and creates smooth, uniform wall surfaces. Wallboard is commonly available in 4 × 8-ft. and 4 × 12-ft. sheets, and in thicknesses ranging from ⅜" to ¾". For general construction, a 4 × 8-ft. sheet is known as a *full sheet*. Some stores also carry half sheets and quarter sheets, or 4 × 4-ft. and 2 × 4-ft. sheets. For easy handling in most applications, use 4 × 8-ft. sheets of ½" thickness. For extra fire protection where building codes require it, or for soundproofing walls and ceilings, use ⅝" wallboard.

Wallboard was once installed using specially designed nails and a wallboard hammer (see photo opposite page, top). Today, wallboard is installed almost exclusively using wallboard screws, which hold better than nails and are more convenient to install and remove.

Wallboard panels are tapered along the long edges, so that adjoining panels form a slightly recessed seam that can be easily covered with paper tape and joint compound. Panels joined end-to-end are difficult to finish; it's best to avoid end-butted seams wherever possible.

Installing and finishing wallboard is a messy job. Wear a dust mask when you cut or sand wallboard to keep the dust out of your lungs and mouth.

Everything You Need:

Tools: Straightedge, hammer, tape measure, wallboard T-square, utility knife, wallboard saw, jig saw, circle cutter, sawhorse scaffolding (page 98), screwgun or drill and driver bits, rented wallboard lifter, caulk gun, wet sander.

Materials: 4 × 8-ft. wallboard panels, 1¼" wallboard screws, panel adhesive.

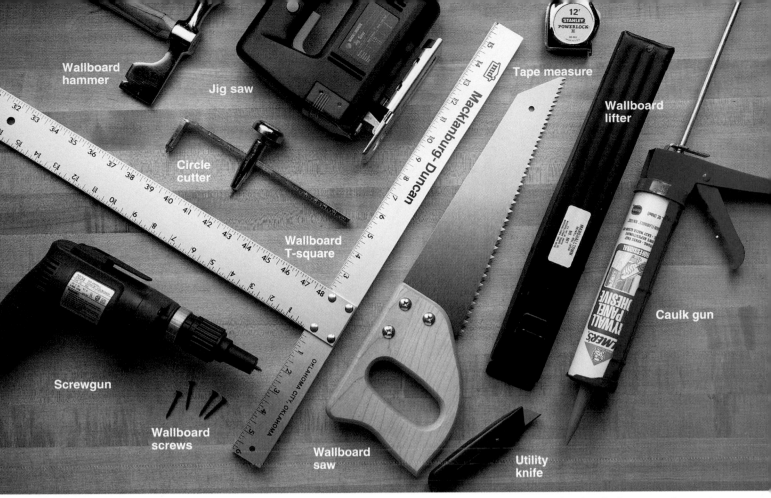

Wallboard installation tools include: jig saw, tape measure, wallboard lifter for positioning wallboard panels, caulk gun and panel adhesive, utility knife, wallboard saw for straight cuts around windows and doors, wallboard T-square, wallboard screws, screwgun with adjustable clutch, circle cutter for making round cutouts for lighting fixtures, wallboard hammer with a convex head. Wallboard hammers, once essential for installing wallboard, now are seldom used.

Tips for Preparing for Wallboard Installation

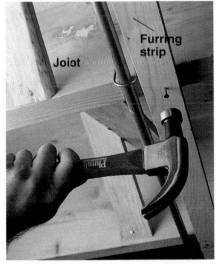

Use protector plates where wires or pipes pass through framing members less than 1¼" from the face. The plates prevent wallboard screws from puncturing wires or pipes.

Nail furring strips to the framing to extend the wall surface beyond any obstructions such as water pipes or heating ducts.

Mark the locations of the studs on the floor with a carpenter's pencil or masking tape. After wallboard covers the studs, the marks indicate where the studs are for easier installation.

How to Cut Wallboard

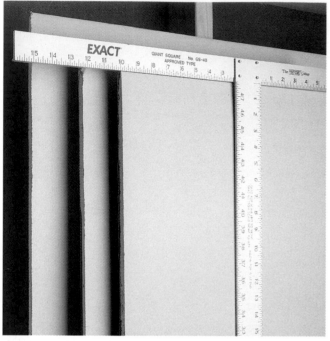

1 Set wallboard upright with smooth side out when cutting panels. Cut and install wallboard panels one at a time. Use a tape measure to find the length of wallboard needed.

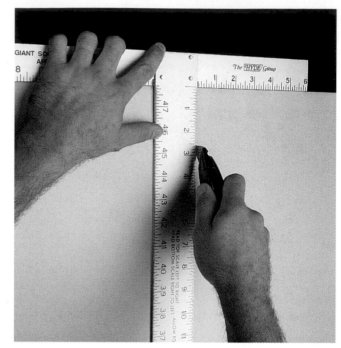

2 Position the wallboard T-square with the short arm flush against the edge. Use a utility knife to score the wallboard face paper along the arm of the square at the length measured in step 1.

3 Bend the scored section with both hands to break the plaster core of the wallboard. Fold back the unwanted piece and cut through the back paper to separate the pieces.

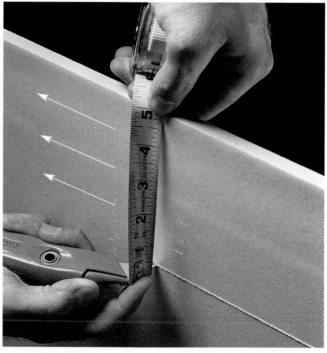

OPTION: For horizontal cuts, extend the tape measure to the width of the desired cut and hook the utility knife blade under the end of the tape. Hold the utility knife tightly in one hand and the tape tightly in the other. Move both hands along the panel to score a cut in the face paper and complete the cut as in step 3.

How to Cut Notches in Wallboard

1 Use a wallboard saw to cut the short sides of the notch. A wallboard saw cuts wallboard easily because it has coarse, wide set teeth that cut quickly without clogging.

2 Use a utility knife to cut the remaining side of the notch, then break the core as shown. Cut the back portion with a utility knife, then separate the unwanted portion.

Cut openings for electrical and telephone outlets and heating ducts by making plunge cuts with a jig saw outfitted with a coarse, wood-cutting blade.

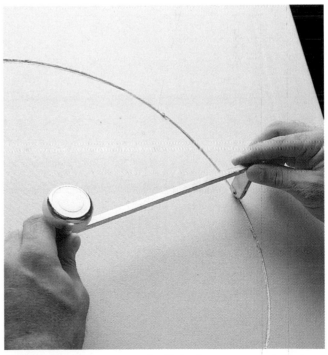

Make circular cutouts for light fixtures or exhaust fans with an adjustable circle cutter. Mark a center point and use the circle cutter to score both sides of the wallboard. Tap the cutout with a hammer to release it from the surrounding panel.

How to Install Wallboard on Ceilings

1 Create a control line by measuring out from the top plate of the adjoining wall. Make a mark on the outermost joists (or rafters) at 48⅛", then snap a chalk line at the marks. The line should be perpendicular to the joists. Use this control line to align the first row of panels and to measure for cutouts.

2 Measure across the joists to make sure the first panel will break on the center of a joist. If necessary, cut the panel from the end that abuts the side wall so that the panel breaks on the next farthest joist. Load the panel onto a rented wallboard lift, and hoist the panel until it rests against the joists.

3 Position the panel so the side edge is even with the control line and the leading end reaches the center of the appropriate joist. Drive a 1¼" wallboard screw every 8" along the edges and every 12" in the field (Consult local building codes for fastening requirements in your area).

4 After the first row of sheets is installed, begin the next row with a half-sheet of wallboard. This ensures that the butted end joints will be staggered between rows.

How to Install Wallboard on Walls

1 Plan wallboard placement so joints do not fall at the corners of doors or windows. Wallboard joints at corners often crack and cause bulges that interfere with miter joints in window or door trim.

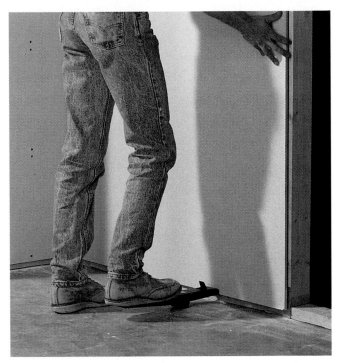

2 Unless the panels are long enough to span the wall, install them vertically to avoid butt joints that are difficult to finish. Plumb the first panel with a level, making sure it breaks on the center of a stud. Lift panels tight against ceiling with a wallboard lifter, then screw them into position.

3 Anchor wallboard panels by driving wallboard screws, spaced every 10", into the framing members. Screw heads should be sunk just below the wallboard surface, but should not tear the paper.

4 Add 1× or 2× backing in situations where additional support is necessary to support wallboard edges. NOTE: In some framing and remodeling projects additional support is necessary to install wallboard properly. (page 172)

How to Tape Wallboard Joints

1 Apply a thin layer of wallboard compound over the joint with a 4" or 6" wallboard knife. To load the knife, dip it into a pan filled with wallboard compound.

2 Press the wallboard tape into the compound immediately, centering the tape on the joint. Wipe away the excess compound and smooth the joint with a 6" knife. Let dry overnight.

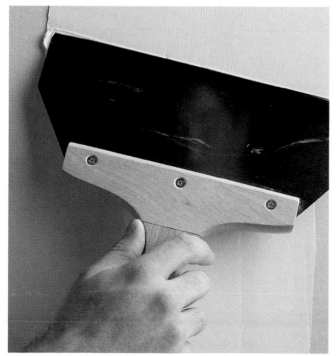

3 Apply a thin finish coat of compound with a 10" wallboard knife. Allow the second coat to dry and shrink overnight. Apply the last coat and let it harden slightly before wet-sanding.

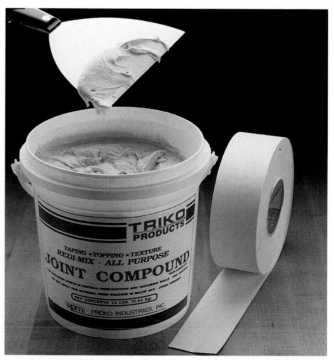

TIP: Use premixed wallboard compound for most taping and finishing jobs to eliminate mixing. Use paper wallboard tape when using premixed wallboard compound.

How to Finish Inside Corners

1 Fold a strip of paper wallboard tape in half by pinching the strip and pulling it between thumb and forefinger. Apply a thin layer of wallboard compound to both sides of the inside corner, using a 4" wallboard knife.

2 Position the end of the folded tape strip at the top of the joint and press the tape into the wet compound with the knife. Smooth both sides of the corner. Finish as described in step 3, page 138.

How to Finish Outside Corners

1 Position corner bead on outside corners. Using a level, adjust bead so corner is plumb. Attach with 1¼" wallboard nails or screws spaced at 8" intervals. (Some corner beads are fastened with wallboard compound.)

2 Cover the corner bead with three coats of wallboard compound, using a 6" or 10" wallboard knife. Let each coat dry and shrink overnight before applying the next coat. Smooth the final coat with a wet sander.

Tip: Sand joints lightly after wallboard compound dries. Use pole sander to reach high areas without a ladder. Wear a dust mask when dry-sanding.

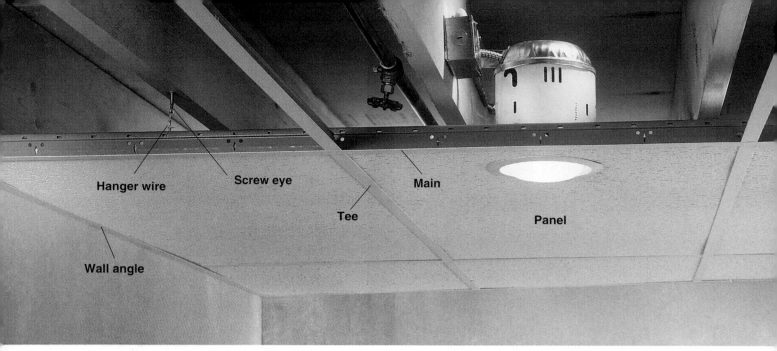

Hanger wire   **Screw eye**   **Main**

Tee   **Panel**

Wall angle

Suspended ceilings are easy to install, provide convenient access to mechanicals, and resolve a variety of ceiling problems. Plan your grid so cut panels are placed on opposite sides of the room, creating a balanced look.

Installing a Suspended Ceiling

A suspended ceiling is a grid framework made of lightweight metal brackets hung on wires attached to an existing ceiling or joists. The frame consists of T-shaped main beams (mains) and cross-tees (tees), and L-shaped wall angles. The grid openings are filled with ceiling panels that rest on the flanges of the framing pieces. Ceiling panels come in 2 × 2 ft. or 2 × 4 ft. sections. They are available in a variety of styles, such as insulated panels and acoustical tiles.

Installing a suspended ceiling is an economical solution when access to plumbing, electrical, or ductwork in a ceiling is necessary. It also compensates for sagging or uneven joists, hides ceiling surfaces, and easily converts a room to a standard 8-ft. height. A lightweight metal system is more durable than a plastic system.

When deciding if a suspended ceiling is right for you, remember that a minimum space (usually about 4") must be left behind the suspended ceiling framework so panel pieces can be inserted into or removed from the brackets. Also, many building codes have minimum ceiling height regulations, so check with your local building inspector.

Before beginning this project, determine the panel layout, based on the width and length of the room. Some panels may require cutting to accommodate the space. Place trimmed panels on opposite sides of your ceiling for a balanced, professional look. You'll also want to make sure

your suspended ceiling is level. Use a water level or a long carpenter's level for marking a level line around a room's perimeter.

Installation is easier with a helper. Low scaffolding also makes installation simpler. Frame around obstructions, such as support beams that hang below the ceiling height (see "Framing Soffits & Chases," pages 127 to 129). Level and attach wall angle pieces to this framed surface at the same time as the perimeter walls. You also can install recessed or incandescent light fixtures or a ceiling fan in a suspended ceiling, although this generally requires additional framing to ensure proper positioning and support for the fixtures.

Everything You Need:

Tools: Water level or 6-ft. carpenter's level, chalk line, drill, tin snips, mason's string, lock-type clamps, screw-eye driver, needlenose pliers, utility knife, straightedge, tape measure.

Materials: Suspended ceiling kit (wall angle, mains, tees), screw eyes, hanger wires, ceiling panels, 1× dimensional lumber, 1½" wallboard screws or masonry nails.

Tips for Installing a Suspended Ceiling

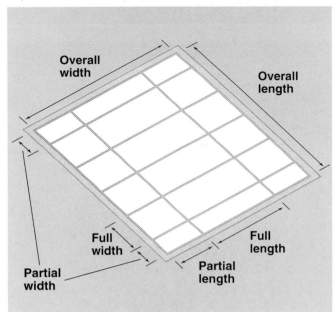

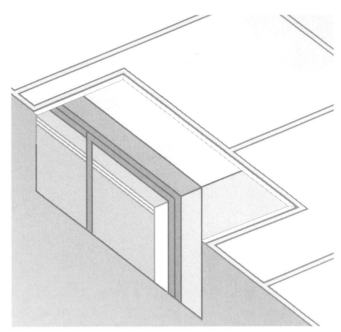

Draw your ceiling layout on paper, based on exact dimensions of the room. Plan so that cut border pieces on opposite sides of the room are of equal width and length (avoid pieces smaller than ½ panel). Be sure to include lighting fixtures in your plan; they must conform to the grid layout.

Build a valance around awning windows in basements with low ceilings so windows can be opened fully. Attach 1x lumber of an appropriate width to joists or blocking, and miter the joints. Install wallboard (or a suspended-ceiling panel trimmed to fit) to the joists inside the valance.

How to Install a Suspended Ceiling

1 Make a mark on one wall to represent the ceiling height plus the height of the wall angle. Use a water level to transfer that mark to both ends of each wall. Snap a chalk line to connect the marks. This line represents the top of the ceiling's wall angle.

2 Attach wall angle pieces to studs on all walls, positioning the top of the wall angle flush with the chalk line. Use 1½" wallboard screws (or short masonry nails driven into mortar joints on concrete block walls). Miter-cut corners with tin snips.

(continued next page)

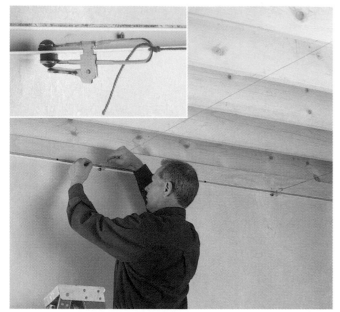

3 Mark the location of each main on the wall angles at the ends of the room. Remember that mains are parallel to each other and perpendicular to ceiling joists. Set up a guide string for each main, using a thin dryline and lock-type clamps (inset). Clamp the strings to the bottom faces of opposing wall angles, stretching them very taut to prevent sagging.

4 Install screw eyes for hanging the mains, using a screw-eye driver. Drill pilot holes and drive the eyes into joists every 4 ft., locating them directly above the guide strings. Attach a support wire to the screw eyes by threading one end through the eye and twisting the wire on itself at least three times. Trim excess, leaving at least 5" hanging below the guide string level.

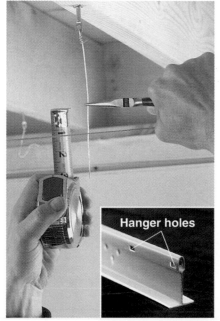

Hanger holes

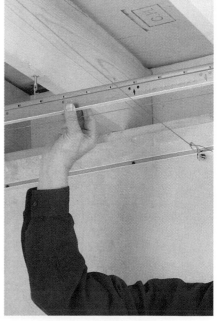

5 Measure the distance from the bottom of a main's flange to the hanger hole in the web (inset). Use this measurement to prebend each hanger wire. Measure up from the guide string and make a 90° bend in the wire, using pliers.

6 Following your layout drawing, mark the placement of the first tee on opposite wall angles at one end of the room. Set up a guide string for the tee, using a dryline and clamps, as before. This string must be perpendicular to the guide strings for the mains.

7 Trim one end of each main so that a tee slot in the main's web is aligned with the tee guide string and the end of the main bears fully on the wall angle. Set the main in place to check the alignment of the tee slot and the string.

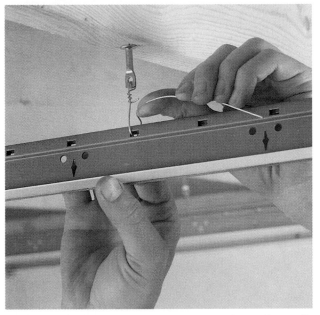

8 Cut the other end of each main to fit, so that it rests on the opposing wall angle. If a single main cannot span the room, splice two mains together, end-to-end (the ends should be fashioned with male-female connectors). Make sure the tee slots remain aligned when splicing.

9 Install the mains by setting the ends on the wall angle and threading the hanger wires through the holes in the webs. The wires should be as close to vertical as possible. Wrap each wire around itself three times, making sure the mains' flanges are level with the main guide strings. Also install a hanger near each main splice. Remove all main guide strings and clamps.

10 Attach tees to the mains, slipping their tabbed ends into slots on mains. Align the first row of tees with the tee guide string; install the remaining rows at 4-ft. intervals. For 2 × 2-ft. panels, also install 2-ft. cross-tees between the midpoints of the 4-ft. tees. Then, cut and install the border tees, placing the tee ends on the wall angles.

11 Place full ceiling panels into the grid first, then install the border panels. Lift the panels in at an angle, and position them so they rest on the frame's flanges. Reach through adjacent openings to adjust the panels, if necessary. To trim partial panels to size, cut them face-up, using a straightedge and a sharp utility knife.

Tongue-and-groove paneling can be installed directly over rafters or joists, or over wallboard. In attic installations, it's important to insulate first, adding a separate vapor barrier if required by building codes. Local code may also require that paper-faced insulation behind a kneewall be covered with drywall or other material.

Everything You Need:

Tools: Tape measure, drill, hammer, jig saw, table saw or circular saw with guide fence, T-bevel, chalk line, nail set.

Materials: Tongue-and-groove boards, 1¾" spiral flooring nails, trim molding.

Paneling an Attic Ceiling

Tongue-and-groove paneling is a pleasing alternative to a wallboard ceiling, particularly in a knee-wall attic. Pine paneling is most common, but any tongue-and-groove material can be used. These materials are typically ⅜ to ¾" thick and are attached directly to ceiling joists and rafters (over faced insulation, when required). Most codes require you to install ⅜" wallboard as a fire stop under ceiling material thinner than ¼".

Allow for waste by purchasing 15% more material than the square footage of the ceiling; add more for waste if the ceiling requires many angled cuts. Since the tongue portion on most pieces slips into the groove on an adjacent piece, square footage is based on the exposed face (called the *reveal*) once the boards are installed. A compound miter saw is the best tool for ensuring clean cuts. This is especially important if the ceiling includes non-90° angles.

Tongue-and-groove boards are attached with

flooring nails driven through the shoulder of the tongue into each rafter (called *blindnailing* because the nail heads are covered by the next board). Nailing through the board face is only necessary on the first and last course and on scarf joints.

Layout is very important to the success of a paneled surface, because the lines clearly reveal flaws such as pattern deviations, misaligned walls, and installation mistakes. Before beginning the installation, measure to see how many boards will be installed (using the reveal measurement). If the final board will be less than 2 inches wide, trim the first, or *starter*, board by trimming the long edge that abuts the wall.

If the angle of the ceiling peak is not parallel to the wall, you must compensate for the difference by ripping the starter piece at an angle so that the leading edge, and every piece thereafter, is parallel to the peak.

How to Panel an Attic Ceiling

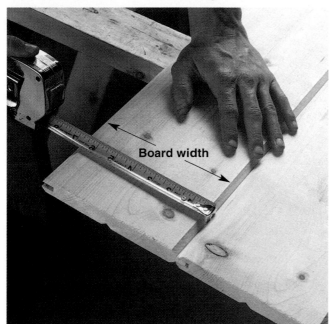

1 To plan your layout, first measure the reveal of the boards—the exposed surface when they are installed. Fit two pieces together and measure from the bottom edge of the upper board to the bottom edge of the lower board. Calculate the number of boards needed to cover one side of the ceiling by dividing the reveal dimension into the overall distance between the top of one wall and the peak.

2 Use the measurement from step 1 to snap a line marking the top of the first row: at both ends of the ceiling, measure down from the peak an equal distance, and make a mark to represent the tongue (top) edges of the starter boards. Keep in mind that the bottom edges must be bevel-cut to fit flush against the wall (see step 4). Snap a chalk line through the marks.

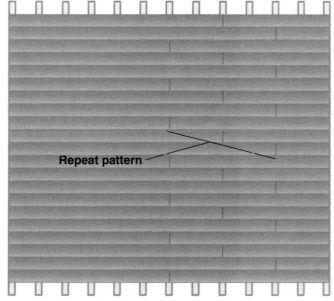

3 If the boards aren't long enough to span the entire ceiling, plan the locations of the seams. Staggering the locations of the seams in a three-step pattern will help hide the seams. Note that each seam must fall in the middle of a rafter.

4 Rip the first starter board to width by bevel-cutting the bottom (grooved) edge with a circular saw. If the starter row will have seams, cut the board to length using a 30° bevel cut on the seam-end only. Two beveled ends joined together form a scarf joint (inset), which is less noticeable than a butt joint. If the board spans the ceiling, square-cut both ends.

(continued next page)

5 Position the starter board so the grooved (or cut) edge butts against the side wall and the tongue is aligned with the control line. Leave a ⅛" gap between the square board end and the wall. Fasten the board by nailing through its face about 1" from the grooved edge, into the rafters. Then, blindnail through the base of the tongue into each rafter, angling the nail backwards at 45°. Drive the nail heads beneath the wood surface, using a nail set.

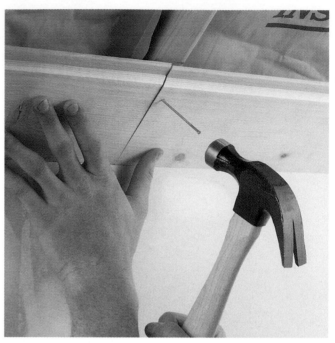

6 Cut and install any remaining boards in the starter row one at a time, making sure the scarf-joint seams fit together tightly. For best appearance, select boards of similar coloring and grain for each row.

7 Cut the first board for the next row, then fit its grooved edge over the tongue of the board in the starter row. Use a hammer and a scrap piece of paneling to tap along the tongue edge, seating the grooved edge over the tongue of the starter board. Fasten the second row of board with blindnails only.

8 As you install successive rows, measure down from the peak to make sure the boards are parallel to the peak. Correct any misalignment by adjusting the tongue-and-groove joint slightly with each row. You can also snap additional control lines to help align the rows.

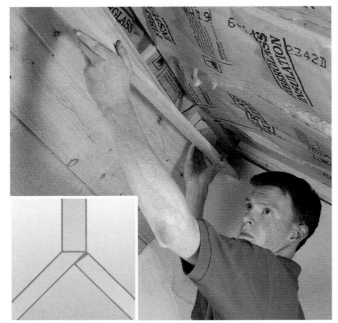

9 Rip the boards for the last row to width, beveling the top edges so they fit flush against the ridge board. Facenail the boards in place. Install paneling on the other side of the ceiling, then custom-cut the final row of panels to form a closed joint at the peak (inset).

10 Install trim molding along walls, at seams, around obstacles, and along inside and outside corners, if desired. (Select-grade 1 × 2s work well as trim along walls.) For trim along the bottom edge, bevel the back of the trim to match the slope of the ceiling.

Tips for Paneling an Attic Ceiling

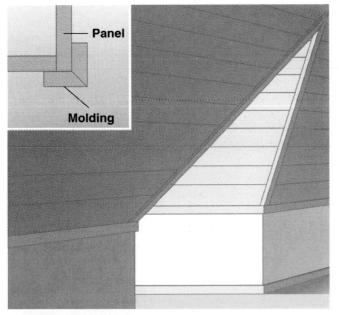

Install trim molding to hide the joints where panels meet at opposing angles, such as on the corners of a dormer. Miter-cut the moldings and install them over the butt joint of the corners to hide the seam. Moldings can also be cut from paneling boards and given a decorative edge with a router and bit.

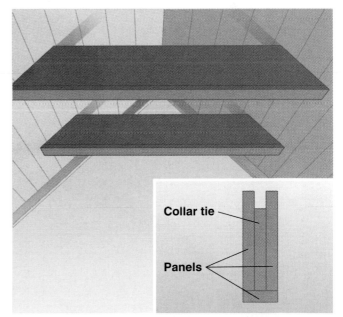

Wrap collar ties or exposed beams with custom-cut panels. Use a T-bevel to determine the angle for mitering the board ends where they meet the ceiling surface. Mitered joints are best when wrapping a collar tie, but if boards are installed with butt joints, make the bottom piece wide enough so that the side pieces will butt against it.

147

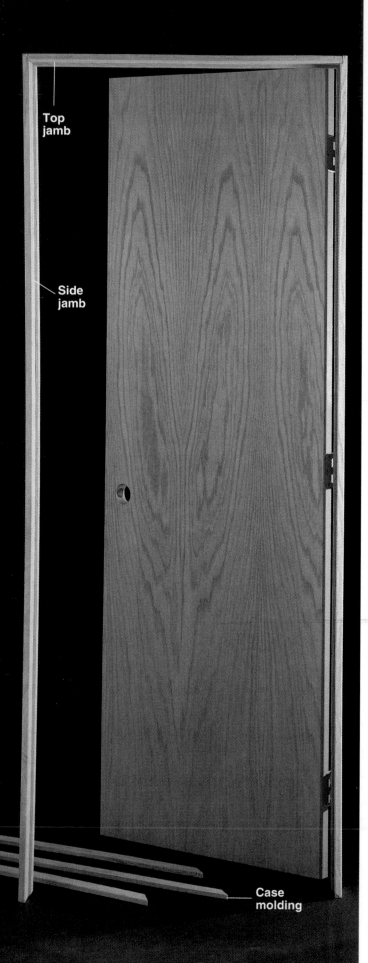

Top
jamb

Side
jamb

Case
molding

Installing a Prehung Interior Door

Install prehung interior doors after the framing work is complete and the wallboard has been installed (see pages 132 to 139). If the rough opening for the door has been framed accurately, installing the door takes about an hour.

Standard prehung doors have 4½"-wide jambs and are sized to fit walls with 2 × 4 construction and ½" wallboard. If you have 2 × 6 construction or thicker wall surface material, you can special-order a door to match, or you can add jamb extensions to a standard-size door (photo, below).

Everything You Need:

Tools: Level, hammer, handsaw.

Materials: Prehung interior door, wood shims, 8d casing nails.

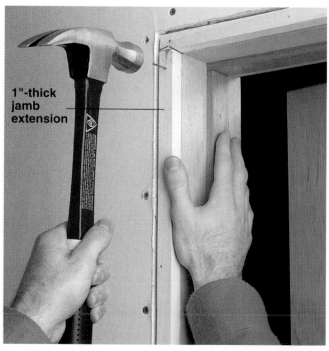

1"-thick
jamb
extension

TIP: If your walls are built with 2 × 6 studs, you'll need to extend the jambs by attaching 1"-thick wood strips to the edges of the jamb after the door is installed. Use glue and 4d casing nails when attaching jamb extensions.

How to Install a Prehung Interior Door

1 Slide the door unit into the framed opening so the edges of the jambs are flush with the wall surface and the hinge-side jamb is plumb.

2 Insert pairs of wood shims driven from opposite directions into the space between the framing members and the hinge-side jamb, spaced every 12". Check the hinge-side jamb to make sure it is still plumb and does not bow.

3 Anchor the hinge-side jamb with 8d casing nails driven through the jamb and shims and into the jack stud.

4 Insert pairs of shims in the space between the framing members and the latch-side jamb and top jamb, spaced every 12". With the door closed, adjust the shims so the gap between door edge and jamb is ⅛" wide. Drive 8d casing nails through the jambs and shims, into the framing members.

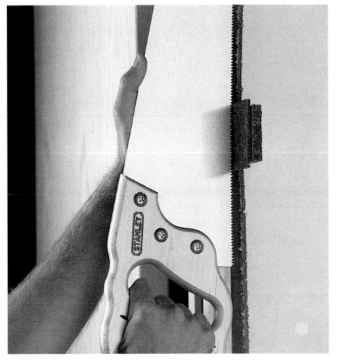

5 Cut the shims flush with the wall surface, using a handsaw. Hold the saw vertically to prevent damage to the door jamb or wall. Finish the door and install the lockset as directed by the manufacturer. See pages 152 to 155 to install trim around the door.

Hollow-core doors have solid wood frames, with hollow center cores. If the entire frame member is cut away when shortening a door, it can be reinserted to close the hollow door cavity. Measure carefully when marking a door for cutting.

Shortening an Interior Door

Prehung interior doors should allow a ¾" gap between the bottom of the door and the floor. This gap lets the door swing without binding on carpet or floor covering. If a thicker carpet or a larger threshold is installed, the door may need to be shortened.

Shortening a hollow-core door requires a few more steps because the door consists of multiple pieces. Depending on the width of the cut, the pieces may need to be cut and then reassembled.

If the door is solid wood, material can usually be removed by planing the edge, using a hand plane or power plane.

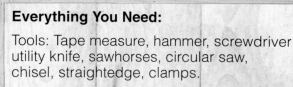

Everything You Need:

Tools: Tape measure, hammer, screwdriver utility knife, sawhorses, circular saw, chisel, straightedge, clamps.

Materials: Carpenter's glue.

How to Cut Off a Hollow-core Interior Door

1 With the door in place, measure ⅜" up from the top of the floor covering and mark the door. Remove the door from the hinges by tapping out the hinge pins with a screwdriver and a hammer.

2 Mark the cutting line. Cut through the door veneer with a sharp utility knife to prevent it from chipping when the door is sawed.

3 Lay the door on sawhorses and clamp a straightedge to the door as a cutting guide.

4 Saw off the bottom of the door. The hollow core of the door may be exposed.

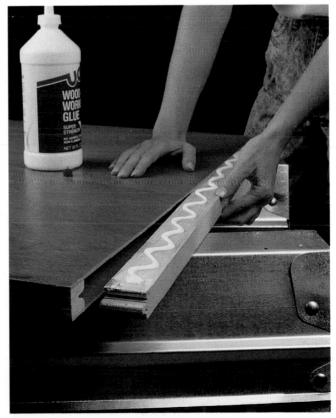

5 To reinstall a cut-off frame piece in the bottom of the door, chisel the veneer from both sides of the removed portion.

6 Apply wood glue to the cut-off frame. Insert the frame piece into the opening of the door and clamp it. Wipe away any excess glue and let the door dry overnight.

Installing Door & Window Casings

Door and window casings provide an attractive border around doors and windows. They also cover the gaps between door or window jambs and the surfaces of surrounding walls.

Install door and window casings with a consistent reveal between the inside edges of the jambs and casings, making sure the casings are level and plumb.

In order to fit casings properly, the jambs and wallcoverings must lie in the same plane. If either one protrudes, the casings will not lie flush. To solve this problem, you'll need to remove some material from whichever surface is protruding.

Use a block plane to shave protruding jambs or a surface forming rasp to shave a protruding wallboard edge (page 84). Wallboard screws rely on the strength of untorn facing paper to support the wallboard. If the paper around the screws is damaged, drive additional screws nearby where the paper is still intact.

Photo courtesy of Andersen Windows, Inc.

Everything You Need:

Tools: Tape measure, pencil, combination square, nail set, level, straight edge, power miter saw, hammer or pneumatic nailer.

Materials: Casing material, plinths and corner blocks (optional), 4d and 6d finish nails, wood putty.

How to Install Mitered Casing on Doors & Windows

1 On each jamb, mark a reveal line ⅛" from the inside edge. The casings will be installed flush with these lines. NOTE: On double-hung windows, the casings are usually installed flush with the edge of the jambs, so no reveal line is needed.

2 Place a length of casing along one side jamb, flush with the reveal line. At the top and bottom of the molding, mark the points where horizontal and vertical reveal lines meet. (When working with doors, mark the molding at the top only).

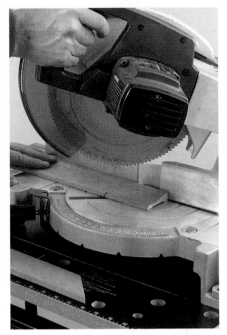

3 Make 45° miter cuts on the ends of the moldings (page 65). Measure and cut the other vertical molding piece, using the same method.

4 Drill pilot holes spaced every 12" to prevent splitting and attach the vertical casings with 4d finish nails driven through the casings and into the jambs. Drive 6d finish nails into framing members near the outside edge of the casings.

5 Measure the distance between the side casings, and cut top and bottom casings to fit, with ends mitered at 45°. If window or door unit is not perfectly square, make test cuts on scrap pieces to find the correct angle of the joints. Drill pilot holes and attach with 4d and 6d finish nails.

6 Locknail the corner joints by drilling pilot holes and driving 4d finish nails through each corner, as shown. Drive all nail heads below the wood surface, using a nail set, then fill the nail holes with wood putty.

How to Install Butted Door Casings

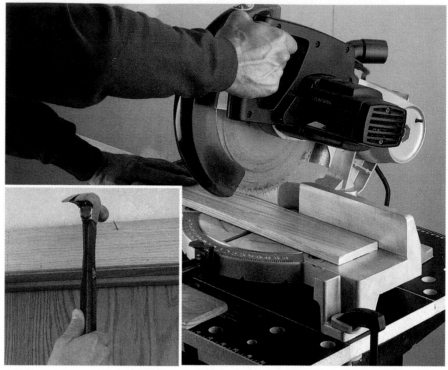

1 On each jamb, mark a reveal line ⅛" from the inside edge. The casings will be installed flush with these lines.

2 Cut the head casing to length. Mark the centerpoint of the head casing and the centerpoint of the head jamb. Align the casing with the head jamb reveal line, matching the centerpoints so that the head casing extends evenly beyond both side jambs. Nail the casing to the wall at stud locations and at the jamb.

3 Hold the side casings against the head casing and mark them for cutting, then cut the side casings to fit.

4 Align the side casings with the side jamb reveal lines, then nail the casings to the jambs and framing members. Set the nails, using a nail set. Fill the nail holes with wood putty.

Options for Installing Door & Window Casings

Combine mitered and butted casings. Form miter joints at the top of the window, then square-cut the bottoms of the side casings. Cut the sill casing to extend 1" beyond the side casings. Hand-sand the ends with 150-grit sandpaper, removing any rough edges.

Mark the sill casing 1" from each end, then invert it so thick edge is up. Attach the sill casing to the wall with finish nails so the pencil marks are aligned with the edges of the side casings.

Dress up door casings by adding plinths. Cut the plinths from 1 × plinth stock and bevel one edge. Nail the plinths to the jambs with 2" finish nails so the beveled edges are aligned with the reveal lines for the casings.

Head casing

Add corner blocks, also known as *rosettes*, at the ends of the head casing. Attach the corner blocks once the side casings are in place, then cut the head casing to fit. Set the nails, using a nailset, after all pieces are installed.

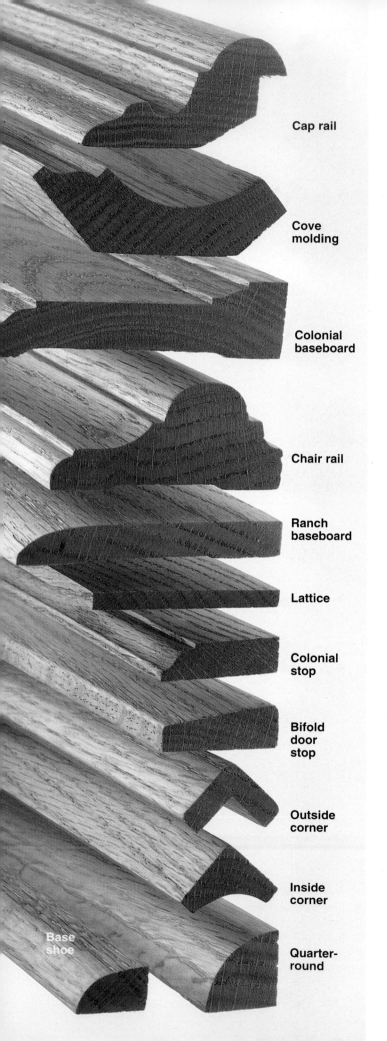

Cap rail

Cove molding

Colonial baseboard

Chair rail

Ranch baseboard

Lattice

Colonial stop

Bifold door stop

Outside corner

Inside corner

Base shoe

Quarter-round

Installing Baseboard & Ceiling Trim

Baseboard and ceiling trim are designed to dress up a room while concealing the joints where the walls meet the ceiling and the floor. Because baseboard and ceiling trim require many miter cuts, you'll need to familiarize yourself with the use of a miter box (page 46) or a power miter saw (pages 62 to 69) for cutting. Practice on scrap materials until you can construct joints that have no discernible gaps when you view them from a distance of 2 to 3 ft. When you're ready to cut pieces for the walls, remember that the corners of walls are seldom perfectly square. You may need to adjust the angle of the miter on some pieces and use caulk after installation to fill small gaps.

When purchasing trim, select straight, solid pieces that are free of knots. Whenever possible, purchase pieces long enough to span an entire wall. To span walls in big rooms or long hallways, you will need to join two pieces of trim with a scarf joint. To avoid problems due to shrinkage after installation, stack trim in the room where it will be installed and allow it to acclimate for several days. Next, apply a coat of primer or sealer to the front, back, and edges of each piece. Let it dry thoroughly before you begin the project. Note: If you choose to paint trim prior to installation, you'll need to add a touch-up coat once the installation is completed.

Everything You Need:

Tools: Pencil, level, chalk line, power miter saw or miter box and back saw, coping saw, drill with bits, stud finder, utility knife, T-bevel, hammer or pneumatic nailer, nail set.

Materials: Trim, primer, 6d finish nails or pneumatic nailer nails, wood putty, paintable caulk.

Baseboard and ceiling trim can consist of one piece or several on each wall. Popular baseboard treatments include a base, shoe, and cap molding. Elaborate crown moldings have five or more parts that form a highly decorative transition between walls and ceilings. Pine or poplar are common choices for baseboard that will be painted. Choose a hardwood, such as oak, for trim that you plan to stain.

Planning a Baseboard or Ceiling Trim Project

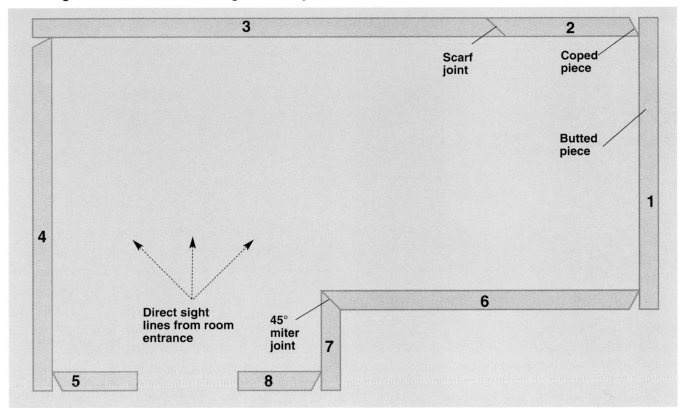

Plan the order of installation for your baseboard or ceiling moldings to save time and improve your results. Start by measuring the walls that are most noticeable—typically walls that are directly opposite entrances to the room. Cut and install the pieces for those walls first so that any gaps in the corners will be out of the direct line of sight when you enter the room. On subsequent pieces, cut the inside corners to size, then hold those pieces in position on the wall and mark the opposite ends for cutting. By doing so, you'll avoid cutting pieces that are too short.

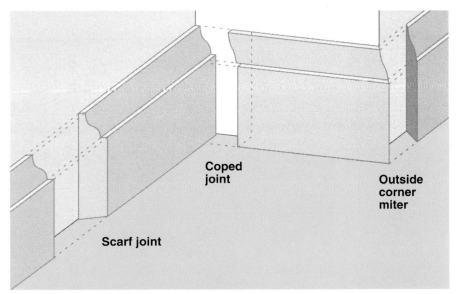

Joints used to install baseboard and ceiling trim depend on where they are located in the room. For joints that run along the length of a wall, use a scarf joint. Interior corners look better when a coped joint is used rather than a miter joint. For outside corners, miter joints look great. TIP: Do not assume that any corner is a true 90° angle. Measure each corner with a T-bevel before making miter cuts.

A pneumatic nailer greatly simplifies tasks such as nailing trim—it frees one hand to support the trim as you nail. A nailer also countersinks each nail automatically, eliminating the need to use a nail set.

157

Planning a Baseboard Trim Project

Dress up simple baseboard stock with cap moldings and base shoe or quarter round. Cap moldings are installed at an angle, like crown moldings. Cut these moldings, as you would ceiling moldings (page 69), using compound miter cuts.

Form butt joints at door casings by square-cutting the baseboard to meet the casing. Whenever possible, select trim with a profile no thicker than the casings, so the two trims will blend well where they meet.

How to Install Baseboard

1 Mark each wall about 1 ft. from the floor to indicate the locations of the studs. Use a stud finder if necessary.

2 Measure each wall and mark baseboard to fit, bearing in mind the order in which you plan to install each piece, and whether it will be mounted flush with the walls at each end or butted against adjacent pieces.

3 To install flat baseboard at inside corners, form simple butt joints by making a square cut on the end of each piece, then mount one piece flush with the adjacent wall and butt the other piece against the first.

4 At outside corners, hold each piece in position and mark them for cutting where the inside edge meets the outside corner of the wall. Set a miter saw to 45°, and make miter cuts.

5 Drill pilot holes and attach the baseboard pieces. Drive nails, slightly offset, at each stud location, ½" from the top and bottom of the piece so the upper nails enter the studs and the lower nails enter the sole plate.

6 Lock-nail the outside corners by driving an additional nail at a slight angle through each piece about 1" from the joint. If you're nailing with a hammer, use a nail set to sink each nail head slightly below the surface. Fill the nail holes with wood putty.

Option: When installing contoured baseboard, butt one piece against the adjacent wall. Miter-cut the overlapping piece at a 45° angle, and cope the edge with a coping saw, following the contour of the piece.

How to Install Crown Molding

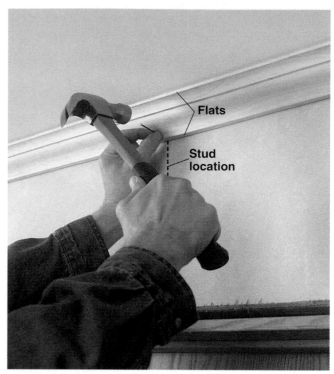

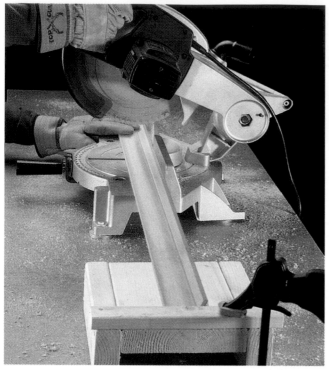

1 Measure and mark a piece of molding for the first wall. In the example shown here, installation begins on a wall that has an inside and an outside corner, so the molding is cut to length with a square cut at one end and a miter cut at the other end.

Flats

Stud location

2 Attach the first piece of molding by positioning it on the wall so the flats are flush against the wall and ceiling, drilling pilot holes, and driving finish nails through the flats of the molding at the stud locations. NOTE: To avoid splitting moldings, slightly offset the nails that will enter the ceiling joists from those that will enter the studs.

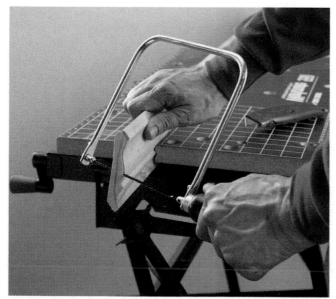

3 On a second piece of molding, make a 45° miter cut on the end that will mate with the previous piece. Cope the mitered edge with a coping saw, back-cutting slightly. Remove any burrs with a utility knife.

4 On the other end, make a miter cut for an outside corner. Attach the piece by driving finish nails as before. Install the remaining pieces, forming coped joints on each inside corner and mitered joints at outside corners. Drive nails to within ⅛" of the wood, then finish with a nail set. Fill the nail holes with wood putty.

160

Tips for Installing Single-piece Cove Molding

When using a standard miter saw, you'll need to position each piece of *sprung* molding upside down for cutting (page 69). With compound miter saws this isn't necessary.

Most ceiling moldings wrap the entire room. However, if it's necessary to stop the molding at some point, miter the end, then conceal the miter by cutting a mitered return piece to fit. Attach it by applying a thin bead of wood glue or hot glue to the mitered edges.

How to Install Chair Rail or Picture Rail

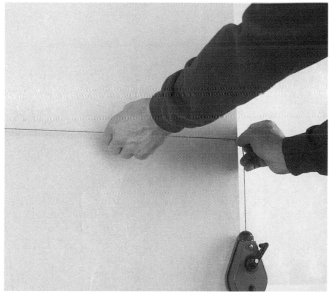

1 Snap level chalk lines to mark the edge of the molding that will be least visible. Cut the pieces as you would cut baseboard (pages 158 and 159).

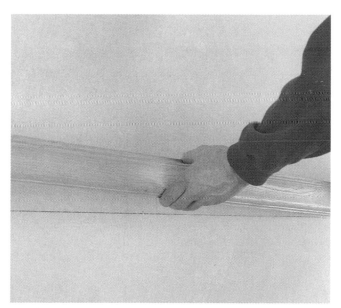

2 Locate and mark the studs, then align the edge of each piece with the chalk line. Nail the pieces to the studs, using finish nails. Use mitered returns (above), as necessary. Set the nails with a nail set, then fill the nail holes with wood putty.

Tongue-and-groove wainscoting boards are milled with smooth faces, or contoured to add additional texture to your walls. For staining, choose a wood species with a pronounced grain. For painting, poplar is a good choice, since it has few knots and a highly consistent grain.

Everything You Need:

Tools: Pencil, level, circular saw, miter saw or miter box, jig saw, hammer, nail set, compass, plane, circuit tester, pry bar, tape measure, paint brush.

Materials: Tongue-and-groove boards, 6d and 4d finish nails, receptacle box extenders (as required), baseboard and cap rail molding, paint or stain.

Installing Tongue-and-groove Wainscoting

Wainscoting refers to virtually any specialized treatment of the lower three to four feet of interior walls. The form demonstrated here, using tongue-and-groove boards, first gained popularity in the early twentieth century. Recently, it has re-emerged as a way to dress up a room.

Typical tongue-and-groove boards for wainscoting are made of pine, fir, or other softwoods and measure ¼ to ¾" thick. Each board has a tongue on one edge, a groove on the other, and usually a decorative bevel or bead on each edge. Boards are cut to length, then attached with nails, most of which are driven through the tongues of the boards. This technique, known as blindnailing (page 77), hides the nails from view.

Once installed, the wainscoting is capped at a height of 30 to 36" with a molding called a *cap rail*. The exact height of the wainscoting is a matter of personal preference. When installed to the height of the furniture in the room, wainscoting provides visual symmetry. It also allows the cap rail to double as a chair rail, protecting the lower portion of the walls from damage.

When installed over finished wallboard, wainscoting usually requires that nailers be fastened to the wall studs to provide a reliable backing for nailing. You can skip this step if you know there is consistent blocking between the studs to substitute for this backing. However, this is usually difficult to confirm unless the walls were framed with tongue-and-groove wainscoting in mind.

Wainscoting can be painted or stained. Oil-based stains can be applied before or after installation, since most of the stain will be absorbed into the wood and won't interfere with the tongue-and-groove joints. If you're painting, choose a latex-based paint; it will resist cracking as the joints expand and contract with changes in the weather.

How to Prepare for a Wainscoting Project

Measure to make a plan drawing of each wall in your project. Indicate the locations of fixtures, receptacles, and windows. Use a level to make sure the corners are plumb. If not, mark plumb lines on the walls to use as reference points.

Condition the planking by stacking it in the room where it will be installed. Place spacers between the planks to let air circulate around each board, allowing the wood to adjust to the room's temperature and humidity. Wait 72 hours before staining or sealing the front, back and edges of each plank.

Remove the baseboard moldings, along with any receptacle cover plates, vent covers, or other wall fixtures within the area you plan to cover. Before you begin, turn off the electricity to the circuits in the area.

Mark the walls with level lines to indicate the top of the wainscoting. Mark a line ¼" from the floor to provide a small gap for expansion at the floor.

(continued next page)

How to Prepare for a Wainscoting Project (continued)

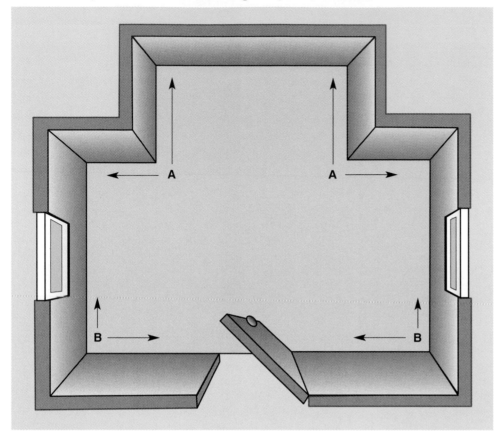

Begin installation at the corners. Install any outside corners (A) first, working your way toward the inside corners. In sections of a room that have no outside corners, start at the inside corners (B), and work your way toward the door and window casings. Calculate the number of boards required for each wall using the measurements on the drawing you created earlier (length of wall ÷ width of one plank). When making this calculation, remember that the tongues are removed from the corner boards. If the total number of boards for a wall includes a fraction of less than ½ of a board, plan to trim the first and last boards to avoid ending with a board cut to less than half its original width.

How to Install Wainscoting at Outside Corners

1 Cut a pair of boards to the widths indicated in the calculations you developed during the planning process.

2 Position the boards at the corner, butting them to create a plumb corner. Facenail the boards in place, then nail the joint, using 6d finish nails. Drive the nails to within ⅛" of the face of the boards, then finish with a nail set.

3 Position a piece of corner trim and nail it in place, using 6d finish nails. Install the remaining boards (opposite, steps 5 and 6).

How to Install Wainscoting at Inside Corners

1 Hold a level against the first board and hold the board flush with the corner. If the wall is out of plumb, trim the board to compensate: Hold the board plumb, position a compass at the inside corner of the wall and use it to scribe a line down the board.

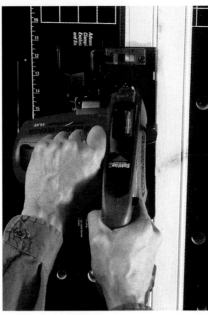

2 Cut along the scribed line with a circular saw.

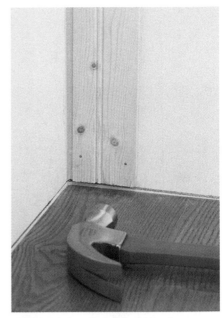

3 Hold the first board in the corner, leaving a ¼" gap for expansion, and facenail into the center of the board at each nailer location, using 6d finish nails. Drive the top nails roughly ½" from the edge so they'll be hidden from view once the cap rail is attached.

4 Install a second board at the corner by butting it against the first one, then facenailing in at least two locations. Nail to within ⅛" of the face of the board, then use a nail set to finish.

5 Position subsequent boards. Leave a ¹⁄₁₆" gap at each joint to allow for seasonal expansion. Use a level to check every third board for plumb. If the wainscoting is out of plumb, adjust the fourth board, as necessary, to compensate.

6 Mark and cut the final board to fit. If you're at a door casing, cut the board to fit flush with the casing (trim off at least the tongue). If you're at an inside corner, make sure it is plumb. If not, scribe and trim the board to fit.

How to Make a Cutout

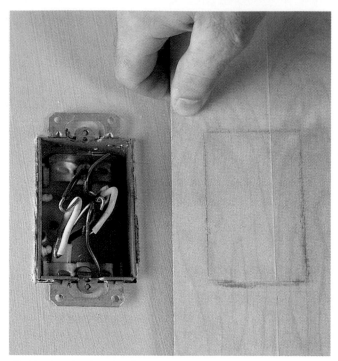

1 Test the receptacle (inset) to make sure the power is off. Then, unscrew and remove the receptacle from the box. Coat the edges of the electrical box with bright colored chalk.

2 Press the back of the board that will be installed over the receptacle directly against the electrical box, to create a cutting outline.

3 Lay the board face-down and drill a large pilot hole near one corner of the outline. Use a jig saw fitted with a fine-tooth woodcutting blade to make the cutout. Be careful not to cut outside the lines.

4 Facenail the wainscoting to the wall, then reattach the receptacle with the tabs overlapping the wainscoting so the receptacle is flush with the opening. You may need longer screws.

TIP: When paneling around a receptacle with thick stock, you will need to attach a receptacle box extender to the inside of the box, then reconnect the receptacle so it is flush with the opening in the paneling.

166

How to Install Wainscoting Around a Window

On casement windows, install wainscoting up to the casings on the sides and below the window. Install ½" cove molding or other trim to finish the edges.

On double-hung windows, install wainscoting up to the side casings. You can notch the wainscoting to fit around the stool, or remove the stool and notch it to fit over the wainscoting. Remove the apron (below the stool) and reinstall it over the wainscoting.

How to Finish a Wainscoting Project

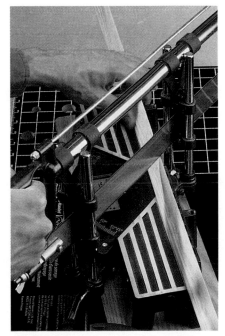

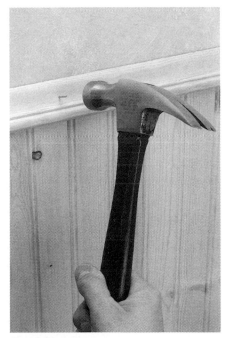

1 Cut baseboard moldings (pages 156 to 159) to fit over the wainscoting and attach them by nailing 6d finishing nails at the stud locations. If you plan to install base shoe, leave a small gap at the floor.

2 Cut cap rail to fit as you would contoured baseboard (page 159). At doors and windows, install cap rail so its edge is flush with the side casings.

3 Attach the cap rail by nailing 4d finish nails through the flats of the moldings at the stud locations. Set the nails with a nail set.

Advanced Projects

Enlarging Openings & Removing Walls

Many carpentry projects actually begin with demolition. When you're remodeling, it's often necessary to cut or enlarge openings for new doors or windows, or even to remove entire walls. The basic procedures for this type of demolition are the same whether you're working with doors and windows on exterior walls or altering interior walls.

Your first step will be to determine how your house was framed (pages 102 and 103). House framing variations will dictate the proper procedures for creating openings in walls or removing walls altogether. Then, you'll need to inspect the walls for hidden mechanicals—wiring, plumbing, and HVAC lines.

After you've rerouted any utility lines, you're ready to remove the interior wall surfaces (pages 172-175). If you're replacing old windows and doors, now is the time to remove them as well (pages 180-181). Where necessary, you can now remove exterior wall surfaces (pages 176-179), but don't remove any framing members yet.

The next step will depend on the nature of your project.

If you are removing a load-bearing wall, or creating a new or enlarged opening in one, you'll need to build temporary supports to brace the ceiling while the work is being done (pages 182-185). This step won't be necessary if you are removing a non-loadbearing wall.

Now you can remove any wall framing members (pages 186-191), following the applicable procedures for load-bearing or non-loadbearing walls.

With the destructive steps of the project completed, you'll be ready for the creative: installing new windows and doors. Information on these subjects begins on page 192.

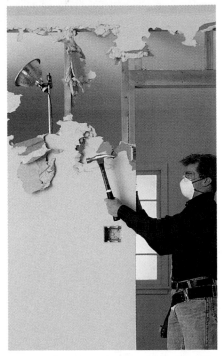

Removing interior wall surfaces is found on pages 172-173 (wallboard) and on pages 174-175 (plaster).

Removing exterior wall surfaces is covered on pages 176 to 179.

Removing interior partition walls between rooms is covered on pages 186 to 188.

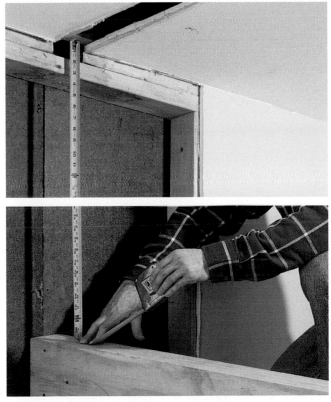

Removing interior load-bearing walls is covered on pages 188 to 191. Make sure to create temporary supports (pages 182-185) before removing or altering load-bearing walls.

Instructions for installing doors and windows begins on page 192.

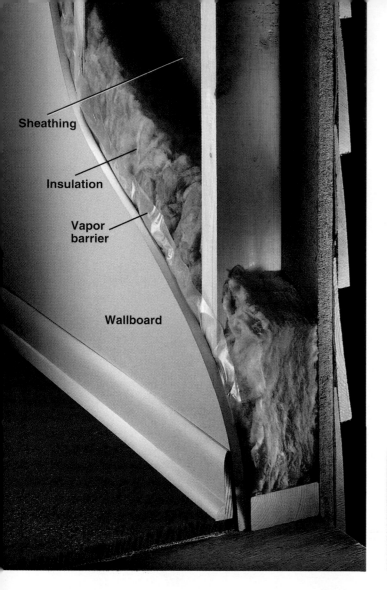

Sheathing

Insulation

Vapor barrier

Wallboard

Removing Wallboard

You must remove interior wall surfaces before starting the framing work for most remodeling projects. Most often, the material you'll be removing is wallboard. Demolishing a section of wallboard is a messy job, but it is not difficult. Before you begin, shut off the power and inspect the wall for wiring and plumbing.

Remove enough surface material so that there is plenty of room to install the new framing members. When framing for a window or door, remove the wall surface from floor to ceiling and all the way to the first wall studs on either side of the planned rough opening. If the wallboard was attached with construction adhesive, clean the framing members with a rasp or an old chisel.

NOTE: If your walls are covered in wood paneling, remove it in full sheets if you intend to reuse it. It may be difficult to find new paneling to match the old style.

Everything You Need:

Tools: Screwdrivers, tape measure, pencil, stud finder, chalk line, circular saw with demolition blade, utility knife, pry bar, protective eye wear, hammer.

How to Remove Wallboard

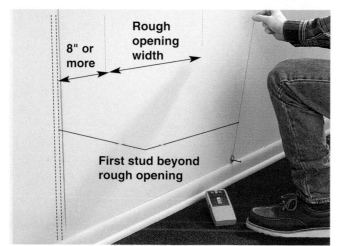

1 Mark the width of the rough opening on the wall and locate the first stud on either side of the planned rough opening. If the rough opening is more than 8" from the next stud, use a chalk line to mark a cutting line on the inside edge of the stud. During framing, an extra stud will be attached to provide a surface for anchoring the new wallboard (page 137).

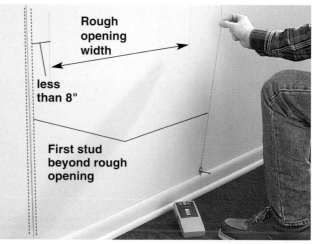

TIP: If the rough opening is less than 8" from the next stud, you will not have room to attach an extra stud. Use a chalk line to mark the cutting line down the center of the wall stud. The exposed portion of the stud will provide a surface for attaching new wallboard when finishing the room.

2 Remove the baseboards and other trim, and prepare the work area (page 109). Make a ¾"-deep cut from floor to ceiling along both cutting lines, using a circular saw. Use a utility knife to finish the cuts at the top and bottom and to cut through the taped horizontal seam where the wall meets the ceiling surface.

3 Insert the end of a pry bar into the cut near a corner of the opening. Pull the pry bar until the wallboard breaks, then tear away the broken pieces. Take care to avoid damaging the wallboard outside the project area.

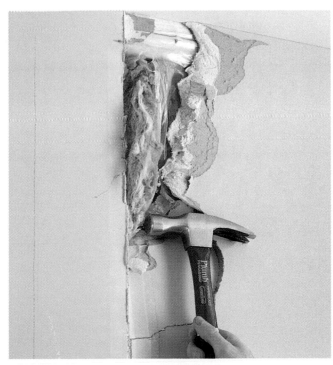

4 Continue removing the wallboard by striking the surface with the side of a hammer, and pulling the wallboard away from the wall with the pry bar or your hands.

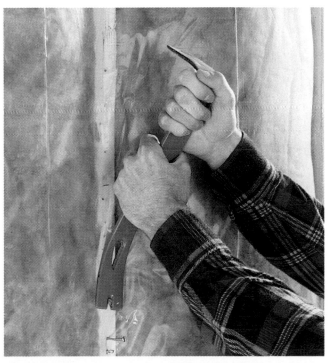

5 Remove nails, screws, and any remaining wallboard from the framing members, using a pry bar. Remove any vapor barrier and insulation.

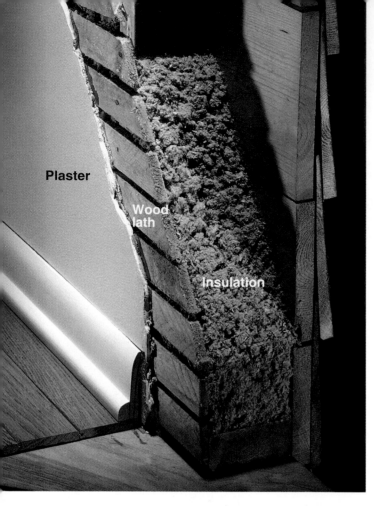

Plaster

Wood lath

Insulation

Removing Plaster

Plaster removal is a dusty job, so always wear eye protection and a particle mask during demolition, and use sheets of plastic to protect furniture and to block open doorways. Plaster walls are very brittle, so work carefully to avoid cracking the plaster in areas that will not be removed.

If the material being removed encompasses most of the wall surface, consider removing the whole interior surface of the wall. Replacing the entire wall with wallboard is easier and produces better results than trying to patch around the project area.

Everything You Need:

Tools: Straightedge, pencil, chalk line, utility knife, particle mask, work gloves, hammer, pry bar, reciprocating saw or jig saw, aviation snips, protective eye wear.

Materials: Masking tape, scrap 2 × 4.

How to Remove Plaster Walls

1 Shut off the power and inspect the wall for wiring and plumbing. Mark the wall area to be removed by following the directions on page 172. Apply a double layer of masking tape along the outside edge of each cutting line.

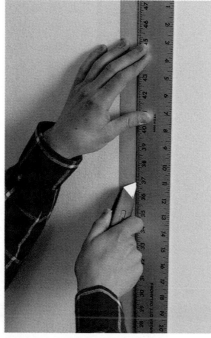

2 Score each line several times with a utility knife, using a straightedge as a guide. Scored lines should be at least ⅛" deep.

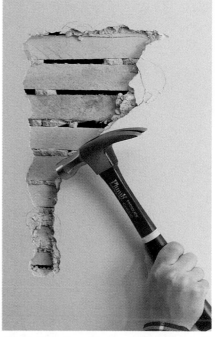

3 Beginning at the top of the wall in the center of the planned opening, break up the plaster by striking the wall lightly with the side of a hammer. Clear away all plaster from floor to ceiling to within 3" of the marked lines.

4 Break the plaster along the edges by holding a scrap piece of 2 × 4 on edge just inside the scored line, and rapping it with a hammer. Use a pry bar to remove the remaining plaster.

5 Cut through the lath along the edges of the plaster, using a reciprocating saw or jig saw.

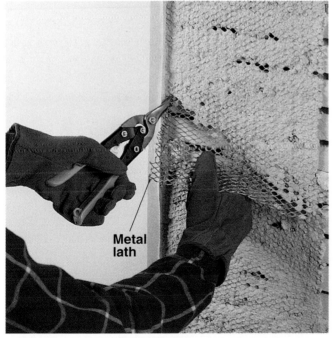

Metal lath

Variation: If the wall has metal lath laid over the wood lath, use aviation snips to clip the edges of the metal lath. Press the jagged edges of the lath flat against the stud. The cut edges of metal lath are very sharp; be sure to wear work gloves.

6 Remove the lath from the studs, using a pry bar. Pry away any remaining nails, and remove any vapor barrier and insulation.

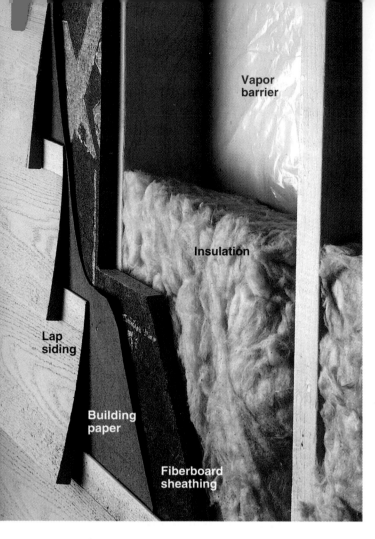

Vapor
barrier

Insulation

Lap
siding

Building
paper

Fiberboard
sheathing

Removing Exterior Surfaces

Exterior surfaces must be removed when you want to create a new opening for a door, window, or room addition in an exterior wall. Start by identifying the surface. If it is lap siding, it may be wood, vinyl, or metal. The same basic method is used for removal of any exterior surface. However, some materials must be cut with a specialty saw blade, such as a metal-cutting blade (page 52).

Always shut off the power and reroute utility lines, remove any interior surfaces, and frame in the new opening before removing an exterior surface. To protect the wall cavities against moisture, enclose the new opening as soon as you remove the old siding.

Everything You Need:

Tools: Drill with an 8"-long, ³⁄₁₆" twist bit; hammer; tape measure; chalk line; circular saw with remodeling blade; reciprocating saw; eye protection.
Materials: 8d casing nails, straight 1 × 4.

How to Make an Opening in Lap Siding

1 From inside the house, drill through the wall at the corners of the framed opening. Push casing nails through the holes to mark their location. For round-top windows, drill holes around the curved outline (see variation, page 179).

2 Measure the distance between the nails on the outside of the house to make sure the dimensions are accurate. Mark the cutting lines with a chalk line stretched between the nails. Push the nails back through the wall.

3 Nail a straight 1 × 4 flush with the inside edge of the right cutting line. Sink the nail heads with a nail set to prevent scratches to the foot of the saw. Set the circular saw to its maximum blade depth.

4 Rest the saw on the 1 × 4, and cut along the marked line, using the edge of the board as a guide. Stop the cuts about 1" short of the corners to keep from damaging the framing members.

5 Reposition the 1 × 4, and make the remaining straight cuts. Drive nails within 1½" of the inside edge of the board, because the siding under this area will be removed to make room for door or window brick moldings.

Variation: For round-top windows, make curved cuts using a reciprocating saw or jig saw. Move the saw slowly to ensure smooth, straight cuts. To draw an outline for round-top windows, use a cardboard template (page 213).

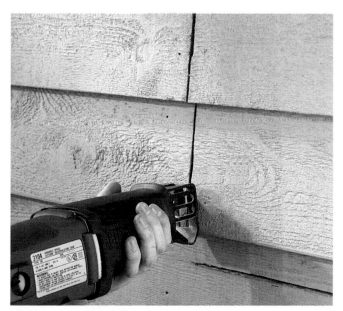

6 Complete the cuts at the corner with a reciprocating saw or jig saw.

7 Remove the cut wall section. If you are working with metal siding, wear work gloves. If you wish, remove the siding pieces from the sheathing and save them for future use.

How to Make an Opening in Stucco

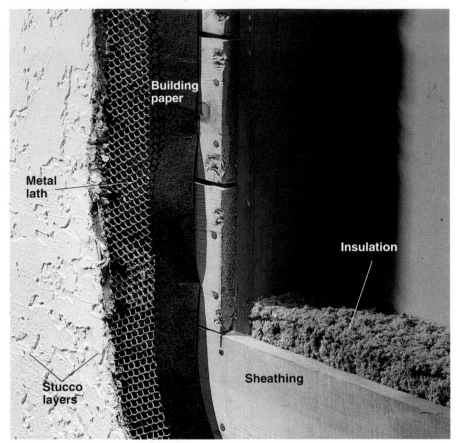

Building paper

Metal lath

Insulation

Sheathing

Stucco layers

TIP: Stucco is a multiple-layer cement product applied to metal lath. Building paper is sandwiched between the metal lath and the sheathing to create a waterproof barrier. Stucco is extremely durable due to its cement base. But if you don't do the removal carefully, it's easy to crack the stucco past the outline for the new window or door.

Everything You Need:

Tools: Drill with an 8" long, ³⁄₁₆" twist and masonry bits, tape measure, chalk line, compass, masonry hammer, eye and ear protection, circular saw and blades (masonry-cutting and remodeling), masonry chisels, pry bar, aviation snips.

Materials: 8d casing nails.

1 From inside the house, drill through the wall at the corners of the framed opening. Use a twist bit to drill through the sheathing, then use a masonry bit to finish the holes. Push casing nails through the holes to mark their locations.

2 On the outside wall, measure the distance between the nails to make sure the rough opening dimensions are accurate. Mark cutting lines between the nails, using a chalk line.

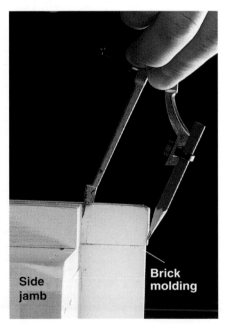

Side jamb

Brick molding

3 Match the distance between the side jambs and the edge of the brick molding on a window or door with the legs of a compass.

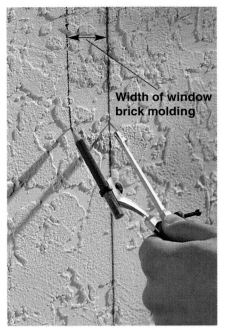

4 Scribe a cutting line on the stucco by moving the compass along the outline, with the compass point held on the marked line. This added margin will allow the brick molding to fit tight against the wall sheathing.

5 Score the stucco surface around the outside edge of the scribed line, using a masonry chisel and masonry hammer. The scored grooves should be at least ⅛" deep to serve as a guide for the circular saw blade.

6 Make straight cuts using a circular saw and masonry-cutting blade. Make several passes with the saw, gradually deepening the cuts until blade just cuts through the metal lath, causing sparks to fly. Stop cuts just ahead of the corners to avoid damaging the stucco past the cutting line; complete the cuts with a masonry chisel.

Variation: For round-top windows, mark the outline on the stucco, using a cardboard template (page 213), and drill a series of holes around the outline, using a masonry bit. Complete the cut with a masonry chisel.

7 Break up the stucco with a masonry hammer or sledgehammer, exposing the underlying metal lath. Use aviation snips to cut through the lath around the opening. Use a pry bar to pull away the lath and attached stucco.

8 Outline the rough opening on the sheathing, using a straightedge as a guide. Cut the rough opening along the inside edge of the framing members, using a circular saw or reciprocating saw. Remove the cut section of sheathing.

Masking tape used to keep windows from shattering

Removing Doors & Windows

If your remodeling project requires removing old doors and windows, do not start this work until all preparation work is finished and the interior wall surfaces and trim have been removed. You will need to close up the wall openings as soon as possible, so make sure you have all the necessary tools, framing lumber, and new window or door units before starting the final stages of demolition. Be prepared to finish the work as quickly as possible.

Doors and windows are removed using the same basic procedures. In many cases, old units can be salvaged for resale or later use, so use care when removing them.

Everything You Need:

Tools: Utility knife, flat pry bar, screwdriver, hammer, reciprocating saw.

Materials: Plywood sheets, masking tape.

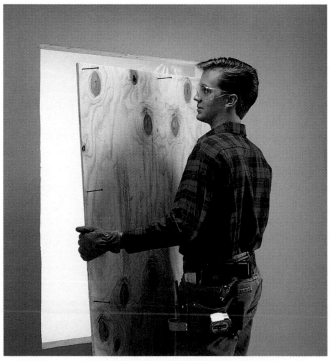

If wall openings cannot be filled immediately, protect your home by covering the openings with scrap pieces of plywood screwed to the framing members. Plastic sheeting stapled to the outside of the openings will prevent moisture damage.

How to Remove Doors & Windows

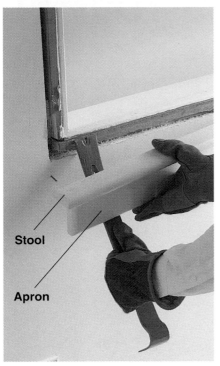

1 Remove the window trim, using a pry bar.

2 For double-hung windows with sash weights, remove the weights by cutting the cords and pulling the weights from the pockets.

3 Cut through the nails holding the window and door frames to the framing members, using a reciprocating saw.

4 Pry the brick moldings free from the framing members, using a pry bar.

5 Pull the unit from the rough opening, using a pry bar, and remove it completely.

Variation: For windows and doors attached with nailing fins, cut or pry loose the siding material or brick moldings, then remove the mounting nails holding the unit to the sheathing.

Temporary supports for a platform-framed house must support the ceiling joists, since the ceiling platform carries the load of the upper floors. Platform framing can be identified by the sole plate to which the wall studs are nailed.

Temporary supports for a balloon-framed house support the wall studs, which carry the upstairs load. The temporary support header, called a *whaler*, is anchored to the wall studs above the planned rough opening, and is supported by wall studs and bracing adjacent to the rough opening. Balloon framing can be identified by long wall studs that pass uncut through the floor to a sill plate resting on the foundation.

Making Temporary Supports

If your project requires you to remove more than one stud in a load-bearing wall, temporary supports will be needed while you do the framing. The technique for making temporary supports varies, depending on what type of construction was used to build your house. See pages 102 to 107 to easily identify wall types and other framing anatomy.

Interior load-bearing walls in a balloon-framed house and any load-bearing wall longer than 12 ft. should only be removed by a professional.

Removal of load-bearing interior walls requires temporary support on both sides of the wall.

To make temporary supports for platform framing, use hydraulic jacks or a temporary stud wall (page 184). The stud wall method is a better choice if the supports must remain in place for more than one day.

If the ceiling and floor joists run parallel to the wall you are working on, use the method shown at the bottom of page 184.

To make temporary supports for balloon framing, use the method shown on page 185.

Everything You Need:

Tools: Tape measure, level, circular saw, hammer, ratchet, drill and spade bit, hydraulic jacks.

Materials: 2 × 4 lumber, shims, 3 & 4" lag screws, 2" wallboard screws, 10d nails, cloth.

How to Support Platform Framing with Hydraulic Jacks (Joists Perpendicular to Wall)

1 Measure the width of the planned rough opening and add 4 feet so the temporary support will reach well past the rough opening. Cut three 2 × 4s to length. Nail two of the 2 × 4s together with 10d nails to make a top plate for the temporary support; the remaining 2 × 4 will be the sole plate. Place the temporary sole plate on the floor, 3 ft. from the wall, centering it on the planned rough opening.

2 Set the hydraulic jacks on the temporary sole plate, 2 ft. in from the ends. (Use three jacks if the opening will be more than 8 ft. wide.) For each jack, build a post by nailing together a pair of 2 × 4s. The posts should be about 4" shorter than the distance between the ceiling and the top of the jacks. Attach the posts to the top plate, 2 ft. from the ends, using countersunk lag screws.

Direction of joists

3 Cover the top of the plate with a thick layer of cloth to protect the ceiling from marks and cracks, then lift the support structure onto the hydraulic jacks.

4 Adjust the support structure so the posts are exactly plumb, and raise the hydraulic jacks until the top plate just begins to lift the ceiling. Do not lift too far, or you may damage the floor and ceiling.

How to Support Platform Framing With a Temporary Stud Wall (Joists Perpendicular to Wall)

1 Build a 2 × 4 stud wall that is 4 ft. wider than the planned wall opening and 1¾" shorter than the distance from floor to ceiling.

2 Raise the stud wall up and position it 3 ft. from the wall, centered on the planned rough opening.

3 Slide a 2 × 4 top plate between the temporary wall and the ceiling. Check to make sure the wall is plumb, and drive shims under the top plate at 12" intervals until the wall is wedged tightly in place.

How to Support Platform Framing (Joists Parallel to the Wall)

1 Follow directions on page 183, except: Build two 4-ft.-long cross braces, using pairs of 2 × 4s nailed together. Attach the cross braces to the double top plate, 1 ft. from the ends, using countersunk lag screws.

2 Place a 2 × 4 sole plate directly over a floor joist, then set hydraulic jacks on the sole plate. For each jack, build a post 8" shorter than the jack-to-ceiling distance. Nail the posts to the top plate, 2 ft. from the ends. Cover the braces with the cloth, and set the support structure on the jacks.

3 Adjust the support structure so the posts are exactly plumb, and pump the hydraulic jacks until the cross braces just begin to lift the ceiling. Do not lift too far, or you may damage the ceiling or floor.

How to Support Balloon Framing

1 Remove the wall surfaces around the rough opening from floor to ceiling (pages 172 to 175). Make a temporary support header (called a whaler) by cutting a 2 × 8 long enough to extend at least 20" past each side of the planned rough opening. Center the whaler against the wall studs, flush with the ceiling. Tack the whaler in place with 2" screws.

2 Cut two lengths of 2 × 4 to fit snugly between the bottom of the whaler and the floor. Slide the 2 × 4s into place at the ends of the whaler, and attach them with nailing plates and 10d nails.

3 Drill two ³⁄₁₆" holes through the whaler and into each stud it spans. Secure the whaler with ⅜ × 4" lag screws.

4 Drive shims between the bottom of each 2 × 4 and the floor to help secure the support structure.

Header made from two pieces of MicroLam®

Post

Post

Spacing blocks

Spacing blocks

Nailing strip

When removing a wall, first shut off and reroute all utilities in the work area. Then, tear off the wall surface, exposing the framing members. Do not cut wall studs until you know whether you are working with a load-bearing wall, or a non-load-bearing (partition) wall (page 109). If the wall is load-bearing, you will need to install temporary supports (pages 182 to 185) before cutting out the studs. After removal of the wall surface, install a permanent header and posts strong enough to carry the structural weight once borne by the wall. The posts will be hidden inside the adjacent walls after the wallboard is patched. The header will be visible, but covering it with wallboard will help it blend in with the ceiling.

Removing Interior Walls

Removing an existing wall is an easy way to create more usable space without the expense of building an addition. Removing a wall turns two small rooms into a large space perfect for family living. Adding new walls in a larger area creates a private space to use as a quiet study or as a new bedroom for a growing family.

The techniques for removing a wall vary, depending on the location and structural function of the wall (see pages 102 to 107).

In addition to defining living areas and supporting the house structure, walls also hold the essential mechanical systems that run through your home. You will need to consider how your project affects the mechanicals of your house. Have a professional make changes to the mechanicals of your house if you aren't confident of your skills.

> ### Everything You Need:
>
> Tools: Tape measure, pencil, drill and bits, reciprocating saw, pry bar, hammer.
>
> Materials (for installing a header): 2" dimension lumber, MicroLam® framing members, 10d nails.

Materials for Building a Header

Beam made from 2 x 12s and plywood: 8-ft. maximum recommended span.

Double 9½" MicroLam® beam: 10-ft. maximum recommended span. MicroLam® framing members are made from thin layers of wood laminate glued together.

Double 11⅜" MicroLam® beam: 11-ft. maximum recommended span.

12" Glue-lam beam: 12-ft. maximum recommended span. Glue-lam beams are made from layers of dimension lumber laminated together.

Manufactured support members are stronger and more durable than 2" dimension lumber, so they work well for building headers to replace load-bearing walls. Always consult your local building inspector or a professional builder when choosing materials and sizes for a support header.

Tips for Installing a Header

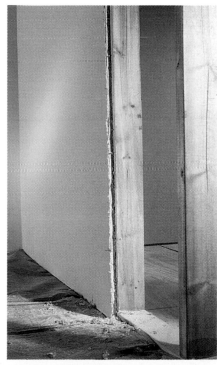

When removing wall surfaces, expose the wall to the first permanent stud at each side of the opening.

Leave a small portion of exposed sole plate to serve as the base for posts. In a load-bearing wall, leave 3" of sole plate to hold the double 2 × 4 post that will support the permanent header. In a non-load-bearing wall, leave 1½" of exposed sole plate to hold one extra wall stud. Remove the top plates over the entire width of the opening.

How to Remove Wall Framing

1 Prepare the project site and remove the wall surfaces. Remove or reroute any wiring, plumbing lines, or ductwork.

2 Remove the surface of the adjoining walls just enough to expose the permanent studs.

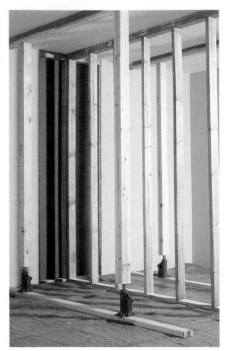

3 Determine if the wall being removed is load-bearing. If the wall is load-bearing, install temporary supports on each side (pages 182 to 185).

4 Remove studs by cutting them through the middle and prying them from the sole and top plates.

Nailing stud

5 Remove the end stud on each end of the wall. If the wall being removed is load-bearing, also remove any nailing studs or blocking in the adjoining walls directly behind the removed wall.

6 Make two cuts through the top plate, at least 3" apart, using a reciprocating saw. Remove the cut section with a pry bar.

7 Remove the remaining sections of the top plate, using a pry bar.

8 Cut out a 3"-wide section of sole plate, using a reciprocating saw. Pry out entire sole plate, using a pry bar. If the removed wall was load-bearing, install a permanent header (below).

How to Remove a Load-Bearing Wall With Platform Framing

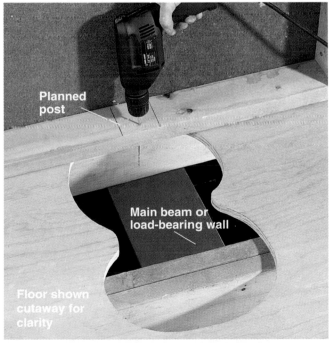

Planned post

Main beam or load-bearing wall

Floor shown cutaway for clarity

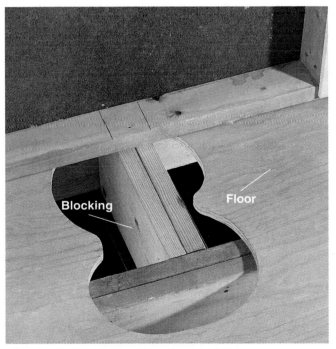

Blocking

Floor

1 Mark the location of the planned support posts on the sole plate. Drill through the sole plate where the support posts will rest to make sure there is a joist directly underneath. If not, install blocking under the post locations (step 2).

2 If necessary, cut and install double 2" blocking between joists. (You may need to cut into a finished ceiling to gain access to this space). Blocking should be the same size lumber as the joists. Attach blocks to joists with 10d nails.

(continued next page)

First ceiling joist

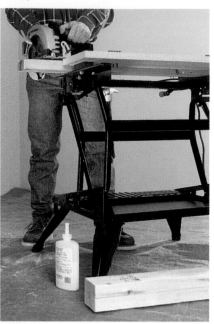

3 Build a support header to span the width of the removed wall, including the width of the support posts. See page 187 for header recommendations. In this project, the header is built with two lengths of MicroLam® joined with 10d nails.

4 Lay the ends of the header on the sole plates. Find the length for each support post by measuring between the top of the header and the bottom of the first ceiling joist in from the wall.

5 Make support posts by cutting pairs of 2 × 4s to length and joining them side by side with wood glue and 10d nails.

6 Measure the thickness (A) and width of the top plate at each end, then notch the top corners of the header to fit around the top plates, using a reciprocating saw (inset).

7 Lift the header against the ceiling joists, then set the posts under the ends of the header. If the header will not fit due to sagging ceiling joists, then raise the joists by jacking up or shimming the temporary supports.

8 Toenail the posts to the header with 10d nails.

9 Check each post for plumb with a level. Adjust the post if necessary by tapping the bottom with a hammer. When post is plumb, mark a reference line on the sole plate, and toenail each post to the sole plate.

10 Cut 2 × 4 nailing strips and attach them to each side of the post and header with 10d nails. Nailing strips provide a surface for attaching new wallboard.

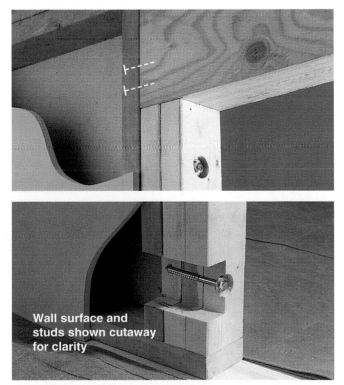

11 Cut and toenail spacing blocks to fit into the gaps between the permanent studs and the nailing strips. Patch and finish the wall and beam as directed on pages 132 to 139.

TIP: When removing a section of a wall, endnail the wall studs to the header with 10d nails, (top) and attach the posts to the wall studs with countersunk lag screws (bottom).

Wall surface and studs shown cutaway for clarity

Framing & Installing Doors

The first step in installing a new door is deciding what size and style you want. Although many styles of doors are carried in stock at home centers, if you want a custom size, you may need to have the home center special-order the doors from the manufacturer. Special orders generally take three or four weeks for delivery.

For easy installation, buy a prehung door, which is already mounted in the jamb. Although unmounted doors are widely available, installing them is a complicated job that is best left to a professional.

When replacing an existing door, choose a new unit the same size as the old door because you'll be able to use the framing members that are already in place.

This section shows:

• Framing an exterior door opening (pages 193 to 197)

• Installing an entry door (pages 198 to 201)

• Installing a storm door (pages 202 and 203)

• Installing a patio door (pages 204 to 209)

The following pages show installation techniques for wood-frame houses with lap siding. If your home exterior is stucco, see pages 178 and 179. For information on interior door installation, see pages 148 and 149.

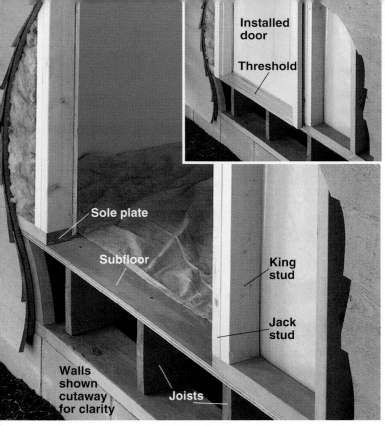

A new door opening in a platform-framed house has studs that rest on a sole plate running across the top of the subfloor. The sole plate is cut away between the jack studs so the threshold for the new door can rest directly on the subfloor.

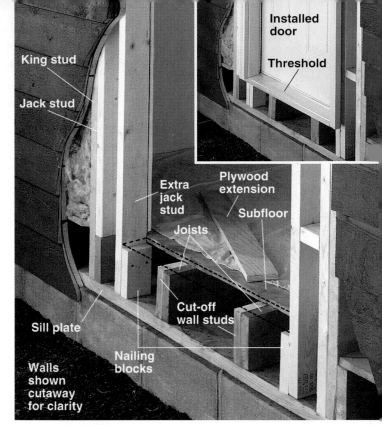

A new door opening in a balloon-framed house has studs extending past the subfloor to rest on the sill plate. Jack studs rest either on the sill plate or on top of the joists. To provide a surface for the door threshold, install nailing blocks, and extend the subfloor out to the ends of the joists, using plywood.

Framing an Exterior Door Opening

The rough opening for a new exterior door should be framed after the interior preparation work is done (pages 172 to 175), but before the exterior wall surfaces are removed. The methods for framing the opening will vary, depending on what type of construction your house was built with (see photos, above).

Make sure the rough opening is 1" wider and ½" taller than the dimensions of the door you plan to install, including the jambs, to allow space for adjustment during installation.

Because exterior walls are always load-bearing, the framing for an exterior door requires doubled studs on each side of the door opening and a larger header than those used for interior partition walls. The double-framed stud construction cuts down on vibration in the wall when the door is opened and closed and ensures adequate support for the larger header.

Local building codes will specify a minimum size for the door header based on the size of your rough opening, but you can get an estimation of what size the header will be on page 104.

Always build temporary supports to hold up the ceiling if your project requires that you cut or remove more than one stud in a load-bearing wall (pages 182 to 185).

When you finish framing, measure across the top, middle, and bottom of the door opening to make sure it is uniform from the top to the bottom. If there are major differences in the opening size, adjust the studs so the opening is uniform.

Everything You Need:

Tools: Tape measure, pencil, level, plumb bob, reciprocating saw, circular saw, handsaw, hammer, pry bar, nippers.

Materials: 2" dimension lumber, ⅜" plywood, 10d nails.

(continued next page)

How to Frame an Exterior Door Opening (Platform Framing)

1 Prepare the project site and re-move the interior wall surfaces (pages 172 to 175).

2 Measure and mark the rough opening width on the sole plate. Mark the locations of the jack studs and king studs on the sole plate. (Where practical, use existing studs as king studs).

3 If king studs need to be added, measure and cut them to fit between the sole plate and top plate. Position the king studs and toenail them to the sole plate with 10d nails.

4 Check the king studs with a level to make sure they are plumb, then toenail them to the top plate with 10d nails.

5 Measuring from the floor, mark the rough opening height on one king stud. For most doors, the recommended rough opening is ½" greater than the height of the door jamb. This line marks the bottom of the door header.

6 Determine the size of the header needed, (pages 104 and 105) and measure and mark where the top of it will fit against a king stud. Use a level to extend the lines across the intermediate studs to the opposite king stud.

7 Cut two jack studs to reach from the top of the sole plate to the rough opening marks on the king studs. Nail the jack studs to the king studs with 10d nails driven every 12". Make temporary supports (pages 182 to 185) if the wall is load-bearing and you are removing more than one stud.

8 Use a circular saw set to maximum blade depth to cut through the old studs that will be removed. The remaining stud sections will be used as cripple studs for the door frame. NOTE: Do not cut king studs. Make additional cuts 3" below the first cuts, then finish the cuts with a handsaw.

9 Knock out the 3" stud sections, then tear out the rest of the studs with a pry bar. Clip away any exposed nails, using nippers.

10 Build a header to fit between the king studs on top of the jack studs. Use two pieces of 2" dimensional lumber sandwiched around ⅜" plywood (page 212). Attach the header to the jack studs, king studs, and cripple studs, using 10d nails.

11 Use a reciprocating saw to cut through the sole plate next to each jack stud, then remove the sole plate with a pry bar. Cut off any exposed nails or anchors, using nippers.

How to Frame a Door Opening (Balloon Framing)

1 Remove the interior wall surfaces (pages 172 to 175). Select two existing studs to use as king studs. The distance between selected studs must be at least 3" wider than the planned rough opening. Measuring from the floor, mark the rough opening height on a king stud.

2 Determine the header size (pages 104 and 105) and measure and mark where the top of it will fit against a king stud. Use a level to extend the line across the studs to the opposite king stud.

3 Use a reciprocating saw to cut open the subfloor between the studs, and remove any fire blocking in the stud cavities. This allows access to the sill plate when installing the jack studs. If you will be removing more than one wall stud, make temporary supports (page 185).

4 Use a circular saw to cut studs along the lines marking the top header. NOTE: Do not cut king studs. Make two additional cuts on each stud, 3" below the first cut and 6" above the floor. Finish cuts with a handsaw, then knock out the 3" sections with a hammer. Remove studs with a pry bar (page 195).

5 Cut two jack studs to reach from top of the sill plate to the rough opening mark on the king studs. Nail the jack studs to the king studs with 10d nails driven every 12".

6 Build a header to fit between the king studs on top of the jack studs, using two pieces of 2" dimension lumber sandwiched around ⅜" plywood (page 212). Attach the header to the jack studs, king studs, and cripple studs, using 10d nails.

7 Measure and mark the rough opening width on the header. Use a plumb bob to mark the rough opening on the sill plate (inset).

8 Cut and install additional jack studs, as necessary, to frame the sides of the rough opening. Toenail the jack studs to the header and the sill plate, using 10d nails. NOTE: You may have to go to the basement to do this.

9 Install horizontal 2 × 4 blocking between the studs on each side of the rough opening, using 10d nails. Blocking should be installed at the lockset location and at the hinge locations on the new door.

10 Remove the exterior wall surface as directed on pages 176 to 179.

11 Cut off the ends of the exposed studs flush with the tops of the floor joists, using a reciprocating saw or handsaw.

12 Install 2 × 4 nailing blocks next to the jack studs and joists, flush with the tops of the floor joists. Replace any fire-blocking that was removed. Patch the subfloor area between the jack studs with plywood to form a flat, level surface for the door threshold.

Installing an Entry Door

Prehung entry doors come in many styles, but all are installed using the same basic methods. Because entry doors are very heavy—some large units weigh several hundred pounds—make sure you have help before beginning installation.

To speed your work, do the indoor surface removal (pages 172 to 175) and framing work (pages 193 to 197) in advance. Before installing the door, make sure you have all the necessary hardware. Protect the door against the weather by painting or staining it and by adding a storm door (pages 202 and 203).

Everything You Need:

Tools: Metal snips, hammer, level, pencil, circular saw, wood chisel, nail set, caulk gun, stapler, drill and bits, handsaw.

Materials: Building paper, drip edge, wood shims, fiberglass insulation, 10d galvanized casing nails, silicone caulk, entry door kit.

How to Install an Entry Door

1 Remove the door unit from its packing. Do not remove the retaining brackets that hold the door closed. Remove the exterior face material inside the framed opening as directed on pages 176 and 177.

2 Test-fit the door unit, centering it in the rough opening. Check to make sure door is plumb. If necessary, shim under the lower side of the door jamb until the door is plumb and level.

Brick molding

3 Trace an outline of brick molding on siding. NOTE: If you have vinyl or metal siding, enlarge the outline to make room for the extra trim moldings required by these sidings. Remove the door unit after finishing the outline.

4 Cut the siding along the outline, just down to the sheathing, using a circular saw. Stop just short of the corners to prevent damage to the siding that will remain.

5 Finish the cuts at the corners with a sharp wood chisel.

6 Cut 8"-wide strips of building paper and slide them between the siding and sheathing at the top and sides of the opening, to shield framing members from moisture. Bend paper around the framing members and staple it in place.

Drip edge

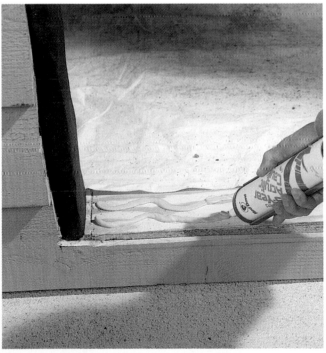

7 To provide an added moisture barrier, cut a piece of drip edge to fit the width of the rough opening, then slide it between the siding and the building paper at the top of the opening. Do not nail the drip edge.

8 Apply several thick beads of silicone caulk to the subfloor at the bottom of the door opening. Also apply silicone caulk over the building paper on the front edges of the jack studs and header.

(continued next page)

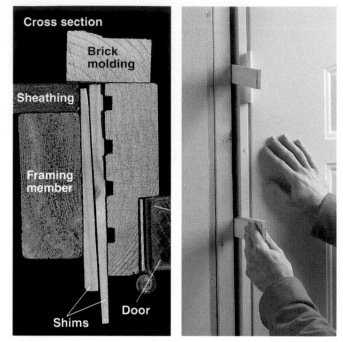

9 Center the door unit in the rough opening, and push the brick molding tight against the sheathing. Have a helper hold the door unit steady until it is nailed in place.

10 From inside, place pairs of hardwood wedge shims together to form flat shims (left), and insert shims into the gaps between the door jambs and framing members. Insert shims at the lockset and hinge locations and every 12" thereafter.

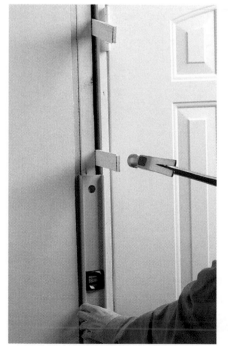

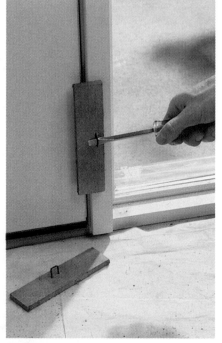

11 Make sure the door unit is plumb. Adjust the shims, if necessary, until the door is plumb and level. Fill the gaps between the jambs and the framing members with loosely packed fiberglass insulation.

12 From outside, drive 10d casing nails through the door jambs and into the framing members at each shim location. Use a nail set to drive the nail heads below the surface of the wood.

13 Remove the retaining brackets installed by the manufacturer, then open and close the door to make sure that it works properly.

14 Remove two of the screws on the top hinge and replace them with long anchor screws (usually included with the unit). These anchor screws will penetrate into the framing members to strengthen the installation.

15 Anchor brick molding to the framing members with 10d galvanized casing nails driven every 12". Use a nail set to drive the nail heads below the surface of the wood.

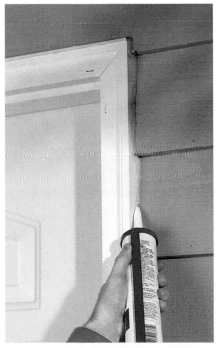

16 Adjust the door threshold to create a tight seal, following manufacturer's recommendations.

17 Cut off the shims flush with the framing members, using a handsaw.

18 Apply silicone caulk around the entire door unit. Fill the nail holes with latex caulk if you plan on painting the area. Finish the door and install the lockset as directed by the manufacturer.

Adjustable sweeps help make storm doors weathertight. Before installing the door, attach the sweep to the bottom of the door. After the door is mounted, adjust the height of the sweep so it brushes the top of the sill lightly when the door is closed.

Installing a Storm Door

Install a storm door to improve the appearance and weather resistance of an old entry door, or to protect a newly installed door against weathering. In all climates, adding a storm door can extend the life of an entry door.

When buying a storm door, look for models that have a solid inner core and seamless outer shell construction. Carefully note the dimensions of your door opening, measuring from the inside edges of the entry door's brick molding. Choose a storm door that opens from the same side as your entry door.

Everything You Need:

Tools: Tape measure, pencil, plumb bob, hacksaw, hammer, drill and bits, screwdrivers.

Materials: Storm door unit, wood spacer strips, 4d casing nails.

How to Cut a Storm Door Frame to Fit a Door Opening

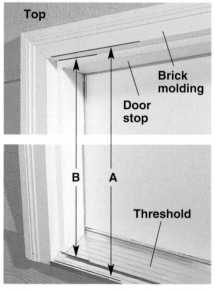

1 Because entry door thresholds are slanted, the bottom of the storm door frame needs to be cut to match the threshold angle. Measure from the threshold to the top of the door opening along the corner of the brick molding (A), then measure along the front edge of entry door stop (B).

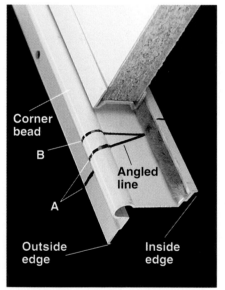

2 Subtract ⅛" from measurements A and B to allow for small adjustments when the door is installed. Measuring from the top of the storm door frame, mark the adjusted points A and B on the corner bead. Draw a line from point A to the outside edge of the frame and from point B to the inside edge. Draw an angled line from point A on corner bead to point B on the inside edge.

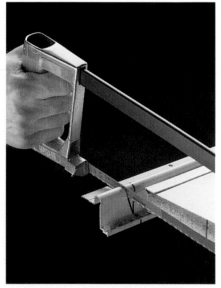

3 Use a hacksaw to cut down through the bottom of the storm door frame, following the angled line. Make sure to hold the hacksaw at the same slant as the angled line to ensure that the cut will be smooth and straight.

How to Fit & Install a Storm Door

Brick molding

Push hinge side tight

1 Position the storm door in the opening and push the frame tight against the brick molding on the hinge side of the storm door, then draw a reference line on the brick molding, following the edge of the storm door frame.

Push latch side tight

2 Push the storm door frame tight against the brick molding on the latch side, then measure the gap between the reference line and the hinge side of the door frame. If the distance is greater than ⅜", spacer strips must be installed to ensure the door will fit snugly.

3 To install spacers, remove the door then nail thin strips of wood to the inside of the brick molding at storm door hinge locations. The thickness of the wood strips should be ⅛" less than the gap measured in step 2.

4 Replace the storm door and push it tight against the brick molding on the hinge side. Drill pilot holes through the hinge side frame of the storm door and into the brick molding spaced every 12". Attach the frame with mounting screws.

5 Remove any spacer clips holding the frame to the storm door. With the storm door closed, drill pilot holes and attach the latch side frame to the brick molding. Use a coin to keep an even gap between the storm door and the storm door frame.

6 Center the top piece of the storm door frame on top of the frame sides. Drill pilot holes and screw the top piece to the brick molding. Adjust the bottom sweep, then attach the locks and latch hardware as directed by the manufacturer.

Installing a Patio Door

For easy installation, buy a patio door with the door panels already mounted in a preassembled frame. Try to avoid patio doors sold with frame kits that require complicated assembly.

Because patio doors have very long bottom sills and top jambs, they are susceptible to bowing and warping. To avoid these problems, be very careful to install the patio door so it is level and plumb and to anchor the unit securely to framing members. Yearly caulking and touch-up painting helps prevent moisture from warping the jambs.

Everything You Need:

Tools: Pencil, hammer, circular saw, wood chisel, stapler, caulk gun, pry bar, level, cordless screwdriver, handsaw, drill and bits, nail set.

Materials: Shims, drip edge, building paper, silicone and latex caulk, 10d casing nails, 3" wood screws, sill nosing, patio door kit, fiberglass insulation.

Screen doors, if not included with the unit, can be ordered from most patio door manufacturers. Screen doors have spring-mounted rollers that fit into a narrow track on the outside of the patio door threshold.

Tips for Installing Sliding Doors

Remove heavy, glass panels if you must install the door without help. Reinstall the panels after the frame has been placed in the rough opening and nailed at opposite corners. To remove and install the panels, remove the stop rail, found on the top jamb of the door unit.

Adjust the bottom rollers after installation is complete. Remove the coverplate on the adjusting screw, found on the inside edge of the bottom rail. Turn the screw in small increments until the door rolls smoothly along the track without binding when it is opened and closed.

Tips for Installing French-style Patio Doors

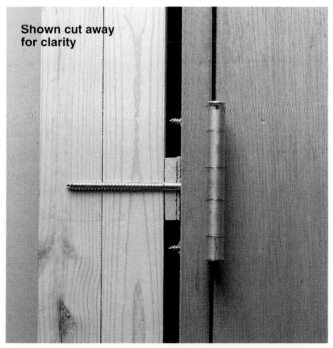

Shown cut away for clarity

Provide extra support for door hinges by replacing the center mounting screw on each hinge with a 3" wood screw. These long screws extend through the side jambs and deep into the framing members.

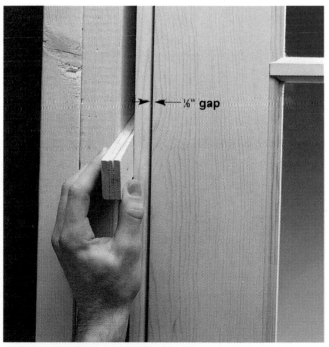

⅛" gap

Keep a uniform ⅛" gap between the door, side jambs, and top jamb to ensure that the door will swing freely without binding. Check this gap frequently as you shim around the door unit.

How to Install a Patio Door

1 Prepare the work area and remove the interior wall surfaces (pages 172 and 173), then frame the rough opening for the patio door (pages 192 and 193). Remove the exterior surfaces inside the framed opening (pages 176 and 177).

2 Test-fit the door unit, centering it in the rough opening. Check to make sure door is plumb. If necessary, shim under the lower side jamb until the door is plumb and level. Have a helper hold the door in place while you adjust it.

3 Trace the outline of the brick molding onto the siding, then remove the door unit. NOTE: If you have vinyl or metal siding, enlarge the outline to make room for the extra trim moldings required by these sidings.

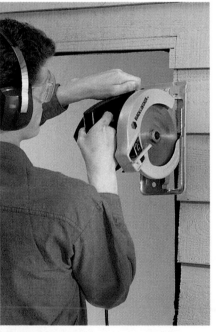

4 Cut the siding along the outline, just down to the sheathing, using a circular saw. Stop just short of the corners to prevent damage to the remaining siding. Finish the cuts at the corners with a sharp wood chisel.

Drip edge

5 To provide an added moisture barrier, cut a piece of drip edge to fit the width of the rough opening, then slide it between the siding and the existing building paper at the top of the opening. Do not nail the drip edge.

6 Cut 8"-wide strips of building paper and slide them between the siding and the sheathing. Bend the paper around the framing members and staple it in place.

7 Apply several thick beads of silicone caulk to the subfloor at the bottom of the door opening.

8 Apply silicone caulk around the front edge of the framing members, where the siding meets the building paper.

9 Center the patio door unit in the rough opening so the brick molding is tight against the sheathing. Have a helper hold the door unit from outside until it is shimmed and nailed in place.

10 Check the door threshold to make sure it is level. If necessary, shim under the lower side jamb until the patio door unit is level.

(continued next page)

11 If there are gaps between the threshold and subfloor, insert shims coated with caulk into the gaps, spaced every 6". Shims should be snug, but not so tight that they cause the threshold to bow. Clear off excess caulk immediately.

12 Place pairs of hardwood wedge shims together to form flat shims. Insert the shims every 12" into the gaps between the side jambs and the jack studs. For sliding doors, shim behind the strike plate for the door latch.

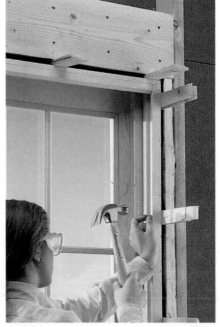

13 Insert shims every 12" into the gap between the top jamb and the header.

14 From outside, drive 10d casing nails, spaced every 12", through the brick molding and into the framing members. Use a nail set to drive the nail heads below the surface of the wood.

15 From inside, drive 10d casing nails through the door jambs and into the framing members at each shim location. Use a nail set to drive the nail heads below the surface of the wood.

16 Remove one of the screws and cut the shims flush with the stop block found in the center of the threshold. Replace the screw with a 3" wood screw driven into the subfloor as an anchor.

17 Cut off the shims flush with the face of the framing members, using a handsaw. Fill gaps around the door jambs and beneath the threshold with loosely packed fiberglass insulation.

18 Reinforce and seal the edge of the threshold by installing sill nosing under the threshold and against the wall. Drill pilot holes and attach the sill nosing with 10d casing nails.

19 Make sure the drip edge is tight against the top brick molding, then apply silicone caulk along the top of the drip edge and along the outside edge of the side brick moldings. Fill all exterior nail holes with silicone caulk. Use latex caulk for the nail holes if you plan to paint over the area.

20 Caulk completely around the sill nosing, using your finger to press the caulk into any cracks. As soon as the caulk is dry, paint the sill nosing. Finish the door and install the lockset as directed by the manufacturer. See pages 132 to 139 and 152 to 155 to finish the walls and trim the interior of the door.

Header

Angled stud

Jambs

Shims

Double rough sill

Cripple studs

Insulation

Jack stud

King stud

Framing & Installing Windows

Many windows must be custom-ordered several weeks in advance. To save time, do the interior framing before the window unit arrives. However, never open the outside wall surface until you have the window and accessories and are ready to install them.

Follow the manufacturer's specifications for rough opening size when framing for a window. The listed opening usually is 1" wider and ½" taller than the actual dimensions of the window unit. The following pages show techniques for wood-frame houses with siding and platform framing. This section shows:

- How to frame a window opening (pages 211 to 213)

- How to install a window (pages 214 to 217)

If your home's exterior is stucco, see pages 178 and 179.

If your house has balloon framing (pages 102 and 103), use the method shown on page 196 (steps 1 to 6) to install a header. Consult a professional to install a window on the second story of a balloon framed house.

If your house has masonry walls, or if you are installing polymer-coated windows, you may want to attach your window using masonry clips instead of nails (page 217).

Everything You Need:

Tools: Tape measure, pencil, combination square, hammer, level, circular saw, handsaw, pry bar, nippers, drill, reciprocating saw, stapler, nail set, caulk gun.

Materials: 10d common nails, shims, 2× lumber, ⅜" plywood, building paper, drip edge, casing nails (10d, 8d), fiberglass insulation, silicone caulk.

How to Frame a Window Opening

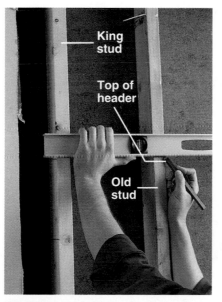

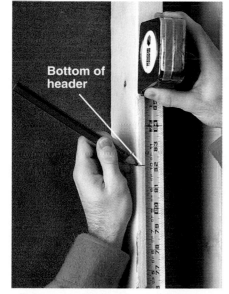

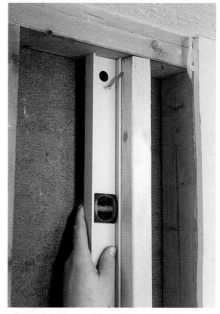

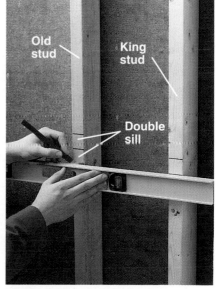

1 Prepare the project site and remove the interior wall surfaces (pages 172 and 173). Measure and mark the rough opening width on the sole plate. Mark the locations of the jack studs and king studs on the sole plate. Where practical, use the existing studs as king studs.

2 Measure and cut the king studs, as needed, to fit between the sole plate and the top plate. Position the king studs and toenail them to the sole plate with 10d nails.

3 Check the king studs with a level to make sure they are plumb, then toenail them to the top plate with 10d nails.

4 Measuring from the floor, mark the bottom of the rough opening on one of the king studs. For most windows, the recommended rough opening is ½" taller than the height of the window frame. This line marks the bottom of the window header.

5 Measure and mark where the top of the window header will fit against the king stud. The header size depends on the distance between the king studs (page 104 and 105). Use a carpenter's level to extend the lines across the old studs to the opposite king stud.

6 Measure down from header line and outline the double rough sill on the king stud. Use a carpenter's level to extend the lines across the old studs to the opposite king stud. Make temporary supports (pages 182 to 185) if removing more than one stud.

(continued next page)

7 Set a circular saw to its maximum blade depth, then cut through the old studs along the lines marking the bottom of the rough sill and along the lines marking the top of the header. Do not cut the king studs. On each stud, make an additional cut about 3" above the first sill cut. Finish the cuts with a handsaw.

8 Knock out the 3" stud sections, then tear out the old studs inside the rough opening, using a pry bar. Clip away any exposed nails, using nippers. The remaining sections of the cut studs will serve as cripple studs for the window.

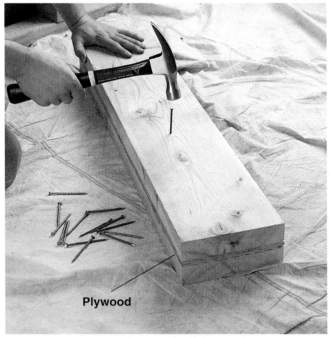

9 Build a header to fit between the king studs on top of the jack studs, using two pieces of 2× lumber sandwiched around ⅜" plywood.

10 Cut two jack studs to reach from the top of the sole plate to the bottom header lines on the king studs. Nail the jack studs to the king studs with 10d nails driven every 12". NOTE: On a balloon-frame house the jack studs will reach to the sill plate.

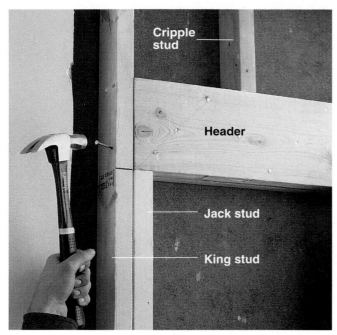

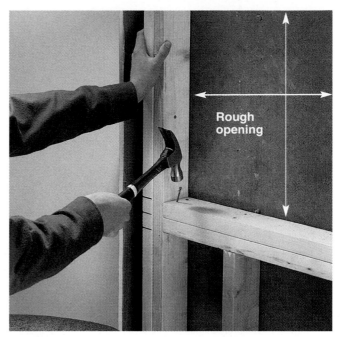

11 Position the header on the jack studs, using a hammer if necessary. Attach the header to the king studs, jack studs, and cripple studs, using 10d nails.

12 Build the rough sill to reach between the jack studs by nailing a pair of 2 × 4s together. Position the rough sill on the cripple studs, and nail it to the jack studs and cripple studs with 10d nails.

Variations for Round-top Windows

Create a template to help you mark the rough opening on the sheathing. Scribe the outline of the curved frame on cardboard, allowing an extra ½" for adjustments within the rough opening. A ¼ × 1¼" metal washer makes a good spacer for scribing the outline. Cut out the template along the scribed line.

Tape the template to the sheathing, with the top flush against the header. Use the template as a guide for attaching diagonal framing members across the top corners of the framed opening. The diagonal members should just touch the template. Outline the template on the sheathing as a guide for cutting the rough opening (pages 176 and 179).

1 Remove the exterior wall surface as directed on pages 176 to 179, then test-fit the window, centering it in the rough opening. Support the window with wood blocks and shims placed under the bottom jamb. Check to make sure the window is plumb and level, and adjust the shims, if necessary.

2 Trace the outline of the brick molding on the siding. NOTE: If you have vinyl or metal siding, enlarge the outline to make room for the extra J-channel moldings required by these sidings. Remove the window after finishing the outline.

3 Cut the siding along the outline just down to the sheathing. For a round-top window, use a reciprocating saw held at a shallow angle. For straight cuts, you can use a circular saw adjusted so the blade depth equals the thickness of the siding, then use a sharp chisel to complete the cuts at the corners (page 199).

4 Cut 8"-wide strips of building paper and slide them between the siding and sheathing around the entire window opening. Bend the paper around the framing members and staple it in place.

5 Cut a length of drip edge to fit over the top of the window, then slide it between the siding and building paper. For round-top windows, use flexible vinyl drip edge; for rectangular windows, use rigid metal drip edge (inset).

6 Insert the window in the opening, and push the brick molding tight against the sheathing.

7 Check to make sure the window is level.

8 If the window is perfectly level, nail both bottom corners of the brick molding with 10d casing nails. If the window is not perfectly level, nail only at the higher of the two bottom corners.

9 If necessary, have a helper adjust the shim under the low corner of the window from the inside, until the window is level.

10 From outside, drive 10d casing nails through the brick molding and into the framing members near the remaining corners of the window.

(continued next page)

11 Place pairs of shims together to form flat shims. From inside, insert shims into the gaps between the jambs and framing members, spaced every 12". On round-top windows, also shim between the angled braces and curved jamb.

12 Adjust the shims so they are snug, but not so tight that they cause the jambs to bow. On multiple-unit windows, make sure the shims under the mull posts are tight.

13 Use a straightedge to check the side jambs to make sure they do not bow. If necessary, adjust the shims until the jambs are flat. Open and close the window to make sure it works properly.

14 At each shim location, drill a pilot hole, then drive an 8d casing nail through the jamb and shims. Be careful not to damage the window. Drive the nail heads below the wood surface with a nail set.

15 Fill the gaps between the window jambs and the framing members with loosely packed fiberglass insulation. Wear work gloves when handling insulation.

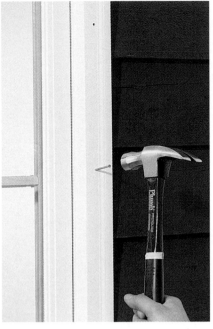

16 Trim the shims flush with the framing members, using a handsaw.

17 From outside, drive 10d galvanized casing nails, spaced every 12", through the brick moldings and into the framing members. Drive all nail heads below the wood surface with a nail set.

18 Apply silicone caulk around the entire window unit. Fill nail holes with caulk. See pages 130 to 139 to finish the walls, and pages 152-155 to trim the interior of the window.

Installation Variation: Masonry Clips

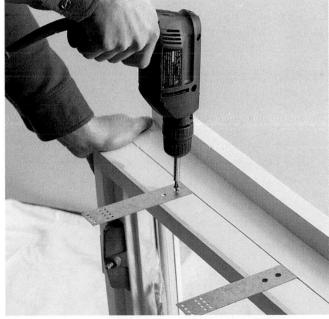

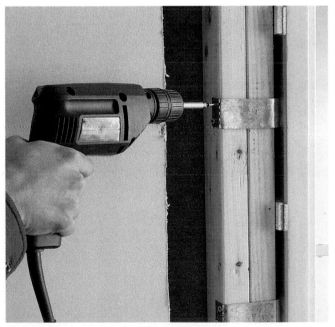

Tip: Use metal masonry clips when the brick molding on a window cannot be nailed because it rests against a masonry or brick surface. The masonry clips hook into precut grooves in the window jambs (above, left), and are attached to the jambs with utility screws. After the window unit is positioned in the rough opening, the masonry clips are bent around the framing members

and anchored with utility screws (above, right). NOTE: masonry clips also can be used in ordinary lap siding installations if you want to avoid making nail holes in the smooth surface of the brick moldings. For example, windows that are precoated with polymer-based paint can be installed with masonry clips so that the brick moldings are not punctured with nails.

Shelves, Cabinets & Countertops

¼" glass

Melamine-covered
particleboard

¾" pine

¾" finish-grade
plywood

¾" hardwood

¾" finish-grade
plywood edged
with 1 × 2
hardwood

Double-layer
plywood edged
with hardwood
molding

Adding Shelves

When making shelves for your floor-to-ceiling shelves (page 222) or utility shelves (page 228), choose shelving materials appropriate for the loads they must support. Thin glass shelves or particleboard can easily support light loads, such as decorative glassware, but only the sturdiest shelves can hold a large television set or heavy reference books without bending or breaking.

The strength of a shelf depends on its *span*—the distance between vertical risers. In general, the span should be no more than 36" long.

Building your own shelves from finish-grade plywood edged with hardwood strips is a good choice for most carpentry projects. Edged plywood shelves are strong, attractive, and much less expensive than solid hardwood shelves.

Everything You Need:

Tools: Right-angle drill guide, drill with bits, marking gauge, router, hammer, nail set.

Materials: Shelving material, scrap pegboard, pin-style shelf supports, metal shelf standards, shelf clips, finish nails.

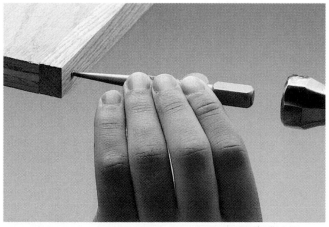

Attach hardwood edging or moldings to the front face of plywood shelves, using wood glue and finish nails. Position the edging so the top is slightly above the plywood surface, then drill pilot holes and drive finish nails. Use a nail set to countersink the nail heads. Sand the edging so it is smooth with the plywood surface before you finish the shelf (pages 244 to 247). For greater strength, edge plywood shelves with 1 × 2 or 1 × 3 hardwood boards (photo, left).

How to Install Pin-style Supports for Adjustable Shelves

1 To make pin-style adjustable supports for floor to ceiling shelves (page 225), mount a drill and ¼" bit in a right-angle guide, with the drill-stop set for ⅜" depth. Align a pegboard scrap along the inside face of each riser to use as a drilling template. Drill two rows of holes in each riser, about 1½" from the edges, using the pegboard holes as a guide.

2 Build shelves that are ⅛" shorter than the distance between risers. To mount each shelf, insert a pair of ¼" pin-style shelf supports in each riser.

How to Install Metal Standards for Adjustable Shelves

1 To use metal standards for adjustable shelves (page 225), mark two parallel lines for dado grooves on the inside face of each riser, using a marking gauge.

2 Cut dadoes to depth and thickness of metal standards, using a router and an edge guide (page 73). Test-fit the standards and remove them.

3 After finishing the built-in, cut metal standards to fit into dadoes, and attach using nails or screws provided by manufacturer. Make sure slots in standards are aligned properly so shelves will be level.

4 Build shelves ⅛" shorter than the distance between risers, then insert shelf clips into the slots on the metal standards, and install shelves.

Building Floor-to-Ceiling Shelves

Floor-to-ceiling shelves are sturdier and make better use of space than freestanding bookcases. When finished and trimmed to match the surrounding room, floor-to-ceiling shelves turn an ordinary room into an inviting den or library.

This project uses finish-grade oak plywood and a solid oak face frame to create the look of an expensive, solid oak shelf unit at a fraction of the cost. The plywood panels are supported and strengthened by an internal framework of 2 × 4 stud lumber.

When installing floor-to-ceiling shelves in a corner, as shown here, add ½" plywood spacers to the support studs that adjoin the wall. Spacers ensure that face frame stiles of equal width can be installed at both shelf ends (see diagram, page opposite).

Everything You Need:

Tools: Tape measure, pencil, level, framing square, plumb bob, drill with drive bits, hammer, circular saw, router, ¾" straight bit.

Materials: See parts list page opposite, finish nails (1½", 2"), utility screws (1¾", 2", 3"), shims, metal shelf standards and clips, finishing materials, ½" plywood scraps, carpenter's glue.

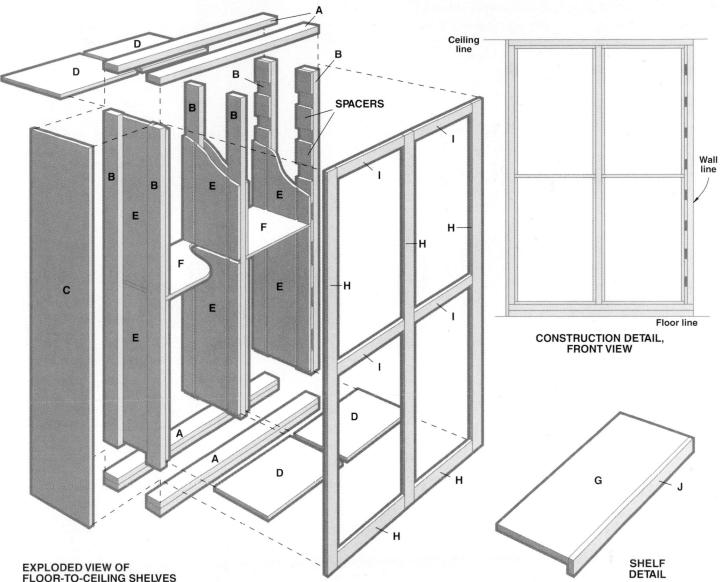

Ceiling line

Wall line

Floor line

SPACERS

CONSTRUCTION DETAIL,
FRONT VIEW

EXPLODED VIEW OF
FLOOR-TO-CEILING SHELVES

SHELF
DETAIL

Parts List: Floor-to-Ceiling Shelves

	Project as Shown				Your Project	
Key	**Part**	**Material**	**Pieces**	**Size**	**Pieces**	**Size**
A	Top and sole plates	2 × 4s	6	59½"		
B	Support studs	2 × 4s	6	91½"		
C	End panel	½" oak plywood	1	95¾ × 13"		
D	Top, bottom panels	½" oak plywood	4	27¼ × 13"		
E	Risers	½" oak plywood	8	44⅞ × 13"		
F	Permanent shelves	¾" oak plywood	2	27¼ × 13"		
G	Adjustable shelves	¾" oak plywood	8	26⅛ × 11⅞"		
H	Stiles and bottom rail	1 × 4 oak	28 linear ft.			
I	Top rail, middle rail	1 × 3 oak	10 linear ft.			
J	Shelf edging	1 × 2 oak	18 linear ft.			

223

How to Build Floor-to-Ceiling Shelves

1 Mark the location for two parallel 2 × 4 top plates on the ceiling, using a framing square as a guide. The front edge of the outer top plate should be 13" from the back wall, and the other top plate should be flush against the wall. Mark the location of the ceiling joists; if necessary, install blocking between joists (page 112) to provide a surface for anchoring the top plates.

2 Measure and cut the 2 × 4 top plates. Position each plate, check to make sure it is level, and install shims if necessary. Attach the plates to the ceiling with 3" screws driven into the joists or blocking.

3 Cut 2 × 4 sole plates and screw them together to form two doubled sole plates. Use a plumb bob suspended from the outside corners of the top plates to align the sole plates. Shim the plates to level, if needed. Anchor the plates by driving 3" screws toenail-style into the floor.

4 Install 2 × 4 support studs between the ends of the top plates and sole plates. Attach support studs with 3" screws driven toenail-style into the top plates and sole plates.

5 Install the center support studs midway between the end support studs. Attach them to the bottom plate first, using 3" screws driven toenail-style. Use a level to make sure that each stud is plumb, then attach the studs to the top plate with 3" screws.

6 Where the shelves fit into a corner, use 2" screws to attach ½" plywood spacers on the inside faces of the support studs, spaced every 4". Make sure spacers do not extend past the front face of the studs.

7 Where the end of the project is exposed, measure and cut a ½" plywood end panel to floor-to-ceiling height. Attach the panel to the support studs so the front edges are flush, using 1¾" screws driven through the support studs and into the end panel.

8 Measure and cut ½" plywood top and bottom panels to fit between the support studs. Attach to the top and sole plates using 1½" finish nails.

9 Measure and cut lower risers from ½" plywood, then cut dadoes for metal shelf standards using an edge guide (page 73).

10 Install lower risers on each side of the 2 × 4 support studs so the front edges are flush with the edges of the studs. Attach risers with 1½" finish nails driven into the support studs. For risers that adjoin the wall, drive nails at spacer locations.

11 Measure and cut permanent shelves from ¾" plywood to fit between the support studs, just above the lower risers. Set the shelves on the risers and attach them with 1½" finish nails driven down into the risers.

(continued next page)

12 Measure and cut upper risers to fit between the permanent shelves and the top panels. Cut dadoes for metal shelf standards, then attach the risers to the support studs with 1½" finish nails.

13 Measure and cut 1 × 3 stiles to reach from floor to ceiling along the front edges of the exposed support studs. Drill pilot holes and attach the stiles to the support studs so they are flush with the risers, using glue and 1½" finish nails driven at 8" intervals.

14 Measure and cut 1 × 3 top rails to fit between the stiles. Drill pilot holes and attach the rails to the top plate and top panels, using carpenter's glue and 1½" finish nails.

15 Measure and cut 1 × 4 bottom rails to fit between the stiles. Drill pilot holes, and attach the rails to the sole plates and bottom panels, using glue and 1½" finish nails. The top edge of the rails should be flush with the top surface of the plywood panels.

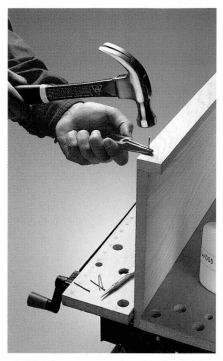

16 Fill nail holes, then sand and finish the wood surfaces (pages 244 to 247).

17 Measure, cut, and install metal shelf standards into the dadoes, using nails or screws provided by the manufacturer.

18 Measure and cut adjustable shelves ⅛" shorter than the distance between metal standards. Cut shelf edging, and attach it with glue and 1½" finish nails. Sand and finish the shelves.

19 Insert shelf clips into the metal shelf standards and install the adjustable shelves at desired heights.

20 Cover gaps between the project and walls and floor with molding that has been finished to match the shelf unit.

Building Utility Shelves

You can build adjustable utility shelves in a single afternoon using 2 × 4s and plain ¾" plywood. Perfect for use in a garage or basement, utility shelves can be modified by adding side panels and a face frame to create a finished look suitable for a family room or recreation area.

The quick-and-easy shelf project shown on the following pages creates two columns of shelves with a total width of 68". You can enlarge the project easily by adding more 2 × 4 risers and plywood shelves (do not increase the individual shelf widths to more than 36"). The sole plates for the utility shelves are installed perpendicular to the wall to improve access to the space under the bottom shelves.

Everything You Need:

Tools: Pencil, tape measure, level, framing square, power screwdriver, plumb bob, powder-actuated nailer, clamps, router with ¾" straight bit, circular saw, stepladder.

Materials: See parts list page opposite, wood glue, shims, utility screws (2½", 3"), finishing materials.

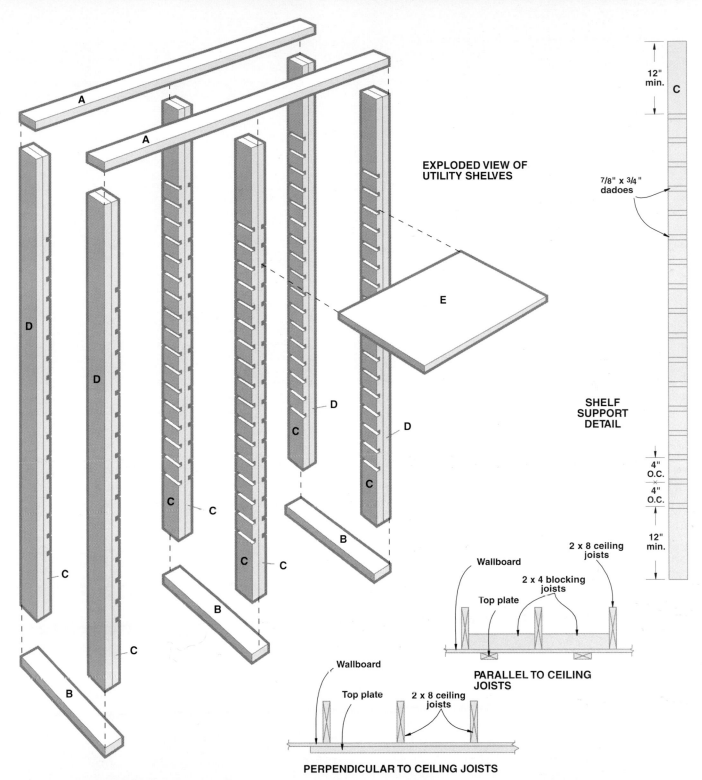

EXPLODED VIEW OF UTILITY SHELVES

12" min.

C

7/8" x 3/4" dadoes

C

SHELF SUPPORT DETAIL

4" O.C.

4" O.C.

12" min.

E

D

C

D

C

C

C

C

C

C

B

D

A

A

D

D

B

B

Wallboard

2 x 8 ceiling joists

2 x 4 blocking joists

Top plate

PARALLEL TO CEILING JOISTS

Wallboard

Top plate

2 x 8 ceiling joists

PERPENDICULAR TO CEILING JOISTS

Parts List: Utility Shelves

Key	Part	Material	Pieces	Size	Pieces	Size
A	Top plates	2 × 4s	2	68"		
B	Sole plates	2 × 4s	3	24"		
C	Shelf risers	2 × 4s	8	93"		
D	End risers	2 × 4s	4	93"		
E	Shelves	¾" plywood	12	30¾ × 24"		

*(Column headers: **Project as Shown** spans Part / Material / Pieces / Size; **Your Project** spans Pieces / Size)*

How to Build Utility Shelves

1 Mark location of top plates on ceiling. One plate should be flush against wall, and the other should be parallel to first plate, with the front edge 24" from the wall. Cut 2 × 4 top plates to full length of utility shelves, then attach to ceiling joists or blocking (page 112), using 3" screws.

2 Mark points directly beneath outside corners of the top plates to find outer sole plate locations, using a plumb bob as a guide (top). Mark sole plate locations by drawing lines perpendicular to the wall connecting each pair of points (bottom).

3 Cut outer 2 × 4 sole plates and position them perpendicular to the wall, just inside the outlines. Shim plates to level if needed, then attach to floor with a powder-actuated nailer or 3" screws. Attach a center sole plate midway between the outer sole plates.

4 Prepare the shelf risers by cutting ⅞"-wide, ¾"-deep dadoes with a router. Cut dadoes every 4" along the inside face of each 2 × 4 riser, with the top and bottom dadoes cut about 12" from the ends of the 2 × 4. Tip: Gang-cut the risers by laying them flat and clamping them together, then attaching an edge guide (page 73) to align the dado cuts. For each cut, make several passes with the router, gradually extending the bit depth until dadoes are ¾" deep.

5 Trim the shelf risers to uniform length before unclamping them. Use a circular saw and a straightedge guide.

6 Build two center shelf supports by positioning pairs of shelf risers back-to-back and joining them with wood glue and 2½" screws.

7 Build four end shelf supports by positioning the back of a dadoed shelf riser against a 2 × 4 of the same length, then joining the 2 × 4 and the riser with glue and 2½" screws.

8 Position an end shelf support at each corner of the shelving unit, between top and sole plates. Attach the supports by driving 3" screws toenail-style into the top plate and sole plates.

9 Position a center shelf support (both faces dadoed) at each end of the center sole plate, then anchor shelf supports to the sole plate using 3" screws driven toenail-style. Use a framing square to align the center shelf supports perpendicular to the top plates, then anchor to top plates.

10 Measure the distance between the facing dado grooves and subtract ¼". Cut the plywood shelves to fit and slide the shelves into the grooves.

Building an Understairs Work Center

The irregular space beneath a staircase can be used for a variety of creative built-in projects. Because the dimensions and angles of understairs areas vary widely, finding stock cabinetry that fits the space is difficult. However, the design shown here can be built to fit almost any area.

The understairs work center, in its simplest form, is a pair of basic cabinets that support a countertop. The basic cabinets are built to a standard height, depending on their use. You can adapt the size of the understairs work center by shortening or lengthening the countertop and connecting shelf. A small cabinet and upper shelves are added to fill out the remaining space. The depth of the countertop also can be adjusted to match the width of your staircase.

Most understairs projects require that you make many angled cuts, but in the project shown

here, you will need to make only a few miters and bevels. Beveled cuts can be made with a power miter saw, circular saw, or table saw.

Everything You Need:

Tools: Pencil, tape measure, level, T-bevel, circular saw or table saw, cordless screwdriver, drill and bits, hammer, router with ¾" straight bit and ⅜" rabbet bit, bar clamps, power miter saw.

Materials: Shims, finish nails (1", 1¼", 2"), utility screws (1", 1¼", 2½"), 1" wire nails, trim molding, finish materials, door and drawer hardware, see parts list (page opposite).

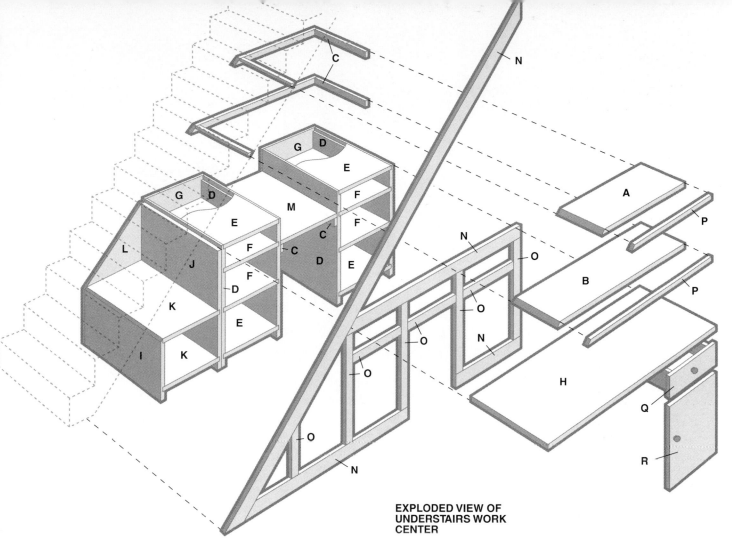

EXPLODED VIEW OF UNDERSTAIRS WORK CENTER

Parts List: Understairs Work Center

		Project as Shown			Your Project	
Key	**Part**	**Material**	**Pieces**	**Size**	**Pieces**	**Size**
A	Top shelf	¾" plywood	1	28 × 18"		
B	Lower shelf	¾" plywood	1	42 × 18"		
C	Shelf cleats	1 × 2	12 linear ft.			
D	Cabinet sides	¾" plywood	4	35½ × 24"		
E	Cabinet base, top panels	¾" plywood	4	24 × 19¼"		
F	Cabinet shelves	¾" plywood	4	24 × 19¼"		
G	Cabinet backs	¼" plywood	2	20 × 35"		
H	Countertop	¾" plywood	1	32 × 64"		
I	Small cabinet side	¾" plywood	1	18 × 24"		
J	Small cabinet side	¾" plywood	1	34½ × 24"		
K	Small cabinet bottom & top	¾" plywood	2	19¼ × 24"		
L	Small cabinet back	¼" plywood	1	20" × 34"		
M	Connecting shelf	¾" plywood	1	27⅞ × 24"		
N	Face frame pieces	1 × 3 oak	26 linear ft.			
O	Face frame pieces	1 × 2 oak	25 linear ft.			
P	Shelf edge strips	¾" plywood	4 linear ft.			
Q	Drawers	see pages 240 to 243				
R	Cabinet doors	purchase to fit				

Project Details

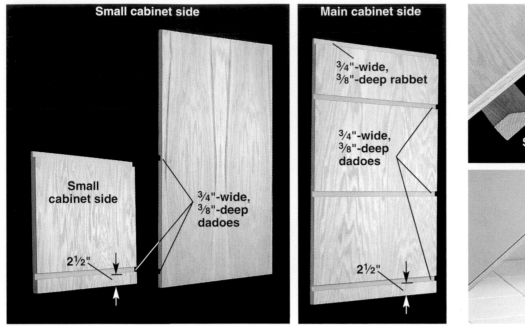

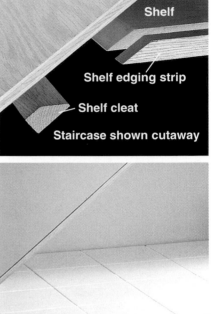

The side panels for the short cabinet (left), made from ¾" plywood, differ in size. A line connecting the tops of the two panels should follow the slope line of the staircase. The side panels for the main cabinets (right), are also made from ¾" plywood, and have dadoes for the cabinet shelves and base, and rabbets for the cabinet top. The taller side panel for the small cabinet fits against a main cabinet side panel when the work center is installed.

Shelves and cleats, made from plywood and 1 × 2 strips, are beveled so they fit flush against the understairs cover. The shelf edging strips are cut from oak 1 × 2, and mitered at the same angle as the shelves.

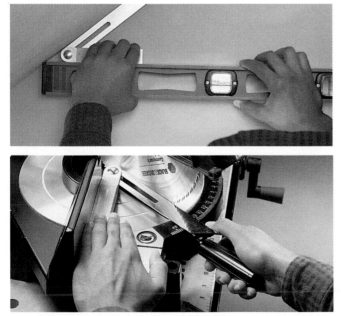

Duplicate the slope of your stairs using a T-bevel. Set one arm of the T-bevel in a level position against the back wall, then align the other arm with the stairs (top photo). Transfer the angle directly to your saw to make mitered and beveled cuts (bottom photo).

Cover stair underside before you install your understairs work center. Panels of 1½" plywood attached to the stringers of the staircase create an understairs cover that can be used to anchor shelf cleats. If you plan to add electrical or plumbing lines, do the work (or hire a professional if you are inexperienced) before installing your built-in.

How to Build an Understairs Work Center

1 Mark the location for the shelf cleats on the walls and understairs cover, using a level as a guide. Butt the 12" cleats against the back wall, and allow at least 12" of clearance between the countertop and the bottom shelf.

2 Measure and cut 1 × 2 shelf cleats to fit along the reference lines on the walls and the understairs cover (see Project Details, page opposite). Bevel the cleats on the understairs cover to match the stair slope angle. Attach the cleats with 2½" screws.

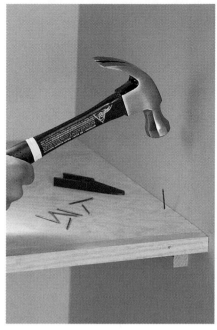

3 Measure and cut ¾" plywood shelves, then attach a ¾" hardwood strip to each shelf edge (see page opposite) using glue and finish nails. Set shelves on cleats and attach with 1½" finish nails driven through pilot holes.

4 Measure and cut ¾" plywood side panels for main cabinets, then use a router and an edge guide (page 73) to cut rabbets for top panels and dadoes for bottom panels and shelves (see Project Details, page opposite).

5 Clamp and glue the cabinet sides to the top and bottom panels and shelves to form rabbet and dado joints. NOTE: If you plan to install center-mounted drawer slides, mount slide tracks before you assemble the cabinet.

6 Reinforce each cabinet joint with 2" finish nails driven at 4" intervals.

(continued next page)

7 Cut a ¼" plywood back panel for each main cabinet. Set each back onto a cabinet frame so that all sides align, then attach them to cabinet side, base, and top panels using 1" wire nails.

8 Position one cabinet so the top panel is pressed against the understairs cover and front face is flush with edge of stairway. Shim if needed, then toenail into the floor through the side panels, using 2" finish nails. For masonry floors, attach with construction adhesive.

9 Position the other cabinet ¾" away from side wall, with front face aligned with first cabinet. Check with a level and shim if needed. Insert ¾" spacers between cabinet and side wall, then anchor to wall with 1½" screws driven into framing members.

10 Cut 1 × 2 cleats for the connecting shelf that fits between the main cabinets. Mark level lines on the inner cabinet sides, then attach shelf cleats to the cabinet sides by driving 1¼" screws through counterbored pilot holes.

11 Measure and cut a ¾" plywood connecting shelf to fit between the cabinets, and attach it to the cleats with 1¼" finish nails. (If you plan to build a drawer using a center-mounted drawer slide, attach the slide track to the shelf before you attach the shelf to the cleats.)

12 Measure and cut a plywood countertop panel that extends all the way to the back wall, with one side flush against the understairs cover. Attach the countertop to top panels of cabinets by driving finish nails down through the countertop.

13 Apply or install any special countertop finishing material, like ceramic tile or plastic laminate. Obtain installation instructions and follow them carefully if you have not installed tile or laminate before.

Back panel

Top panel   Side panel

14 Build a small cabinet the same width and depth as the main cabinets (steps 4 to 7). Adjust the height of the side panels to follow the stair slope (see Project Details, page 234). Cut a ¼" plywood back panel, with the top edge sloped at the same angle as the line between the side panel tops. Attach the back panel to the cabinet with 1" wire nails.

15 Position the small cabinet so the taller side panel is flush against the main cabinet. Align the face of the small cabinet with the face of the main cabinet, then check with a level, shimming if necessary. Connect the cabinets by drilling pilot holes, and driving 1¼" screws through the side panels.

(continued next page)

How to Build an Understairs Work Center (continued)

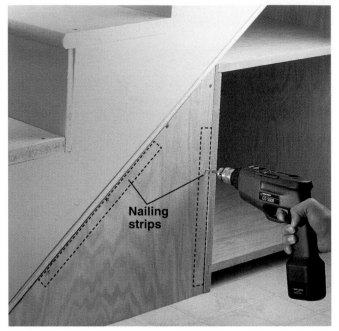

If the corner is open at the bottom of the stairs, attach nailing strips to the understairs cover and cabinet sides, then cut a 1½" plywood panel to fit the space, and attach it to the nailing strips with 1" screws.

16 Measure and cut 1 × 3 bottom rails for the cabinets. Also cut a long, diagonal rail to fit along the edge of the understairs cover. Miter the ends of the diagonal rail to fit against the floor and the side wall, and miter the longer bottom rail to form a clean joint with the diagonal rail. Test-fit the rails, then attach them with glue and 2" finish nails driven through pilot holes.

17 Measure and cut 1 × 3 rails to cover the edges of the connecting shelf and the countertop. Miter the end of the countertop rail that joins the long, diagonal rail. Attach the shelf and countertop rails flush with the countertop and shelf surfaces, using glue and 2" finish nails driven through pilot holes.

18 Measure and cut 1 × 2 stiles for the front edges of the cabinets. Attach the stiles, flush with the edges of the cabinet sides, using glue and 2" finish nails driven through pilot holes.

19 Measure and cut 1 × 2 rails to fit between the stiles, so they cover the cabinet shelf edges and are flush with the shelf tops. Attach the rails, using glue and 2" finish nails driven through pilot holes.

20 Cut base-shoe molding to cover gaps along wall and floor surfaces, mitering the corners. Tack the molding, using 1" finish nails. Sand, fill, and finish the understairs center (pages 244 to 247).

21 Attach slide tracks for side-mounted drawer slides, according to the manufacturer's directions.

22 Build, finish, and install drawers (see pages 240 to 243) and drawer hardware. Purchase or build and finish cabinet doors and hang them using ⅜" semi-concealed hinges.

Define the style of your project with drawer pulls and knobs. If your project also includes cabinet doors with handles or pulls, buy the hardware at the same time to ensure a good match. For drawers wider than 24", install knobs or pulls.

Building Drawers

In its simplest form, a drawer is simply a wooden box that slides back and forth on a permanent shelf. By adding drawer slide hardware, a hardwood drawer face, and attractive pulls, you can make drawers look and feel more professional.

Drawers can be built in many styles, but the drawer shown here is simple to build and works well for the understairs work center project. This design is called an "overlay" drawer because it features a hardwood drawer face that overhangs the cabinet face frame by ½".

Ready-made hardwood drawer faces are sold by companies specializing in cabinet refacing products. You can make your own drawer faces by cutting hardwood boards and using a router to give them decorative edges.

Everything You Need:

Tools: Combination square, marking gauge, cordless screwdriver, tape measure, hammer, pencil, router with ¼" straight bit and decorative edging bit, nail set, bar clamps.

Materials: ¼", ½" finish-grade plywood, ¾" hardwood, 1" wood screws, wire nails, 2" finish nails, center-mounted drawer slides.

Tips for Building Drawers

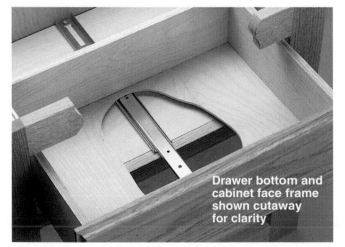

Drawer bottom and cabinet face frame shown cutaway for clarity

Choose center-mounted drawer slides with steel ball-bearing rollers. Center-mounted slides are easier to install than side-mounted slides, and those with steel ball bearings are much more durable than those with plastic rollers. Specify the depth of your drawers when buying drawer slides.

Make your own drawer faces by cutting hardwood boards to the proper size, then routing ornamental edges on them with a decorative router bit, such as an *ogee* bit. To ensure smooth edges, make several passes with the router; begin with the bit set to a shallow depth, then gradually extend the bit until you achieve the desired appearance.

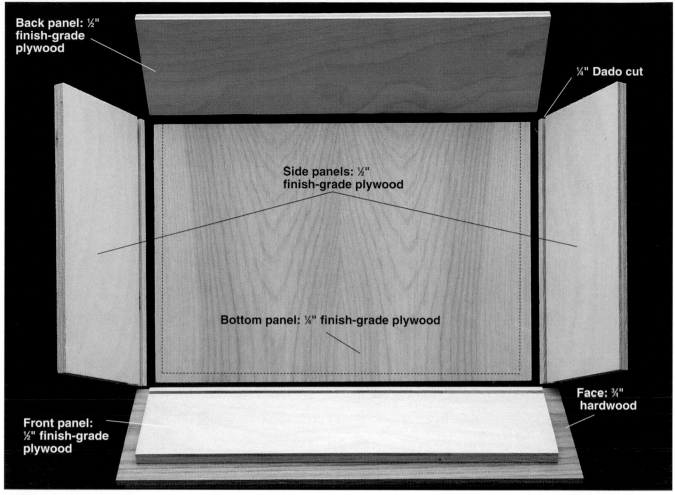

Back panel: ½" finish-grade plywood

¼" Dado cut

Side panels: ½" finish-grade plywood

Bottom panel: ¼" finish-grade plywood

Face: ¾" hardwood

Front panel: ½" finish-grade plywood

Anatomy of an overlay drawer: The basic drawer box is made using ½" plywood for the front, back, and side panels, with a ¼" plywood bottom panel. The bottom panel fits into ¼" dadoes cut near the bottom of the front and side panels and is nailed to the bottom edge of the back panel. The hardwood drawer face is screwed to the drawer front from the inside and is sized so it overhangs the face frame by ½" on all sides. NOTE: This drawer is designed to be mounted with a center-mounted drawer slide attached to the bottom of the drawer (page opposite). If you use different hardware, like side-mounted drawer slides, you will need to alter this design according to the slide manufacturer's directions.

How to Measure for an Overlay Drawer

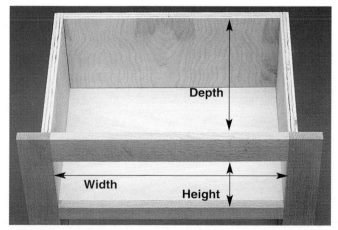

Depth

Width   **Height**

Part		Measurement
Sides	length	Depth of opening, minus 3"
	height	Height of opening, minus ½"
Front	length	Width of opening, minus 1½"
	height	Height of opening, minus ½"
Back	length	Width of opening, minus 1½"
	height	Height of opening, minus 1"
Bottom	length	Width of opening, minus 1"
	depth	Depth of opening, minus 2¾"
Face	length	Width of opening, plus 1"
	height	Height of opening, plus 1"

1 Measure the width and height of the face frame opening, and the depth of the cabinet from face frame to back panel.

2 Calculate the size or dimensions for each drawer part using the table above. Cut and assemble the parts by following the directions on the following pages.

How to Build & Install an Overlay Drawer

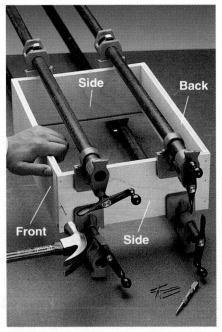

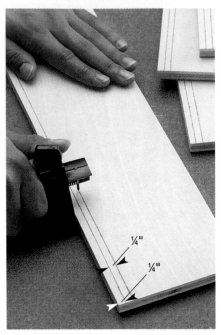

1 Install the track for the center-mounted drawer slide, as directed by the manufacturer. If the slide track will rest on a permanent shelf (left), it is easiest to install it on the shelf before assembling the project. If the slide will be supported by the face frame and the back panel (right), mount the slide using the rear bracket included with the drawer slide kit.

2 Measure the drawer opening, then cut the drawer pieces to size (page 223). Outline ¼" dado grooves on the inside faces of the side and front panels, ¼" from the bottom edges, using a marking gauge as a guide.

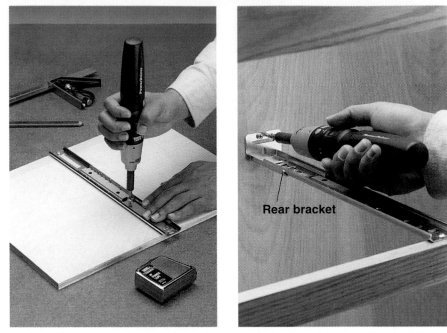

3 Cut ¼" deep dadoes along the marked outlines, using a router and a ¼" straight bit. Use a router edge guide to ensure straight cuts.

4 Clamp and glue the front, back, and side panels together, so the front and back panels are between the side panels, and the top edges of the panels are aligned. Reinforce each corner with 2" finish nails driven through the joints.

5 Let the glue dry, then remove the clamps. From the back of the drawer box, slide the drawer bottom panel fully into the dado grooves. Do not apply glue to the dadoes or the bottom panel.

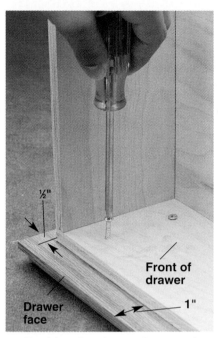

6 Attach the rear edge of the bottom panel to the back panel with wire nails spaced every 4".

7 Position the drawer box against the back side of the drawer face, so the face overhangs by ½" on the sides and bottom, and 1" on the top. Attach the face with 1" screws driven into the drawer face from inside the drawer box.

8 Lay the drawer upside down, then measure and mark a center line along the bottom panel from front to back.

½"

Front of drawer

Drawer face

1"

9 Center the drawer slide insert over the marked center line, and attach it with a 1" screw driven through the drawer bottom and into the back panel, and another screw driven diagonally into the drawer front panel.

10 Install the drawer by lining up the insert with the track, then gently pushing the drawer in until the insert and track lock together. Attach drawer pulls or knobs, if desired.

Finishing Projects

Careful finishing work is as important as good construction, because it improves the appearance of a project, protects the wood, and hides small errors and imperfections.

Finishing work consists of three stages: filling gaps and nail holes; sanding and cleaning; and applying a top coat of tinted oil or stain. All wood products require sanding and cleaning before they are top-coated.

Generally, it is easiest to apply finish or paint after the project is assembled, but for projects with deep shelves and hard-to-reach areas, consider sanding and finishing the pieces individually before assembly.

A traditional wood finish is made from successive coats of sealer, stain, and several coats of varnish or shellac; but a variety of newer, one-step finishes produce excellent results, and are easier to apply. For heavy-use surfaces, like dining counters, cover a one-coat finish with a layer of clear polyurethane.

One-step wood finishes include (from left to right): rubbing oil/finish—a combination of tinted penetrating oil and semigloss tung oil; pure tung oil finish—a clear, semigloss finish often used to protect bare wood; and Danish oil—a penetrating, nongloss oil available in many tints. When choosing a tinted one-step finish, choose a color that matches other woodwork in your home, and always test the finish on scrap wood before you begin.

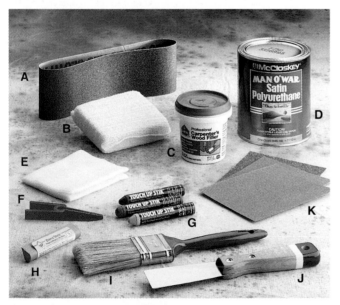

Specialty tools and materials for finishing work include: 120-grit sanding belt (A), staining pad (B), untinted wood filler (C), clear polyurethane (D), tack cloth (E), finish-nail holder (F), tinted filler sticks (G, H), paintbrush with blended bristles (I), putty knife (J), and sandpaper in 80-, 120-, and 220-grit sheets (K).

Painted finishes require a primer coat of sanding sealer to provide a smooth undercoat, followed by one or two coats of latex enamel or oil-base enamel. Latex enamel is easy to apply and clean up, but better grades of oil-base enamel create a smoother finished surface.

Finishing Tips

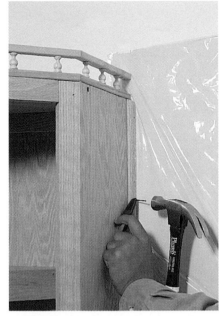

Protect walls from stains by sliding a sheet of wax paper or plastic between the trim moldings and the wall before applying oil finish or paint.

Scrape away dried glue before painting or finishing, using an old chisel with the corners rounded off. Finishing oils and paint will not penetrate glue, so any excess must be removed completely before finish is applied.

Use a toothbrush to apply finishes to hard-to-reach areas, like spindle-and-rail moldings and other ornamental trim pieces.

Protect surfaces that will be glued if you are finishing pieces before assembling the project. Glue will not bond to oiled or stained wood, so cover joint areas with masking tape before applying finishing materials.

Use a tinted filler stick to fill nail holes in finished wood. Filler sticks come in many tones, but if none matches the finish of your project exactly, blend putty from different sticks to create the color you need.

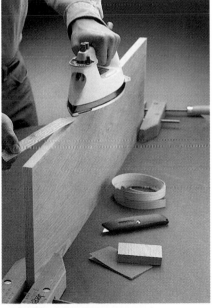

Use heat-activated veneer tape to cover unfinished edges of plywood or particleboard panels on shelves without face frames. Bond the tape with a household iron, then rub the tape with a block of hardwood. Trim the overhang with a utility knife, then lightly sand the edges to smooth them.

Preparation Tips

Fill nail holes and gaps in wood surfaces, using untinted wood filler. Let the filler dry completely before sanding the surfaces. On plywood surfaces that will be painted, fill any void areas along exposed edges.

Sand hardwood face frames to smooth the joints and remove surface defects. First, sand with a belt sander and 80-grit sanding belt (left), using light pressure to avoid gouging the wood. Then sand with a pad sander and 120-grit sandpaper (right). Change to 220-grit sandpaper for the final sanding. Always move the sander in the same direction as the wood grain, and replace sanding sheets as they become worn.

Sand edged plywood shelves carefully. To avoid sanding through the veneer, make light pencil marks on the plywood next to the hardwood edging, then sand across the top of the edging until the pencil marks are removed.

Use a hand sanding block and 220-grit sandpaper to sand corners and other areas where the pad sander will not fit.

Clean all sanded surfaces with a brush and vacuum, then wipe them with a tack cloth.

How to Apply One-step Finishes

Danish oil: Shake container thoroughly, then apply a heavy coat of oil to all wood surfaces, using a lint-free cloth. Wait 30 minutes, then apply more oil. Wait 15 minutes, then wipe the wood dry with clean rags.

Tung oil: Wipe a thin layer of tung oil onto the wood surface with a clean, folded cloth, rubbing in the direction of the wood grain. Wait 5 minutes, then buff the surface with a clean, lint-free cloth. Let the finish harden for 24 hours, then apply a second coat of tung oil.

Rubbing oil/finish: Shake container thoroughly, then apply a heavy coat to all surfaces, using a staining pad. Wait 5 minutes, then wipe away excess with a clean rag. Let the finish harden for 2 hours, then apply a second coat. Apply extra coats, 2 hours apart, if you wish to darken the finish.

How to Apply Enamel Paint

1 After sanding and cleaning wood surfaces, apply a thick coat of sanding sealer to all surfaces that will be painted. Let the sealer dry for 3 hours.

2 Sand surfaces with 220-grit sandpaper, and wipe away all dust with a tack cloth. Apply additional coats of sealer, sanding after each coat, until wood grain feels perfectly smooth to the touch. Open-grain woods, like pine, require several coats of sealer.

3 Wipe surfaces clean of all sanding dust, then apply enamel paint, brushing in the same direction as the wood grain. Let the paint dry according to the manufacturer's suggestion, then sand lightly with 220-grit sandpaper and apply a second coat of paint.

Adding Cabinets

Stud finder

Sanded high area

Filled-in low area

Kitchens are the most likely room for new cabinets, but other rooms such as laundries, bathrooms, and basements can also have cabinets. Although the example shown on the following pages takes place in a kitchen, the installation techniques apply to nearly any room.

Installing new cabinets is easiest when the room is completely empty. Disconnect the plumbing and wiring, and remove all furniture and appliances.

For information on removing old cabinets, see page 250 and 251. If the room requires plumbing or electrical changes, now is the time to have this work done. If you are replacing the flooring, do it before installing the cabinetry.

Cabinets should be installed plumb and level. Using a level as a guide, draw reference lines on the walls to indicate cabinet location. If the floor is uneven, find the highest point of the floor area that will be covered by base cabinets. Measure up from this point to draw reference lines.

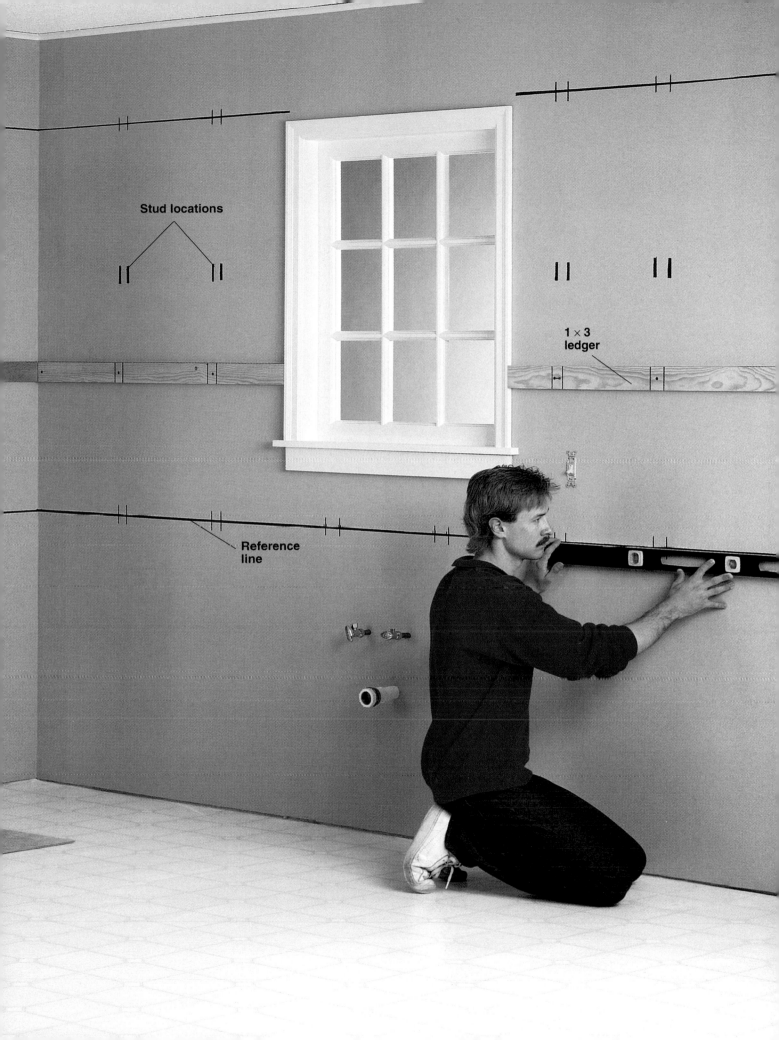

Stud locations

1 × 3 ledger

Reference line

Removing Trim & Old Cabinets

Trim and old cabinetry are almost always reusable, so use care when removing them. Old cabinets can create extra storage space in basements, garages, laundry rooms, and workshops.

Trim pieces should also be saved for later use, especially those with unusual profiles that may no longer be available. Your house may use similar trim in other rooms, and having some extra lengths on hand will make it easier to replace damaged sections.

Everything You Need:

Tools: Pry bar or putty knife, drill with driver bits, reciprocating saw.

Materials: Scrap wood.

Remove trim moldings at edges and tops of cabinets with a flat pry bar or putty knife.

Tips for Removing Trim

Remove vinyl base trim. Work a pry bar or putty knife underneath and peel off the vinyl.

Remove baseboards and base shoe moldings with a pry bar. Protect wall surfaces with scraps of wood.

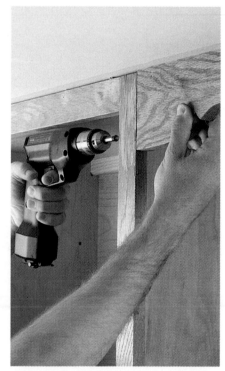

Remove valances. Some are attached to cabinets or soffits with screws. Others are nailed and must be pried loose.

How to Remove Cabinets

1 Remove doors and drawers to make it easier to get at interior spaces. You may need to scrape away old paint to expose hinge screws.

2 Remove any screws holding the cabinets to the back wall. Cabinets can be removed as a group, or can be disassembled.

3 Detach individual cabinets by removing screws that hold face frames together.

TIP: Cut built-in cabinets into manageable pieces with a reciprocating saw for easy removal and installation into a new area.

Preparing for New Cabinets

Preparing walls for new cabinetry is one of the most important steps of cabinet installation. Walls that are not flat and plumb will make the installation difficult and affect the overall appearance of the cabinets once the installation is complete.

Make sure that you take the time to identify any high and low spots on the walls, and install the temporary ledger as level as possible.

Everything You Need:

Tools: Stud finder, tape measure, carpenter's level, pencil, drill with driver bit, trowel, sandpaper.

Materials: 1 × 3 dimensional lumber, a straight 2 × 4, wallboard compound, 2½" wallboard screws.

How to Prepare Walls

1 Find the high and low spots on the wall surfaces, using a long, straight 2 × 4. Sand any high spots flush with the wall.

2 Fill in any low spots of the wall. Apply wallboard taping compound with a trowel, and sand it lightly after the compound dries.

3 Locate and mark the wall studs, using an electronic stud finder. The cabinets will be hung by driving screws into the studs through the back of the cabinets.

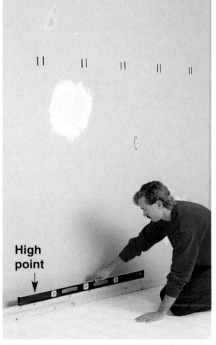

High point

4 Check to see if the floor is level by placing a level on a long, straight 2 × 4, and moving them along the floor. If it is uneven, mark the wall at the floor's highest point.

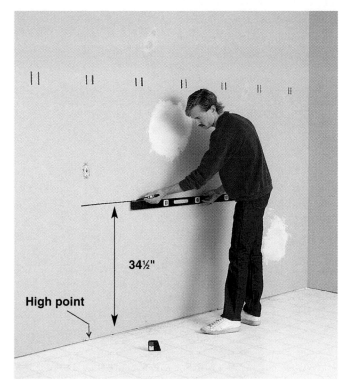

5 Measure up 34½" from the high-point mark. Use a level to mark a reference line on the walls. The base cabinets will be installed with the top edges flush against this line.

34½"

High point

6 Measure up 84" from the high-point mark and draw a second reference line. When installed, the top edges of the wall cabinets wll be flush on this line.

7 Measure down 30" from the wall-cabinet reference line and draw another level line where the bottom of cabinets will be. Temporary ledgers will be installed against this line.

30"

8 Install 1 × 3 temporary ledgers with the top edge flush against the reference line. Attach the ledgers with 2½" wallboard screws driven into every other stud. Mark the stud locations on the ledgers. The cabinets will rest on the ledgers during installation.

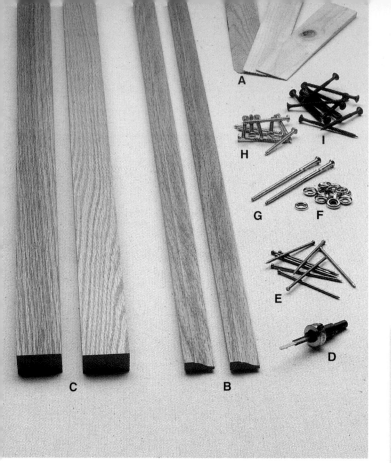

Specialty tools & supplies include: wood shims (A), trim moldings (B), filler strips (C), No. 9 counterbore drill bit (D), 6d finish nails (E), finish washers (F), No. 10 gauge 4" wood screws (G), No. 8 gauge 2½" sheetmetal screws (H), 3" wallboard screws (I).

Installing Cabinets

Cabinets should be firmly anchored to wall studs, and must be exactly plumb and level so that the doors and drawers operate smoothly. Number each cabinet and mark its position on the wall. Remove the cabinet doors and drawers, and number them so they can be easily replaced after the cabinets are installed.

Begin with the corner cabinets, making sure they are installed plumb and level. Adjacent cabinets are easily aligned once the corner cabinets have been correctly positioned.

Everything You Need:

Tools: Tape measure, pencil, stud finder, handscrew clamps, level, hammer, utility knife, nail set, stepladder, drill with ³⁄₁₆" twist bit and counterbore bit, cordless screwdriver, jig saw with wood cutting blade.

Materials: Cabinets, toe-kick molding, valance, wood putty, cleats, specialty supplies (photo, left).

Before installation, test-fit corner and adjoining cabinets to make sure doors and handles do not interfere with each other. If necessary, increase the clearance by pulling the blind cabinet away from side wall by no more than 4" (C). To maintain even spacing between the edges of doors and cabinet corner (A, B), cut a filler strip and attach it to the adjoining cabinet. Measure distance (C) as a reference when positioning the blind cabinet against the wall.

How to Install Wall Cabinets

1 Position the corner cabinet on the ledger. Drill ³⁄₁₆"
pilot holes into studs through the hanging strips at
rear of cabinet. Attach to wall with 2½" sheetmetal
screws. Do not tighten fully until all cabinets are hung.

2 Attach filler strip to adjoining cabinet, if needed
(see page opposite). Clamp filler in place, and
drill pilot holes through cabinet face frame near hinge
locations, using a counterbore bit. Attach the filler to
the cabinet with 2½" sheetmetal screws.

3 Position adjoining cabinet on ledger, tight against
blind corner cabinet. Check face frame for plumb.
Drill ³⁄₁₆" pilot holes into wall studs through the hanging
strips in rear of cabinet. Attach the cabinet with 2½"
sheetmetal screws. Do not tighten wall screws fully until all cabinets are hung.

4 Clamp the corner cabinet and the adjoining cabinet together at the top and bottom of the cabinets.
Handscrew clamps will not damage the wood face
frames.

(continued next page)

5 Attach the blind corner cabinet to the adjoining cabinet from inside the corner cabinet. Drill pilot holes through the face frames and join the cabinets with sheetmetal screws.

6 Position and attach each additional cabinet. Clamp the frames together, and drill pilot holes through the sides of the face frames. Join the cabinets with sheetmetal screws. Drill ³⁄₁₆" pilot holes in the hanging strips, and anchor the cabinets to the wall studs.

Join frameless cabinets with No. 8 gauge 1¼" wood screws and finish washers. Each pair of cabinets should be joined by at least four screws.

7 Fill small spaces between a cabinet and a wall or appliance with a filler strip. Cut the strip to fit the space and wedge it into place with wood shims. Drill counterbored pilot holes through the side of the cabinet face frame. Attach filler with sheetmetal screws.

8 Remove the temporary ledger. Check the cabinet run for plumb, and adjust it if necessary by placing wood shims behind the cabinet, near the stud locations. Tighten the wall screws completely. Cut off the shims with a utility knife.

9 Use trim moldings to cover any gaps between the cabinets and walls. Stain or paint the moldings to match the cabinet finish.

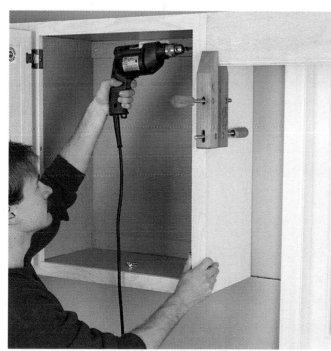

10 Attach a decorative valance above the sink. Clamp the valance to the edge of the cabinet frames, and drill counterbored pilot holes through the cabinet frames into the end of the valance. Attach it with sheetmetal screws.

11 Install the cabinet doors if necessary, and adjust the hinges so that the doors are straight and plumb.

How to Install Base Cabinets

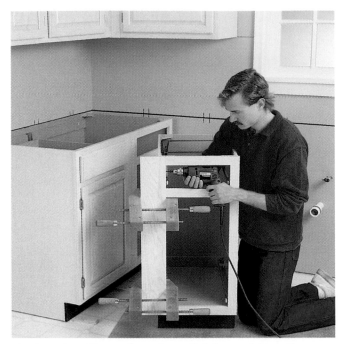

1 Begin installation by positioning the corner cabinet so that the top is flush with the reference line. Make sure the cabinet is plumb and level. If necessary, adjust it by driving wood shims under the base. Be careful not to damage flooring. Drill ³⁄₁₆" pilot holes through hanging strip into the wall studs and attach the cabinet loosely to wall with sheetmetal screws.

2 Attach a filler strip to the adjoining cabinet, if necessary (page 254). Clamp the filler in place, and drill counterbored pilot holes through the side of the face frame. Attach the filler with sheetmetal screws.

3 Clamp the adjoining cabinet to the corner cabinet. Make sure the cabinet is plumb, and drill counterbored pilot holes through corner-cabinet face frame into the filler strip (page 256, step 5). Join the cabinets with sheetmetal screws. Drill ³⁄₁₆" pilot holes through the hanging strips into the wall studs. Attach the cabinets loosely with sheetmetal screws.

4 Use a jig saw to cut any cabinet openings needed for plumbing, wiring, or heating ducts.

5 Position and attach the additional cabinets, making sure the frames are aligned. Clamp the cabinets together, and drill counterbored pilot holes through the sides of the face frames. Join the cabinets with sheetmetal screws. Frameless cabinets are joined with No. 8 gauge 1¼" wood screws and finish washers (page 256).

6 Make sure all the cabinets are level. If necessary, adjust them by driving wood shims underneath the cabinets. Place the wood shims behind the cabinets near the stud locations wherever there is a gap. Tighten the wall screws and cut the shims flush with the cabinetry with a utility knife.

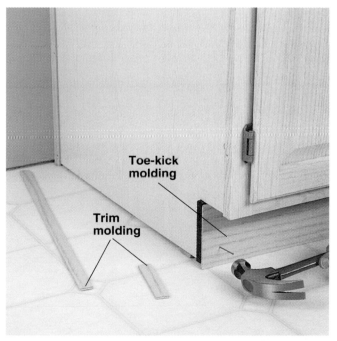

Toe-kick molding

Trim molding

7 Use trim moldings to cover the gaps between the cabinets and the wall or floor. The toe-kick area is often covered with a strip of vinyl or hardwood finished to match the cabinets.

8 If a corner has a void area not covered by cabinets, screw 1 × 3 cleats to the back wall, flush with the reference line. The cleats will help support the countertop.

How to Install a Ceiling-hung Cabinet to Joists

1 Cut a cardboard template to the same size as the top of the cabinet. Use template to outline position of the cabinet on the ceiling. Mark the position of the cabinet face frame on the outline.

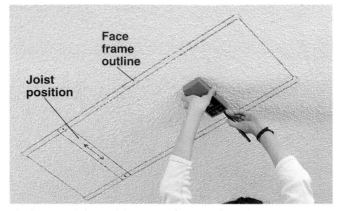

2 Locate joists with a stud finder. If the joists run parallel to the cabinet, install blocking between the them to hang cabinet (below). Measure the joist positions and mark the cabinet frame to indicate where to drive the screws.

3 Have one or more helpers position cabinet against the ceiling. Drill ³⁄₁₆" pilot holes through top rails into the ceiling joists. Attach cabinets with 4" wood screws and finish washers (right).

Shown in cutaway: The cabinet is attached to the joists with wood screws and finish washers.

How to Attach a Ceiling-hung Cabinet to Blocking (joists must be accessible)

1 Drill reference holes through the ceiling at each corner of the cabinet outline. From above the ceiling, install 2 × 4 blocks between the joists. Blocking can be toenailed or end-nailed to the joists.

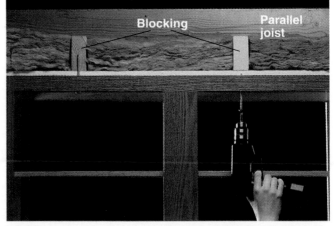

2 Measure the distance between each block and the reference holes. Mark the cabinet frame to indicate where to drive anchoring screws. Drill pilot holes and attach the cabinet to the blocking with 4" wood screws and finish washers, as shown in cutaway (above).

How to Install a Base Island Cabinet

1 Set the base cabinet in the correct position, and lightly trace the cabinet outline on the flooring. Remove the cabinet.

2 Attach L-shaped 2 × 4 cleats to the floor at opposite corners of the cabinet outline. Allow for the thickness of the cabinet walls by positioning cleats ¾" inside the cabinet outline. Attach the cleats to the floor with 3" wallboard screws.

3 Lower the base cabinet over the cleats. Check the cabinet for level, and shim under the base if necessary.

4 Attach the cabinet to the floor cleats using 6d finish nails. Drill pilot holes for nails, and recess nail heads with a nail set. Fill the holes with tinted wood putty to match your cabinets.

Custom laminate

Post-form

Ceramic tile

Solid surface

Choosing Countertops

Countertops provide the main workspace in many rooms, so they must be made from durable and easy-to-clean materials. Countertops add color, pattern, texture, and shape to a room, so choose a style that harmonizes with the other elements in the room.

Custom laminate countertops are built by gluing sheet laminates to particleboard. Laminates are available in hundreds of colors and patterns to match any decorating scheme. Special edge treatments can be added to customize a laminate countertop (page 268 to 275).

Post-form countertops are made of sheet laminates glued to particleboard and come from the factory ready to install. Post-form countertops have pre-attached backsplashes and front edge treatments. They are manufactured in a variety of colors and styles.

Ceramic tile is especially durable and creates a beautiful surface that resists spills and stains. Tile is available in a wide variety of styles and prices, and creating a ceramic tile countertop can be a creative do-it-yourself project.

Solid surface materials are increasing in popularity. Manufactured from acrylic or polyester resins mixed with additives and formed into sheets, they are available in many styles and colors. Solid surface materials are expensive, durable, and installed only by professionals.

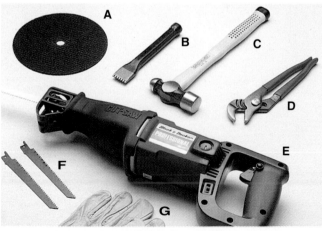

Specialty tools & supplies for removing countertops include: masonry-cutting circular saw blade (A), masonry chisel (B), ball peen hammer (C), channel-type pliers (D), reciprocating saw (E) with coarse wood-cutting blade (F), work gloves (G).

How to Remove an Old Countertop

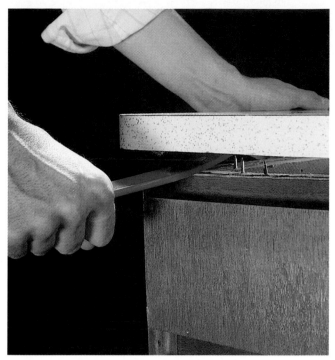

1 Remove all plumbing fixtures. Remove any brackets or screws holding the countertop to the cabinets. Unscrew the take-up bolts on mitered countertops.

2 Use a utility knife to cut caulk beads along backsplash and edge of countertop. Remove any trim. Using a flat pry bar, try to lift countertop away from base cabinets.

3 If countertop cannot be pried up, use a reciprocating saw or jig saw with coarse wood-cutting blade to cut the countertop into pieces for removal. Be careful not to cut into the base cabinets.

TIP: To remove a ceramic tile countertop, chisel tile away from the base with a masonry chisel and ball peen hammer. Wear eye protection. A tile countertop that has a mortar bed can be cut into pieces with a circular saw and abrasive masonry-cutting blade.

Installing a Post-form Countertop

Post-form laminate countertops come in stock lengths, and are cut to fit your space. Pre-mitered sections are available for two- or three-piece countertops that continue around corners. If the countertop has an exposed end, you will need an endcap kit that contains a preshaped strip of matching laminate.

For a precise fit, the backsplash must be trimmed to fit any unevenness in the back wall. This process is called *scribing*. Post-form countertops have a narrow strip of laminate on the backsplash for scribing.

Everything You Need:

Tools: Tape measure, framing square, pencil, straightedge, C-clamps, hammer, level, caulk gun, jig saw, belt sander, drill and spade bit, cordless screwdriver.

Materials: Post-form countertop sections.

Specialty Tools & Materials: See photo, page opposite.

How to Install a Post-form Countertop

1 Measure the span of the base cabinets, from the corner to the outside edge of the cabinet. Add 1" for overhang if end will be exposed. If an end will butt against an appliance, subtract ¹⁄₁₆" to prevent scratches.

Specialty tools & supplies include: wood shims (A), take-up bolts (B), wallboard screws (C), wire brads (D), household iron (E), endcap laminate (F), endcap battens (G), silicon caulk (H), file (I), adjustable wrench (J), carpenter's glue (K), buildup blocks (L), scribing compass (M).

2 Use a framing square to mark a cutting line on the bottom surface of the countertop. Cut off the countertop with a jig saw, using a clamped straightedge as a guide. NOTE: Laminate cutting blades are available for cutting laminate countertops without ruining the surface. If you are using a laminate cutting blade, cut the countertop with bottom side down.

3 Attach the battens from an endcap kit to the edge of the countertop, using carpenter's glue and small brads. Sand out any unevenness with a belt sander.

(continued next page)

4 Hold the endcap laminate against the end, slightly overlapping the edges. Activate the adhesive by pressing an iron set at medium heat against the endcap. Cool it with a wet cloth, then file the endcap laminate flush with the edges.

5 Position the countertop on the base cabinets. Make sure the front edge of countertop is parallel to the cabinet face. Check the countertop for level. Make sure that the drawers and doors open and close freely. If needed, adjust the countertop with wood shims.

6 Because walls are usually uneven, use a compass to trace wall outline onto backsplash scribing strip. Set compass arms to match widest gap, then move compass along length of the wall to transfer outline to scribing strip.

7 Remove the countertop. Use a belt sander to grind the backsplash down to the scribe line.

8 Mark a cutout for a self-rimming sink. Position the sink upside down on the countertop and trace an outline. Remove the sink and draw a cutting line ⅝" inside the sink outline.

9 Mark a cutout for a cooktop with the frame. Position the metal frame on the countertop, and trace an outline around the edge of the vertical flange. Remove the frame.

10 Drill pilot hole just inside cutting line. Make cutouts with jig saw. Support cutout area from below so that falling cutout does not damage the cabinet.

11 Apply a bead of silicone caulk to the edges of the mitered countertop sections. Force countertop pieces tightly together.

12 From underneath cabinet, install and tighten miter take-up bolts. Position the countertop tightly against wall and fasten to cabinets by driving wallboard screws up through corner brackets into the countertop. Screws should be long enough to provide maximum holding power, but not long enough to puncture laminate surface.

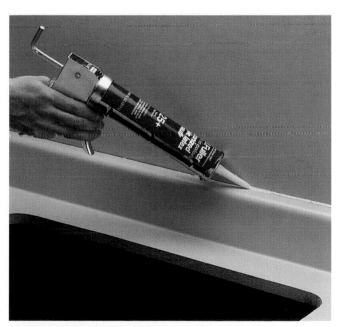

13 Seal the seam between the backsplash and the wall with silicone caulk. Smooth the bead with a wet fingertip. Wipe away excess caulk.

Building a Custom Laminate Countertop

Build your own durable, beautiful countertop with plastic sheet laminates. Plastic laminates are available in hundreds of colors, styles, and textures. A countertop made with laminates can be tailored to fit any space.

Laminates are sold in 6-, 8-, 10-, or 12-foot lengths that are about $\frac{1}{20}$" thick. Laminate sheets range in width from 30" to 48". Most laminates are made by bonding a thin surface layer of colored plastic to a core of hardened resins. Another type of laminate has consistent color through the thickness of the sheet. Solid-color laminate countertops do not show dark lines at the trimmed edges, but they chip more easily than traditional laminates and must be handled carefully.

Choose nonflammable contact cement when building a countertop, and thoroughly ventilate your work area.

Everything You Need:

Tools: Tape measure, framing square, pencil, straightedge, clamps, caulk gun, circular saw with combination blade, cordless screwdriver, belt sander, router, specialty tools & supplies: photo, page opposite.

Materials: $\frac{3}{4}$" particleboard, sheet laminate.

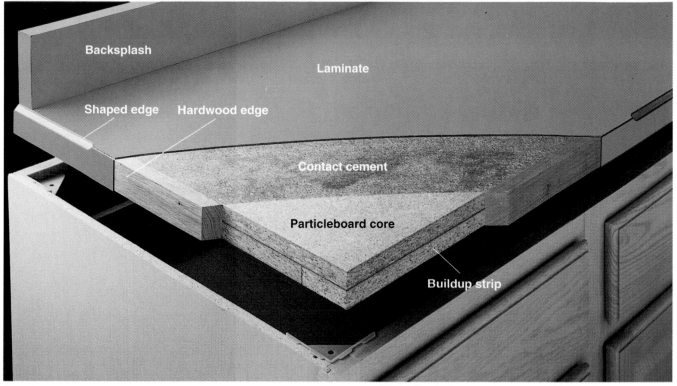

Laminate countertop: Countertop core is ¾" particleboard. Perimeter is built up with strips of particleboard screwed to the bottom of the core. For decorative edge treatments, hardwood strips can be attached to core.

Laminate pieces are bonded to the countertop with contact cement. Edges are trimmed and shaped with a router.

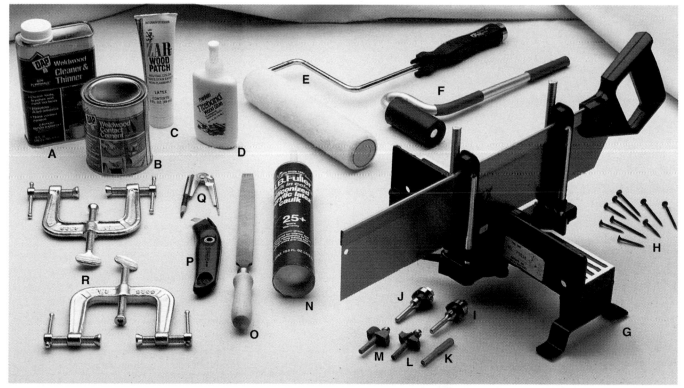

Specialty tools & supplies include: contact cement thinner (A), contact cement (B), latex wood patch (C), carpenter's glue (D), paint roller (E), J-roller (F), miter box (G), wallboard screws (H), flush-cutting router bit (I),

15° bevel-cutting router bit (J), straight router bit (K), corner rounding router bit (L), cove router bit (M), silicone caulk (N), file (O), scoring tool (P), scribing compass (Q), 3-way clamps (R).

How to Build a Custom Laminate Countertop

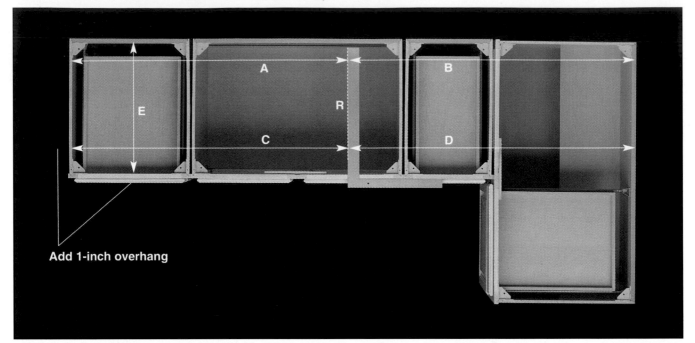

Add 1-inch overhang

1 Measure along tops of base cabinets to determine size of countertop. If wall corners are not square, use a framing square to establish a reference line (R) near middle of base cabinets, perpendicular to front of cabinets. Take four measurements (A, B, C, D) from reference line to cabinet ends. Allow for overhangs by adding 1" to the length for each exposed end, and 1" to the width (E). If an end butts against an appliance, subtract 1/16" from length to prevent scratching appliance.

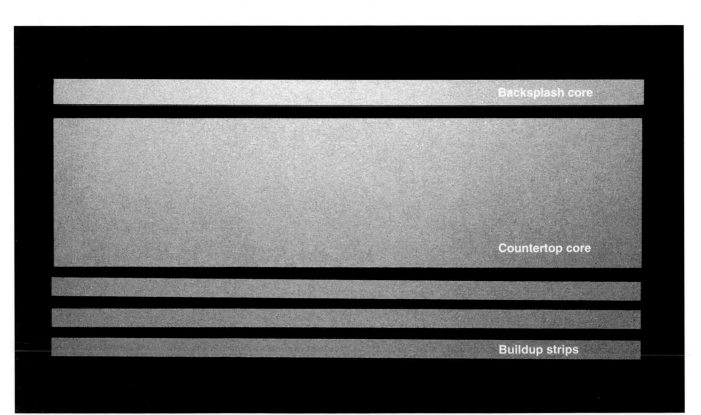

Backsplash core

Countertop core

Buildup strips

2 Transfer measurements from step 1, using a framing square to establish a reference line. Cut core to size using a circular saw with a clamped straight-edge as a guide. Cut 4" strips of particleboard for the backsplash, and for joint support where sections of the countertop core are butted together. Cut 3" strips to use as edge buildup.

Joint support

Buildup strips

3 Join the countertop core pieces on the bottom side. Attach a 4" particle board joint support across the seam, using carpenter's glue and 1¼" wallboard screws.

4 Attach 3" edge buildup strips to bottom of countertop, using 1¼" wallboard screws. Fill any gaps on outside edges with latex wood patch, then sand edges with belt sander.

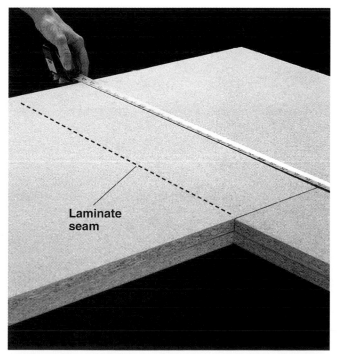

Laminate seam

5 To determine the size of the laminate top, measure countertop core. For strength, laminate seams should run opposite to core seam. Add ½" trimming margin to both the length and width of each piece. Measure laminate needed for face and edges of backsplash, and for exposed edges of countertop core. Add ½" to each measurement.

6 Cut laminate by scoring and breaking it. Draw a cutting line, then etch along the line with a scoring tool. Use a straightedge as a guide. Two passes of scoring tool will help laminate break cleanly.

(continued next page)

How to Build a Custom Laminate Countertop (continued)

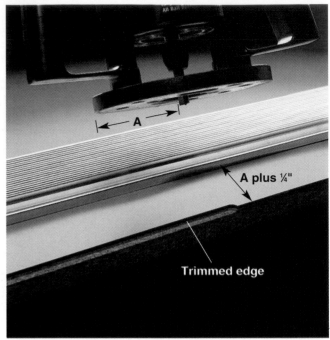

7 Bend laminate toward the scored line until the sheet breaks cleanly. For better control on narrow pieces, clamp a straightedge along scored line before bending laminate. Wear gloves to avoid being cut by sharp edges.

8 Create tight-fitting seams with plastic laminate by using a router and a straight bit to trim edges that will butt together. Measure from cutting edge of the bit to edge of the router baseplate (A). Place laminate on scrap wood and align edges. To guide the router, clamp a straightedge on the laminate at distance A plus 1/4", parallel to laminate edge. Trim laminate.

9 Apply laminate to sides of countertop first. Using a paint roller, apply two coats of contact cement to edge of countertop and one coat to back of laminate. Let cement dry according to manufacturer's directions. Position laminate carefully, then press against edge of countertop. Bond with J-roller.

10 Use a router and flush-cutting bit to trim edge strip flush with top and bottom surfaces of countertop core. At edges where router cannot reach, trim excess laminate with a file. Apply laminate to remaining edges, and trim with router.

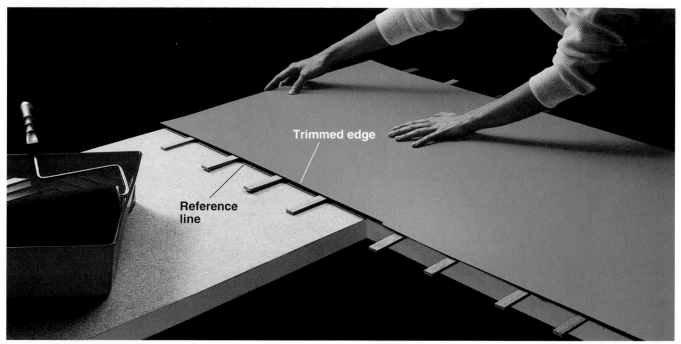

11 Test-fit laminate top on countertop core. Check that laminate overhangs all edges. At seam locations, draw a reference line on core where laminate edges will butt together. Remove laminate. Make sure all surfaces are free of dust, then apply one coat of contact cement to back of laminate and two coats to core. Place spacers made of ¼"-thick scrap wood at 6" intervals across countertop core. Because contact cement bonds instantly, spacers allow laminate to be positioned accurately over core without bonding. Align laminate with seam reference line. Beginning at one end, remove spacers and press laminate to countertop core.

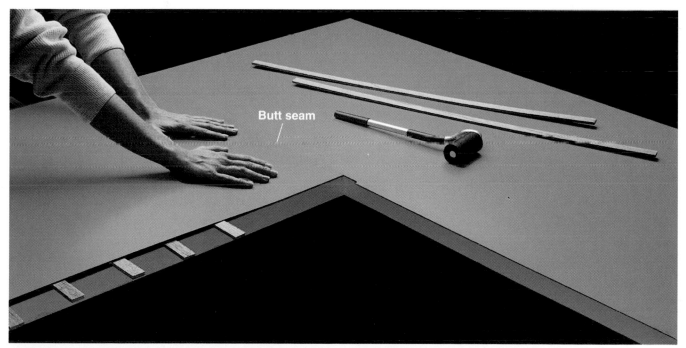

12 Apply contact cement to remaining core and next piece of laminate. Let cement dry, then position laminate on spacers, and carefully align butt seam. Beginning at seam edge, remove spacers and press laminate to countertop core.

(continued next page)

13 Roll entire surface with J-roller to bond laminate to core. Clean off any excess contact cement with a soft cloth and contact cement thinner.

14 Remove excess laminate with a router and flush-cutting bit. At edges where router cannot reach, trim excess laminate with a file. Countertop is now ready for final trimming with bevel-cutting bit.

15 Finish-trim the edges with router and 15° bevel-cutting bit. Set bit depth so that the bevel edge is cut only on top laminate layer. Bit should not cut into vertical edge surface.

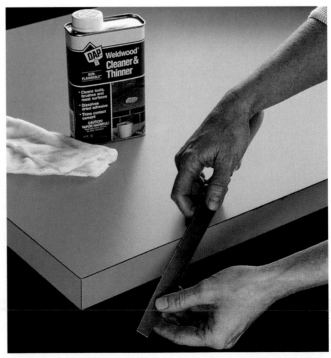

16 File all edges smooth. Use downward file strokes to avoid chipping the laminate.

17 Cut 1¼"-wide strips of ¼" plywood to form over-hanging scribing strip for backsplash. Attach to top and sides of backsplash core with glue and wallboard screws. Cut laminate pieces and apply to exposed sides, top, and front of backsplash. Trim each piece as it is applied.

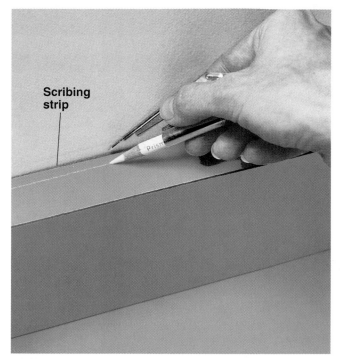

18 Test-fit countertop and backsplash. Because walls may be uneven, use compass to trace wall outline onto backsplash scribing strip. Use a belt sander to grind backsplash to scribe line (page 266).

19 Apply bead of silicone caulk to the bottom edge of the backsplash.

20 Position the backsplash on the countertop, and clamp it into place with bar clamps. Wipe away excess caulk, and let dry completely.

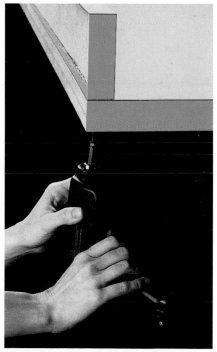

21 Screw 2" wallboard screws through countertop into backsplash core. Make sure screwheads are countersunk completely for a tight fit against the base cabinet.

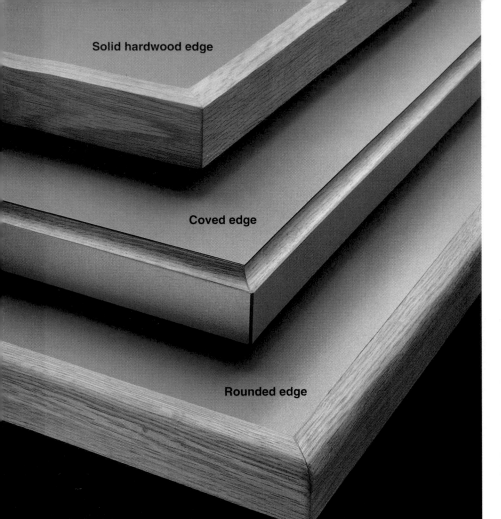

Solid hardwood edge

Coved edge

Rounded edge

Custom Wood Countertop Edges

For an elegant, added touch on a laminate countertop, add hardwood edges and shape them with a router. Rout the edges before attaching the backsplash to the countertop.

Everything You Need:

Tools: 3-way clamps, belt sander, router with edging & cove bit, J-roller, miter box.

Materials: 1 × 2 hardwood strips, wood glue, ¾" particleboard, sheet laminate, 4d finish nails.

How to Build Solid Hardwood Edges

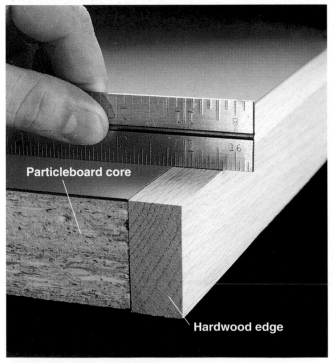

Particleboard core

Hardwood edge

Laminate top of countertop before attaching edge strip. Attach the edge strip flush with the surface of laminate, using carpenter's glue and finish nails (page opposite).

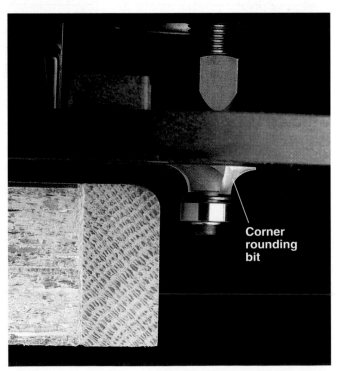

Corner rounding bit

Mold top and bottom edges of strip with router and edging bit, if desired. Stain and finish wood as desired.

How to Build Coved Hardwood Edges

1 Cut 1 × 2 hardwood strips to fit edges of countertop. Sand strips smooth. Miter-cut inside and outside corners.

2 Attach edge strips to countertop with carpenter's glue and 3-way clamps. Drill pilot holes, then attach strip with finish nails. Recess nail heads with a nail set.

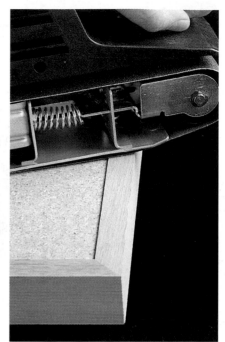

3 Sand edge strips flush with top surface of countertop, using a belt sander and 12-grit sandpaper.

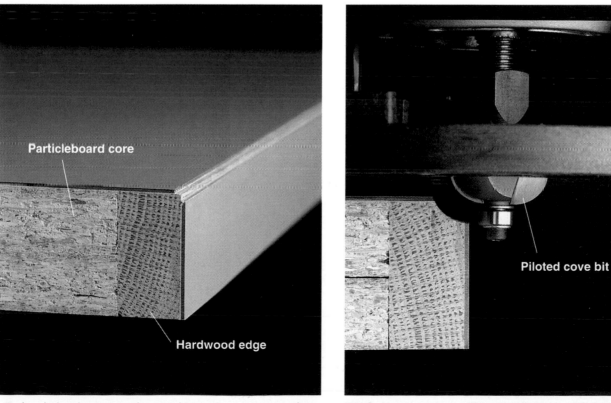

Particleboard core

Hardwood edge

Piloted cove bit

4 Apply laminate to edge and top of countertop after hardwood edge has been sanded flush.

5 Cut cove edge with a router and cove bit with ball-bearing pilot. Smooth cove with 220-grit sandpaper. Stain and finish exposed wood as desired.

Glossary

Balloon framing — a type of framing construction in which the studs run from the sill plate on the foundation to the roof framing in one continuous piece. Used most commonly in house construction before 1930.

Base-shoe molding — a strip of molding nailed to baseboard at the floor to conceal gaps and add a decorative edge.

Beam — a term that applies to any horizontal member such as a joist or header.

Bevel cut — an angled cut through the width or thickness of a board or other piece of stock.

Blindnailing — a nailing technique used in the installation of tongue-and-groove panels where the nail head is hidden from view by the groove of the next panel.

Blocking — a piece of dimensional lumber used between framing members for additional support and for use as a nailer in the installation of finish materials.

Box nail — a nail similar in appearance to a common nail, but with a thinner shaft. Box nails are used for lighter construction and on materials that split easily.

Brick molding — the molding used between the exterior surface of a house and a window or door frame.

Building codes — a set of building regulations and ordinances governing the way a house may be built or modified. Most building codes are controlled by the local municipality.

Casing — any trim around a window, door, or other opening.

Casing nail — similar to a finishing nail, but with a slightly larger dimpled head for better holding power.

Cat's paw — a type of prying tool used primarily in demolition, good for extracting nails.

Chalk box — also known as a chalk line, used to mark straight lines over long areas, or as a plumb bob.

Collet — a collar on a router used to hold a router bit shank in place when tightened.

Common nail — a heavy-shaft nail used primarily for framing carpentry work and concrete forms, available from 2d to 60d.

Coped joint — a joint between two pieces of molding where one piece is cut to match the profile of another.

Coping saw — a handsaw with a flexible blade and fine teeth for cutting intricate curves and bends in wood.

Cripple stud — a short stud that is normally located above or below window and door openings.

Crosscut — to cut a piece of wood perpendicular to its grain.

Crown moldings — a concave piece of molding used to cover the joint between the wall and ceiling; sometimes referred to as *cove molding*.

Drip edge — a piece of molding placed over any exterior opening so that water runs or drips away from the opening.

Easy reader — a tape measure with a fractional readout along the gradation scale to make measurements easier to read.

Endnailing — joining two boards at a right angle by driving nails through the face of one board into the end of another.

Facenailing — joining two parallel boards by driving nails through the faces of both boards.

Finish nail — a nail with a small, dimpled head, used for fastening wood trim and other detail work.

Flush — arranging two or more items so that their surfaces create a level plane.

Full-, Half-, Quarter-sheet — referring to the size of a piece of sheet good relative to a 4 × 8-ft. sheet. A half-sheet is 4 × 4-ft., a quarter-sheet is 2 × 4-ft.

Furring strips — strips of wood, normally 2 × 2 or 1 × 2, that are used to even out a wall or prepare it for finishing with wallboard.

GFCI receptacle — a receptacle outfitted with a ground-fault circuit-interrupter. Also used on some extension cords to reduce the possibility of electric shock when operating an appliance or power tool.

Glue laminate — a type of engineered lumber specifically created for headers or support beams, in which layers of wood are bonded to form a solid unit.

Header — a piece of lumber used as a support beam over a doorway or window opening.

Iron — another name for the blade of a plane

Jamb — the top and side pieces that make up the finished frame of a door or window.

Jack stud — a wall-framing member used to support a header in a doorway or window opening.

Joist — a piece of dimensional lumber used to support a ceiling or floor.

Kerf — a saw cut in wood. The set of the teeth—the degree of outward angle—determine the width of a kerf.

King studs — the first studs on either side of a framed opening to span from the sole plate to the top plate.

Ledger board — a piece of dimensional lumber used to mount cabinets and other elements on a wall.

Level — a line or plane that is parallel to the surface of still water.

Load-bearing wall — any wall (interior or exterior), that bears some of the structural weight of a house. All exterior walls are load-bearing.

Locknailing — strengthening a miter joint in window or door casings by driving nails through the middle of the joint from the outer edge of the casing. This technique also works well with picture frames.

Mandrel — the drill bit tip in the center of a hole saw, used in the cutting of an opening for a doorknob in a door.

MicroLam® — a structural member made of thin layers of wood glued together; used for joists and beams

Miter cut — a 45° bevel cut in the end of a piece of molding or a framing member.

O.C. (on center) O.C. refers to the distance from the center of one framing member to center of the next.

Partition wall — an interior, non-load-bearing wall.

Penny weight — a measure used to indicate nail size and length, commonly shown as a lower case "d."

Platform framing — a type of framing construction in which the studs only span a single story, and each floor acts as a platform to build and support the next higher level. Most common framing method in modern home construction.

Plumb — standing perfectly vertical. A plumb line is exactly perpendicular to a level surface.

Plumb bob — a device consisting of a pointed weight on the end of a string, used to determine whether a surface is exactly vertical, or to transfer marks along a vertical plane.

Plunge cut — a cut that begins in the field of a board or piece of plywood by slowly Pivoting the blade into the wood.

Post — a vertical timber used to support any structural member such as a rafter or header.

Powder actuated nailer — a fastening device used to drive hardened nails into concrete and steel with the aid of gunpowder.

Pre-hung door — a door unit that is sold pre-hung in its jambs for easier installation.

Reciprocating saw — a type of power saw that cuts with a back and forth action through wood, metal, and plastic.

Rip — to cut a piece of wood parallel to the grain.

Rough opening — the opening of the rough framing for a window or door.

STC — (sound transmission class) A rating system referring to how well sound is contained within a room due to the construction. Normal wall construction has a rating of 32 STC.

Scarf joint — a joint made by beveling the ends of two pieces of lumber or molding and nailing them together so that they appear to be seamless.

Shim — a thin wedge of wood used to make slight adjustments in doors or windows during installation.

Sister joist — dimensional lumber attached alongside an existing joist to provide additional strength.

Soffits & chases — boxes made with dimensional lumber and plywood or wallboard to cover up existing mechanicals or other obstructions.

Sole plate — a piece of dimensional lumber (normally 2 × 4) that supports the studs of a wall.

Standout — the distance a tape measure can be drawn out before the tape bends under its own weight.

Stud — a vertical framing member used in the framework of a house or building.

Toenailing — joining two boards at a right angle by driving nails at a 45° angle through the side of one board into the face of another.

Top plate — a piece of dimensional lumber (normally 2 × 4) that rests on top of the studs in a wall and supports the ends of rafters.

Tongue-and-groove paneling — a type of lumber with a machined tongue on one side and a groove on the other, so that when pushed together, the groove of one board fits snugly over the tongue of the adjacent board.

Treated wood — lumber that has been impregnated with chemicals to make it resistant to pests and rot.

VSR — (variable speed reversing) an option available in most drills sold today, allowing you to control drill speed and direction.

Wainscotting — matching panels or boards installed on the lower portion of a wall.

Wallboard — also known as drywall; flat panels available in various sizes made of gypsum covered with durable paper. Used for most interior wall and ceiling surfaces.

Whaler — a temporary support beam used in the modification of balloon framing.

Reference Charts

Converting Measurements

To Convert:	To:	Multiply by:
Inches	Millimeters	25.4
Inches	Centimeters	2.54
Feet	Meters	0.305
Yards	Meters	0.914
Square inches	Square centimeters	6.45
Square feet	Square meters	0.093
Square yards	Square meters	0.836
Cubic inches	Cubic centimeters	16.4
Cubic feet	Cubic meters	0.0283
Cubic yards	Cubic meters	0.765
Ounces	Milliliters	30.0
Pints (U.S.)	Liters	0.473 (Imp. 0.568)
Quarts (U.S.)	Liters	0.946 (Imp. 1.136)
Gallons (U.S.)	Liters	3.785 (Imp. 4.546)
Ounces	Grams	28.4
Pounds	Kilograms	0.454

To Convert:	To:	Multiply by:
Millimeters	Inches	0.039
Centimeters	Inches	0.394
Meters	Feet	3.28
Meters	Yards	1.09
Square centimeters	Square inches	0.155
Square meters	Square feet	10.8
Square meters	Square yards	1.2
Cubic centimeters	Cubic inches	0.061
Cubic meters	Cubic feet	35.3
Cubic meters	Cubic yards	1.31
Milliliters	Ounces	.033
Liters	Pints (U.S.)	2.114 (Imp. 1.76)
Liters	Quarts (U.S.)	1.057 (Imp. 0.88)
Liters	Gallons (U.S.)	0.264 (Imp. 0.22)
Grams	Ounces	0.035
Kilograms	Pounds	2.2

Lumber Dimensions

Nominal - U.S.	Actual - U.S.	METRIC
1 × 2	¾ × 1½"	19 × 38 mm
1 × 3	¾ × 2½"	19 × 64 mm
1 × 4	¾ × 3½"	19 × 89 mm
1 × 5	¾ × 4½"	19 × 114 mm
1 × 6	¾ × 5½"	19 × 140 mm
1 × 7	¾ × 6¼"	19 × 159 mm
1 × 8	¾ × 7¼"	19 × 184 mm
1 × 10	¾ × 9¼"	19 × 235 mm
1 × 12	¾ × 11¼"	19 × 286 mm
1¼ × 4	1 × 3½"	25 × 89 mm
1¼ × 6	1 × 5½"	25 × 140 mm
1¼ × 8	1 × 7¼"	25 × 184 mm
1¼ × 10	1 × 9¼"	25 × 235 mm
1¼ × 12	1 × 11¼"	25 × 286 mm
1½ × 4	1¼ × 3½"	32 × 89 mm
1½ × 6	1¼ × 5½"	32 × 140 mm
1½ × 8	1¼ × 7¼"	32 × 184 mm
1½ × 10	1¼ × 9¼"	32 × 235 mm
1½ × 12	1¼ × 11¼"	32 × 286 mm
2 × 4	1½ × 3½"	38 × 89 mm
2 × 6	1½ × 5½"	38 × 140 mm
2 × 8	1½ × 7¼"	38 × 184 mm
2 × 10	1½ × 9¼"	38 × 235 mm
2 × 12	1½ × 11¼"	38 × 286 mm
3 × 6	2½ × 5½"	64 × 140 mm
4 × 4	3½ × 3½"	89 × 89 mm
4 × 6	3½ × 5½"	89 × 140 mm

Liquid Measurement Equivalents

1 Pint	= 16 Fluid Ounces	= 2 Cups
1 Quart	= 32 Fluid Ounces	= 2 Pints
1 Gallon	= 128 Fluid Ounces	= 4 Quarts

Converting Temperatures

Convert degrees Fahrenheit (F) to degrees Celsius (C) by following this simple formula: Subtract 32 from the Fahrenheit temperature reading. Then, multiply that number by $\frac{5}{9}$. For example, 77°F - 32 = 45. 45 × $\frac{5}{9}$ = 25°C.

To convert degrees Celsius to degrees Fahrenheit, multiply the Celsius temperature reading by $\frac{9}{5}$. Then, add 32. For example, 25°C × $\frac{9}{5}$ = 45. 45 + 32 = 77°F.

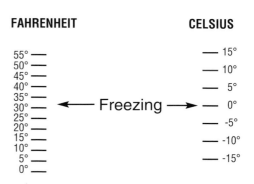

Drill Bit Guide

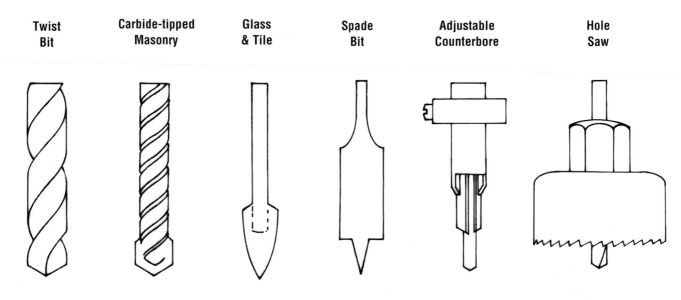

Twist Bit	Carbide-tipped Masonry	Glass & Tile	Spade Bit	Adjustable Counterbore	Hole Saw

Counterbore, Shank & Pilot Hole Diameters

Screw Size	Counterbore Diameter for Screw Head	Clearance Hole for Screw Shank	Pilot Hole Diameter	
			Hard Wood	Soft Wood
#1	.146 (9/64)	5/64	3/64	1/32
#2	1/4	3/32	3/64	1/32
#3	1/4	7/64	1/16	3/64
#4	1/4	1/8	1/16	3/64
#5	1/4	1/8	5/64	1/16
#6	5/16	9/64	3/32	5/64
#7	5/16	5/32	3/32	5/64
#8	3/8	11/64	1/8	3/32
#9	3/8	11/64	1/8	3/32
#10	3/8	3/16	1/8	7/64
#11	1/2	3/16	5/32	9/64
#12	1/2	7/32	9/64	1/8

Saw Blades

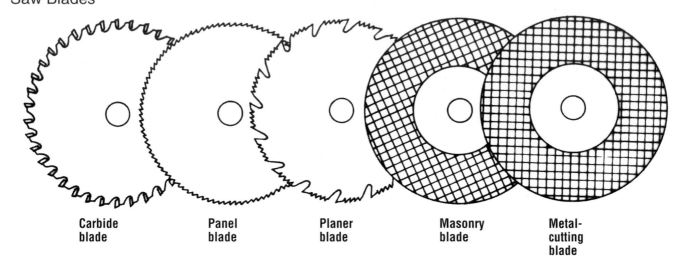

Carbide blade | Panel blade | Planer blade | Masonry blade | Metal-cutting blade

Adhesives

Type	Characteristics	Uses
White glue	**Strength:** moderate; rigid bond **Drying time:** several hours **Resistance to heat:** poor **Resistance to moisture:** poor **Hazards:** none **Cleanup/solvent:** soap and water	**Porous surfaces:** Wood (indoors) Paper Cloth
Yellow glue (carpenter's glue)	**Strength:** moderate to good; rigid bond **Drying time:** several hours; faster than white glue **Resistance to heat:** moderate **Resistance to moisture:** moderate **Hazards:** none **Cleanup/solvent:** soap and water	**Porous surfaces:** Wood (indoors) Paper Cloth
Two-part epoxy	**Strength:** excellent; strongest of all adhesives **Drying time:** varies, depending on manufacturer **Resistance to heat:** excellent **Resistance to moisture:** excellent **Hazards:** fumes are toxic and flammable **Cleanup/solvent:** acetone will dissolve some types	**Smooth & porous surfaces:** Wood (indoors & outdoors) Metal Masonry Glass Fiberglass
Hot glue	**Strength:** depends on type **Drying time:** less than 60 seconds **Resistance to heat:** fair **Resistance to moisture:** good **Hazards:** hot glue can cause burns **Cleanup/solvent:** heat will loosen bond	**Smooth & porous surfaces:** Glass Plastics Wood
Cyanoacrylate (instant glue)	**Strength:** excellent, but with little flexibility **Drying time:** a few seconds **Resistance to heat:** excellent **Resistance to moisture:** excellent **Hazards:** can bond skin instantly; toxic, flammable **Cleanup/solvent:** acetone	**Smooth surfaces:** Glass Ceramics Plastics Metal
Construction adhesive	**Strength:** good to excellent; very durable **Drying time:** 24 hours **Resistance to heat:** good **Resistance to moisture:** excellent **Hazards:** may irritate skin and eyes **Cleanup/solvent:** soap and water (while still wet)	**Porous surfaces:** Framing lumber Plywood and paneling Wallboard Foam panels Masonry
Water-base contact cement	**Strength:** good **Drying time:** bonds instantly; dries fully in 30 minutes **Resistance to heat:** excellent **Resistance to moisture:** good **Hazards:** may irritate skin and eyes **Cleanup/solvent:** soap and water (while still wet)	**Porous surfaces:** Plastic laminates Plywood Flooring Cloth
Silicone sealant (caulk)	**Strength:** fair to good; very flexible bond **Drying time:** 24 hours **Resistance to heat:** good **Resistance to moisture:** excellent **Hazards:** may irritate skin and eyes **Cleanup/solvent:** acetone	**Smooth & porous surfaces:** Wood Ceramics Fiberglass Plastics Glass

Photo Credits

Andersen Windows Inc.
www.andersenwindows.com
800-426-4261

Armstrong Ceilings
www.ceilings.com
800-233-3823

Delta Machinery
www.deltamachinery.com
901-668-8600

Kraftmaid Cabinetry, Inc.
www.kraftmaid.com
440-632-5333

Western Red Cedar Lumber Association
www.wrcla.com
604-684-0266

Additional Resources

Behr Process Corp.
Santa Ana, CA 92704
800-854-0133

**Chimney Safety Institute
of America**
8752 Robbins Rd.
Indianapolis, IN 46268
800-536-0118
www.csia.org

Gypsum Association
810 First St., NE, #510
Washington DC 2002
202-289-5440
www.gypsum.org

Kwikset Corporation
516 East Santa Ana St.
Anaheim, CA 92803
714-535-8111
www.blackanddecker.com

Larson Doors
800-352-3360
www.larsondoors.com

Minwax
10 Mountainview R.
Upper Saddle River, NJ 07458
www.minwax.com

**National Lighting Bureau
Communications Office**
8811 Colesville Rd.
Suite G106
Silver Spring, MD 20910
301-587-9572
www.nlb.org

**National Wood Flooring
Association**
800-422-4556
www.woodfloors.org

Quikrete
2987 Clairmont Rd.
Suite 500
Atlanta, GA 30329
404-634-9100
www.quikrete.com

Tile Council of America
P.O. Box 1787
Clemson, SC 29633
864-646-8453
www.tileusa.com

**U.S. Environmental
Protection Agency**
Indoor Air Quality
www.epa.gov/iedweb00/pubs/
insidest.html

INDEX

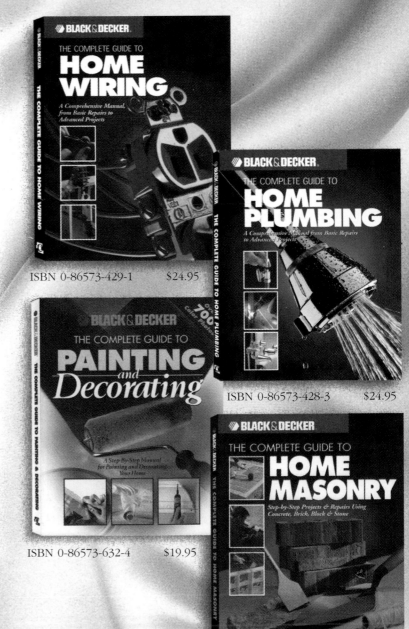